Mexican Politics During the Juárez Regime
1855-1872

Mexican Politics During the Juárez Regime
1855-1872

Walter V. Scholes

University of Missouri Press
Columbia, Missouri

University of Missouri Studies Volume XXX
SBN 8262-0581-X
Copyright © 1957, 1969 by
The Curators of the
University of Missouri
Library of Congress Card Number 57-63240
Manufactured in the United States of America

For France V. Scholes

PUBLISHER'S FOREWORD

Mexican Politics During the Juárez Regime, 1855–1872, was first published in 1957, some 62 years after Bernard Moses launched the first formal course in Latin American studies at Berkeley. In the years after the Berkeley start, the state and status of Latin American studies in this country improved substantially, but still on a curve that indicated no perception of a special urgency or of a particular application such studies might have to serving the national interests of the United States.

Castro and the Dominican conflict changed all that; in the early 60s, Latin American affairs became a "crisis" area for study, much of which was based on a political pragmatism, and most of which took a "current events" approach.

The shadow of the crisis approach is still with us, nearly a decade after Castro marched down from the Sierra Maestra. But there are overwhelming signs that the substantial instructional and research machinery created in the early 60s in response to the crisis is turning itself from the study and teaching of Latin American subjects for special, nationalist reasons. Instead, we may now again be able to approach such studies — but with better facilities and funding — for their intrinsic worth, as lessons in a civilization similar and dissimilar to ours. In that respect, the focus and the momentum residual from the crisis may yet work to the benefit of our culture in the intellectual sense.

Mexican Politics During the Juárez Regime is, of course, a pre-crisis work. Though it continued in distribution through the 60s, its tone and approach are clearly at variance with the "current events" approach. It is history and serves only the purposes of history; because it does, it seems entirely appropriate to the direction of Latin American studies that it be reprinted now in an inexpensive edition for student use.

ACKNOWLEDGMENT

I wish to express my appreciation for the assistance given to me at the libraries of the Universities of Texas, California, Missouri, and Stanford, and at the Biblioteca Nacional in Mexico City. The National Archives gave excellent service on microfilm and the Library of Congress was a great help in obtaining microfilm of Mexican newspapers. I also wish to thank the Graduate Research Council of the University of Missouri for its financial help. Mrs. Mary Ann Ott did the typing. Finally, my wife knows better than anyone else the part she played.

I want to give credit to the *Hispanic American Historical Review* for permission to use material published in my article, "A Revolution Falters: Mexico, 1856-1857," (XXXII, No. 1); and to the *Americas* for material in my two articles entitled: "Church and State at the Mexican Constitutional Convention, 1856-1857," (IV, No. 2); and "EL MENSAJERO and the Election of 1871 in Mexico," (V, No. 1); and also for the use of material from "The Positivist Philosophy in Mexican Education, 1867-1873," (VI, No. 1) by Albert Delmez.

WVS

CONTENTS

Publisher's Foreword vii
I   A Revolution Falters 1
II   War of Reform 25
III   The Government's Program and the Reform Laws 43
IV   1861-1863 56
V   Intervention 92
VI   1867-1870 118
VII   The Presidential Election of 1871 149
VIII The Last Term 166
Bibliography 179
Index 186

This is not the story of Maximilian but rather a consideration of the Mexican national political scene from 1855 through 1872 and of the influences of the Reform Program.

Chapter I

A REVOLUTION FALTERS

On March 1, 1854, a revolt officially began against the egotistical dictator of Mexico, Santa Anna. To the man in power, revolts were nothing new. He had seized and had been driven from the presidency so often that such a situation seemed almost chronic. But this revolt was going to be different, although it is doubtful that even the participants realized in the beginning what its ultimate consequences would be. For when it was over and Santa Anna was ousted forever in 1855, the forces behind the new movement unleashed a decade and a half of turmoil and change. Internal disputes erupted into civil war; foreigners established their rule in parts of Mexico; relations with the United States improved; nationalism, with President Juárez as its symbol, became more pronounced; ideas of capitalism gained a strong foothold; and the cult of science developed.

Attempts had been made in the previous thirty years to bring about fundamental changes, but for various reasons these efforts were unsuccessful. Though many of their ideas were not new to Mexico, the second and third-generation Mexicans were going to have a try. In the past writers, dealing with the period 1855-1872, have stressed the church-state quarrel and the French Intervention. But in so doing they have neglected many of the fundamental internal issues. Now, the Intervention did in fact threaten Mexico's national existence and her success in repelling the invasion did much to strengthen democracy in this hemisphere. Laws did deprive the church of its lands, its special privileges, and did establish religious toleration. But to let the matter rest there is to miss the really dynamic aspect of the period—the attempt to introduce democratic capitalism. Most of the activities of the liberal leaders in the period under study will be devoted to putting this ideal into effect.

In spite of the fact that constant reference will be made to specific aspects of their plan, it might be well to give a brief explanation of what democratic capitalism meant to the Mexican liberals. Equality before the law, republican institutions, and laissez-faire were the three key concepts. Freedom of press and speech, expanded educational facilities, and middle class land ownership, were among the specific goals, as was the desire to inculcate in the Mexicans a belief in hard work and thrift. In short, this was to be the Mexican middle class revolution.

The movement against Santa Anna was supported by most Mexicans. The president obviously was doing little to bring about the improvements that liberals and conservatives felt the country needed. They agreed that something must be done to improve transportation and agricultural and mineral production, for which foreign capital would be needed.[1] Both groups likewise felt it essential to cut the cost of government and advocated an end to the government's dealing with loan sharks as a step in this direction. In addition, the elimination of personal political parties and the development of an esprit d'corps among government employees, liberals and conservatives hoped, would make for more stable and less corrupt administrations. They also wanted strong action to end the Indian raids in the frontier states and greater security for property. They favored liquidation of the national debt.

Liberal thinking, however, went beyond the position held by the conservative. The liberals felt that capitalism could not function properly without additional measures, most of which, directly or indirectly, affected the church. That institution had to be deprived of its land which would be divided into small individual holdings. In addition the clergy would be disenfranchised and parochial obventions abolished. In this sense many of the early reforms would be negative. They sought to remove what they considered to be abuses at the start. Republican institutions, founded on natural rights, sovereignty of the people, and universal suffrage, would rule the country. The government so established would guarantee freedom of speech and the press and religious toleration. One of the tasks of the government would be to encourage immigration from non-Catholic countries.

This movement in Mexico was not atypical. Liberals throughout Latin America were making almost identical demands in the hope of changing their countries. Nor was Mexican liberal thought out

1. "Material improvements" became one of the catch phrases; in fact one newspaper in Campeche in 1859 took the title *Las Mejoras Materiales*. The phrase was overused and when by 1869-1870 economic conditions became extremely depressed the phrase was used in derision by the opposition.

of line with that of Europe. With the variation of a few years, many countries in Europe went through similar phases. As far as the church is concerned, one might easily apply Binkley's statement on the church in Europe to that of the church in Mexico: the Roman Catholic Church entered the 1850's in close collaboration with the dominant elements in society, and was left in 1871 standing isolated and alone. This transition was associated with every one of the principal currents of change, intellectual, economic, and political.[2] The state, rather than the church, was becoming the agency for ruling man.

However, bitter differences of opinion prevailed among the liberals themselves. The Reform period saw a continuation of the split between the radicals (*puros*) and moderates (*moderados*). The radicals favored quick and energetic measures to solve Mexico's problems while the moderates urged a more cautious approach. As might be expected, it is often extremely difficult to differentiate between the two, since on many fundamental issues they agreed on the ends and differed simply on the means. At the same time, personal political parties cut across these two simple classifications. Thus the terms *lerdista, porfirista, juarista,* etc. were not necessarily synonymous with either of the two broad divisions.

The revolt against Santa Anna epitomizes in many ways the complexity of the political scene. The elements opposing the dictator were not coordinated and the various leaders represented all shades of opinion. The whole thing technically began in the state of Guerrero which Juan Alvarez, somewhat of a radical, had controlled for some time. Alvarez brooked no outside interference with his domain and when Santa Anna gave indications of intruding the old leader prepared to fight. He was joined by Ignacio Comonfort whose correspondence indicates that he was basically a moderate. A wily opportunist (many would apply a more forceful term), Santiago Vidaurri, led the fight in northern Mexico. San Luis Potosí contributed a disgruntled conservative, Haro y Tamariz, and Guanajuato a moderate, Manuel Doblado, to complete the leadership of the rebels against Santa Anna. To this group residing in Mexico must be added the men who had lived in exile during the last Santa Anna administration. Benito Juárez, Melchor Ocampo, José María

2. R. C. Binkley, *Realism and Nationalism, 1852-1871* (New York, 1935), 57.

Mata, Ponciano Arriaga, and others now returned to join the new movement.

After Santa Anna's departure from the country in August, 1855, the remnants of his army in and around Mexico City came under the control of Manuel Carrera, a conservative. Carrera had not revolted against the dictator but now, having control of the capital and some troops, he wanted the presidency for himself.[3] Whatever judgment may be passed on Comonfort's later actions, he was the main factor in drawing the diverse elements together. Except for Vidaurri, with whom he could temporarily do nothing, he brought the leaders under control and ended the revolt.[4]

With the success of the rebellion, its leaders faced a much greater challenge—that of evolving a positive program to put their theories into effect. The nominal head of the revolt, Alvarez, was chosen acting president after a meeting in Cuernavaca early in October, 1855. In many ways the choice was unfortunate. Although Alvarez had been battling for certain democratic ideas ever since the independence period, he was now an old man and not too efficient. In his past, like so many believers in federalism, he had opposed centralism in order to keep an iron hold on his own state. Moreover, indications are that he was not above accepting financial help for favors. His supporters (*pintos*) we e a rather crude bunch who caused continual trouble in Mexico City. But, as he had lived so long, he was the symbol temporarily needed for unity. This must have been the reasoning of those who gathered at Cuernavaca and voted him the temporary presidency, for many outsiders believed Comonfort would be the choice.[5]

3. For a summary see Richard A. Johnson, *The Mexican Revolution of Ayutla, 1854-1855* (Rock Island, Ill., 1939), 45-62; 100-112.
4. Antonio Gibaya y Patron claims that the real force behind the new movement was the Masonic order. *Comentario crítico, histórico, auténtico a las revoluciones sociales de México* (5 vols., México, 1926-1934), IV & V. Many men in the movement were Masons, but evidence is lacking to show that the ideas of freemasonry played a vital role in guiding political actions. Arriaga, Anastasio Zereceno, León Guzmán, Ocampo, Juárez, Santos Degollado, Francisco Zarco, Miguel Lerdo de Tejada, and Ignacio Altamirano all were Masons. José María Mateos, *Historia de la masonería en México desde 1806 hasta 1884* (México, 1884), 108-226.
5. Ceballos, Mexico, October 3, 1855, to Doblado. Genaro Garcia, ed., *La revolución de Ayutla según el archivo del General Doblado* in *Documentos inéditos o muy raros para la historia de México*, XXVI, 225-227. Hereinafter this set will be referred to as García, *Raros*. Evidence shows that no preparation was made ahead of time to insure Alvarez' election. Gadsden, November 17, 1855, to Marcy. William R. Manning, ed., *Diplomatic Correspondence of*

It is difficult to define a Mexican cabinet. The numbers in it will vary. Generally the Minister of Relations is considered the key post but at times the Minister of War is more important. Alvarez's cabinet, composed of Ocampo in Relations, Guillermo Prieto in Treasury, Juárez in Justice, and Comonfort in War, exemplified the division among the liberals. A poet and a wonderful gossip who had held many government posts, Prieto probably could be classified as a radical in this period. Juárez, at this time, as earlier in his life, was swaying between the moderates and the radicals. Ocampo wanted far-reaching reforms put into effect immediately.[6] Comonfort, on the other hand, bitterly opposed any immediate change, fearing that it would turn the conservatives and many moderates against the new regime. Because Ocampo was unsuccessful in making his own views prevail, he left the cabinet after serving only a fortnight and shortly thereafter so did Prieto. The resignation of these two men made it increasingly evident that the moderates were winning control of the new government.

Although Alvarez was in power from October until early December, 1855, about the only positive legislation during these months was the law reorganizing the judicial system, limiting the special judicial privileges of the military and the clergy and abolishing the special mercantile courts. Published on November 23, the law is generally known as the Ley Juárez. It is important to remember in connection with it that liberal objectives included equality before the law and they regarded the Ley Juárez as a step in that direction. Certainly it bears a close relationship to the later attempts to provide equality of opportunity as a consequence of abolishing monopolies. Later, for example, in 1856 states were appointing and paying lawyers to defend Indians in their complaints of loss of land.[7] The thought here is, of course, that, given juridical equality, there will, in turn, be equality of opportunity.

But the law has been misunderstood and has usually been regarded as being directed specifically against the clergy.[8] In 1855

the United States: Inter-American Affairs, 1831-1860 (12 vols., Washington, 1932-1939), IX, 796. Hereinafter cited as Manning, Mexico.
6. For Ocampo's position see his "Mi quince días de ministro," Angel Pola, ed., Obras completas de D. Melchor Ocampo (3 vols., México, 1900-1901, II, 73-112.
7. See for example, Siglo XIX, August 3 and September 3, 1856.
8. Law is in Manuel Dublán and José María Lozano, Legislación mexicana o colección completa de las disposiciones legislativas expedidas desde la inde-

the liberals gave little indication of being anti-church. For example, the newspaper *Siglo XIX*, usually considered as reflecting the liberal position, revealed no tendencies in this direction. Editor Francisco Zarco made it plain that he favored no anti-church measures, while holding sincerely to his belief in the ideas of capitalism and political and juridical equality. A small part of the press did betray an anti-church bias but papers such as *Revolución*[9] never lasted long and never assumed the stature of *Siglo*.

Nevertheless, the Ley Juárez created a furor. This, plus the fact that the Alvarez government had been immobilized by the division in the cabinet, led many people to feel that Alvarez must surrender the presidency to Comonfort. After much maneuvering, Alvarez resigned and Comonfort took over early in December, 1855. In the new president's cabinet were Luis de la Rosa, Ezequiel Montes, José M. Yáñez, Manuel Siliceo, José María Lafragua, and Manuel Payno. The moderates had triumphed, and their victory became more apparent as Siliceo's influence grew. But much more important than which faction controlled the government was the fact that there now was a government and one with a program.[10]

The government envisioned legislation establishing a temporary organic statute, individual guarantees, a law on the press, more freedom in the municipalities; in general, however, specific action on political matters was to be left to the constitutional convention or the temporary statute of government. The program included a vague statement on the church, but the most important items dealt with economic matters. Under a new tariff law commerce would be as free from government regulation as was consistent with the protection of national industry. The government would provide funds for internal improvements and planned to take a census of real estate. The program observed that under the prevailing system of entailed estate the division of large estates was almost impossible and promised reforms to make such action easier. Under another law, foreigners would find it easier to acquire real estate.

pendencia de la república (34 vols., México, 1876-1904), VII, 565-626. Hereinafter cited as D y L, *Legislación*.
9. For example its issue of October 8, 1855, suggested that clerical property be used to finance the building of roads and canals, that the noviciates be secularized, that religious toleration and civil marriage be legalized. Cited in Gerardo Decorme, *Historia de la Compañía de Jesús en la república mexicana durante el siglo xix* (2 vols., Guadalajara, 1914-1921), II, 73. Prieto wrote to Doblado on September 1, 1855, that his views and those of Arriaga and Ocampo could be found in *Revolución*. García, *Raros*, XXVI, 136-138.
10. Program given in *Pensamiento Nacional*, December 25, 1855.

A Revolution Falters 7

Comonfort's government had to walk the line carefully to maintain itself, since confusion and conflict were the keynote of the day. The administration had to check both radicals and conservatives and, at the same time, show initiative and boldness, especially in economic matters. For a time Comonfort seemed likely to succeed, because when he took control the current uprisings were only minor affairs. But unhappily, something bigger was brewing in Puebla and what had been discontent in December became a full-scale revolt in January, 1856. Although conservatives, including Haro y Tamariz, and certain clergymen led the revolt, it must be emphasized that not all the churchmen in the Puebla diocese joined the rebels. In fact, the Bishop of Puebla advised the rebellious clergy to make their peace with the government.[11] The Archbishop of Mexico reproached those clergymen who were abusing the pulpit by promoting disobedience and encouraging revolution.[12] When efforts to stop the revolt proved futile, Comonfort decided to lead the troops against the rebels himself. Joined by Doblado and others, in early March, 1856, he laid siege to the city and forced it to surrender on March 22. Because of clerical participation in the rebellion, the government decided to assess an indemnity against the holdings of the church in Puebla.[13]

When news of the assessment reached Puebla, an attempt apparently was made to buy off the government, for the Bishop of Puebla on April 24, 1856, wrote to Mariano Riva Palacio commissioning him to arrange a loan of 200,000 pesos to the government to be paid in monthly installments. Until these payments were completed, the diocese of Puebla would be exempt from other contributions levied by the government; if, for any reason, the government disposed of the wealth of the diocese or impeded the administration of the church, the payments would stop.[14] Since this proposal to forestall an indemnity failed, the clergy in Puebla con-

11. José M. Vigil, *La Reforma*, in Vicente Riva Palacio, ed., *México a través de los siglos* (Mexico, 1940 ed.), V, i, 101.
12. *Siglo*, January 22, 1856. Comonfort himself held that the clergy should not take part in any political activity, but at the same time he believed that there should be uniformity of religious belief in Mexico.
13. For the exchange of notes on this subject between the Minister of Justice and the Bishop of Puebla see Francisco Zarco, ed., *Historia del congreso estraordinario constituyente de 1856 y 1857* (2 vols., México, 1857), I, 183-205. For the difficulties in collection see A. Carrion, *Historia de la ciudad de la Puebla de los Angeles* (2 vols., México, 1897), II, 435-438.
14. Mariano Riva Palacio Correspondence, MSS, University of Texas.

tinued to denounce the government from the pulpit. The bishop reversed his earlier stand, and, in addition to using the pulpit to air his political views, he refused to comply with the decree granting the national authorities power to collect the indemnity. Under the circumstances the government felt it necessary on May 12 to decree his exile.[15] Such action showed that even though Comonfort was a moderate he intended to stand firmly against the conservatives and to tolerate no interference with what he considered the legitimate progress of his government. He held to this position for a year and a half and then finally succumbed.

But in this period, as in 1861-1862 and 1867-1872, one of the major factors influencing the political situation was the relationship of the executive to the radicals. It was not cordial and a study of the constitutional convention, which held its first session on February 18, 1856, shows clearly the basic differences in their thinking.[16] The debates soon indicated that congress did not intend to be a rubber stamp for the executive, the radicals especially being critical of the government's policies. The extraordinary powers held by Comonfort caused much uneasiness, and on February 21 the deputies debated with considerable fervor the decree making him substitute president.

The split between congress and the executive showed itself on other occasions. One of the most serious quarrels came over the status of Santiago Vidaurri who was virtually an independent ruler in the north. Entirely on his own initiative, he decreed that Coahuila was to be joined with Nuevo León. On April 15 the national government declared the union illegal and referred the matter to congress for final decision. The report of a special congressional committee, certainly influenced by Ignacio Ramírez, approved Vidaurri's actions. The committee based its conclusion

15. Vigil, *Reforma*, 136-138. Later in 1856 another revolt occurred in Puebla. Plumb, writing from Mexico City on October 31, 1856, to his friend Allen, reported that he had been in Puebla on October 22 and found that the clergy had purchased a sufficient number of the small garrison to effect a *pronunciamiento*. To increase their numbers they had bought *léperos* from the street at one peso per day. Plumb Papers, MSS, Stanford.

16. The convention served also as a regular legislative body. On the basis of the material available it is extremely difficult to determine how the elections for this congress were managed. Apparently, the national government did not have time to organize the elections and state governors controlled them. Emilio Rabasa, *La organizacion politica de México. La constitución y la dictadura* (Madrid, 1917?), 44-45. There were no conservatives at the convention.

on the absurd idea that following the success of the Ayutla revolution a state of nature existed in Mexico; therefore, since no government had been functioning, the peoples of Coahuila and Nuevo León had been free to make their own choice. Ramírez, in his speech before congress upholding the committee's interpretation, used part of his time to belittle Comonfort's administration. Congress, however, rejected the resolution and sent it back to committee.[17]

Radical suspicions of the executive flared up again over two matters of governmental organization. The government issued a decree reinstating the Council of Government on which Comonfort wished to place his own men.[18] Most of those whom he named were moderates. In June, congress finally considered the matter and showed its dissatisfaction by declaring itself "not ready for the question."[19] The quarrel became more acute when, on May 15, the government presented its Organic Statute which set up a rather highly centralized temporary government. Members of congress attacked the law sharply, and local authorities in some states, as in Oaxaca where Juárez was governor, refused to publish it.

To these incidents many others might be added, but finally the proverbial "cooler heads" took over, and congress appointed a special committee to iron matters out with the executive. Essentially, the radicals in congress feared the establishment of a new dictatorship by Comonfort. He, in turn, did not trust congress because of the extreme statements made by many radicals. But both sides finally recognized that each needed the other to survive and a temporary truce resulted. On the basis of past history congress had a right to distrust any executive, but by executive decree Comonfort had, on paper at least, achieved quite impressive results. He had granted money for railroads, established a limited freedom of the press, abolished the tobacco monopoly, decreed a

17. Zarco, *Congreso*, I, 56-61; 271-277; 336-359.
18. The Council had been named by Alvarez under powers granted to him by Ayutla. It had protested the legality of the decree naming Comonfort substitute president and had not met since then.
19. *Ibid.*, 362-369. There is a great deal of evidence to show the dissension. Siliceo, on May 24, 1856, wrote to Doblado telling him of the differences between the executive and the legislature. García, *Raros*, XXXI, 191-193. John S. Cripps wrote to Marcy on June 5, 1856: "During the last ten days, the Cabinet and Congress have been driven into almost open rupture. . . ." Manning, *Mexico*, IX, 836. The newspapers in Mexico City in May and June, 1856, reflected the tension between the two branches of government.

new tariff granting more freedom of trade, opened discussion on interoceanic communications across the Isthmus of Tehuantepec,[20] provided for schools, adopted the French metric system, created a bank in Mexico City, and forced the clergy to sell its lands.[21]

During all this time congress, in addition to its discussions of the matters introduced by the executive, was also carrying on its other function—the framing of a new constitution. The debates in the press and in congress on the proposed articles revealed the philosophies underlying the policies of the various factions and their practical measures for putting these policies into effect. Three interrelated problems were the big questions of the period: theory of government, theory of economy, and status of the clergy.

In his theory of government, the liberal, taking his cue and belief from the Enlightenment, denounced the doctrine of original sin and stressed the perfectibility of man. He felt that the federal form of government based on the liberty and freedom of the individual, on natural rights, and on popular sovereignty, offered the optimum conditions for achieving this perfection.[22] How, the liberals asked, could freedom prevail under a centralized state? Some moderates argued that the liberals had had their chance with the federal constitution of 1824 and had failed. José M. Iglesias replied that that constitution had not been given a fair trial; the bastard interests had overthrown it in the 1830's and since then— calamity.[23] For the liberals, progress and federalism were closely linked together.

The liberals succeeded in including certain features of their federalism and natural rights in the new constitution. They es-

---

20. On this last point see J. Preston Moore, "Correspondence of Pierre Soulé: the Louisiana Tehuantepec Company," *Hispanic American Historical Review*, February, 1952, 59-72. (The title of this journal will be abbreviated to *HAHR*). Apparently Soulé found it necessary to bribe government officials, particularly Siliceo, to get a concession.
21. Decrees in D y L, *Legislación*, VII, 633-691; VIII, 5-647.
22. The temporary constitutions of the states and territories set up after the overthrow of Santa Anna reflected these same concepts. See, for example, those of Oaxaca, Zacatecas, Querétaro, Michoacán, Tlaxcala, San Luis Potosí, Guerrero, Tehuantepec, Baja California, Sinaloa, and Nuevo León in *Siglo*, October 1, 7, 10, 23; December 27, 1855; and February 3, 4, 28, 1856. All spoke of the natural rights of the individual such as liberty, equality before the law, property, and freedom of the press and speech with some limitations regarding attacks on religion and private affairs. Most of the constitutions said nothing about religious toleration. Querétaro, however, specified that the Roman Catholic religion would be the only one allowed.
23. *Ibid.*; March 28, 1856.

tablished a federal system with the three branches of government. Stress, however, was placed on a single house legislative body. The rights of man were the first subjects considered. Article I declared: The Mexican nation recognizes that the rights of man are the base and the object of social institutions; consequently all the laws and all the authorities of the country must respect and defend the guarantees granted under this constitution. The liberals went on in a total of twenty-nine articles to define the rights of man. Under the constitution no man could be enslaved nor could he be imprisoned for debt; education was to be free; every man could embrace the profession, industry or work he desired; personal service should receive just payment; within certain limits, freedom of press, of speech, and of association would prevail; any man who wished to do so could carry arms; titles of nobility were prohibited; everyone had the right to enter and leave Mexico as he desired; no special tribunals were to be erected nor retroactive laws passed; the death penalty was abolished for political crimes; with some exceptions monopolies were prohibited; the right of petition and assembly was guaranteed; judicial costs were abolished; property was sacred except in the case of eminent domain. The final clause provided that in times of grave crises these guarantees could be suspended.

Most of these propositions excited little controversy. Real debate came, however, over two rejected items—trial by jury and religious toleration. Those who opposed the establishment of the jury system contended that it was incompatible with procedure under Roman law. They emphasized even more strongly their belief that the Mexican people were not yet ready for such an innovation. On the vote, trial by jury was defeated 42-40.[24]

No debates were more bitter than those over religious toleration for on this point the liberals were divided. The Comonfort administration refused to support the measure and members of the government spoke against it. But the economic and political motivation behind the liberals' attack against the church is most clearly shown in these debates.[25]

Many liberals, both moderate and radical, wanted the article in-

---

24. Zarco, *Congreso*, II, 159-183; 993-997.
25. See the author's summary in "Church and State at the Mexican Constitutional Convention, 1856-1857," *Americas*, IV, No. 2.

cluded in the constitution, and in his speech to the congress on July 29, José Antonio Gamboa touched on the main arguments of those who favored it. He began by affirming his Catholic faith and declaring that he spoke as a Catholic. He then presented religious toleration as having two aspects: does man have the right to choose how he will worship God and would the country be better off if religious freedom existed. These were the social, humanitarian, and political ideologies involved. Gamboa regarded the first question as already answered; the age of Torquemada had passed and society was living in the century of liberty and the brotherhood of man.

To the second question, he replied that for Mexico toleration was a matter of life and death since upon it depended immigration, and without immigration Mexico could never exploit her great riches. Indeed Gamboa doubted that the country could hold together for very long under existing conditions. A small population was scattered over a vast territory and because of their isolation Mexicans lacked the feeling of national unity. In addition there was no internal unity because there were no roads; no agriculture because of the lack of farm hands, and no industry because of the lack of capital.

The conservatives, he charged, were satisfied with the status quo and in order to prevent changes they wanted to stop all reforms and keep the people ignorant. But the liberal party would lead the people forward to liberty and progress. To aid in the task they should call on their European brothers, who would bring strength and ingenuity, and in return Mexico would give them riches and a future. But how could they be invited without freedom of religion? What Mexican would go to a country without a Catholic church? To blame lack of immigration on a lack of security was incorrect, for the Germans had migrated to the United States at an early period in its history. Moreover, when such peoples as the Germans moved, they always went in large numbers under the guidance of a clergyman who was their leader. Protestants lived in Mexico, it was true, but with their foot in the stirrup as it were. They could not be happy nor take root, for Mexican law did not even recognize their marriages. The Europeans living in Mexico did not settle permanently and the wealth they produced returned to Europe thus impoverishing the country. Increased population through immigration was necessary not only to Mexico's economic life but to its very national existence, for only by increasing its population could Mexico stop the territorial advances of the United States. The basic argument on which the liberals rested their case was this: religious toleration would result in the arrival of hard-working Protestant immigrants from Europe who would promote and stimulate economic development and who would communicate to the Mexicans that desire for individual improvement so lacking at present.

A speech by Marcelino Castañeda included most of the arguments used by those who spoke against religious toleration. He felt that the Mexican people did not want religious toleration and as the convention represented those people, the delegates should follow their wishes and proclaim the Catholic religion as that of the nation. To pass legislation of which the people disapproved would be absurd, for such a law could never be enforced. If the convention did so, it would only be adding another element of discord. Other speakers had claimed, said Castañeda, that without freedom of religion Mexico would not have immigration, without immigration it would not have population, without population it would not have roads, and without all these it would have neither agriculture nor industry. Religious toleration would not solve these problems. First must come peace, justice, good government, and guarantees of order and security. Then would come prosperity; then Mexico would have both capital and industry.

Thus those opposed to the article used the argument that religious toleration, by encouraging Protestants to settle in Mexico, would introduce new discord into an already divided country. What Mexico needed above all else was peace, and only with internal peace and stability could it hope for immigrants and foreign capital. The statement of the opposition, "now is not the time," was probably the most telling argument against religious toleration.

After days of debate, the convention finally decided by a vote of 65-44 that it was not ready to consider the question. When the results became known there was a great deal of commotion. In the galleries there were shouts of Viva Religion! Death to the Heretics! Death to the Cowards! The galleries had to be cleared before order could be restored and the article sent back to committee.

On January 24, 1857, at the close of the day's session when many deputies were getting ready to leave, the committee asked permission to retire the article completely. The proposal created quite a discussion as to whether there could be such a proposal. After some disorder a vote was decided upon, but since a quorum was not present the decision had to be postponed. Two days later by a vote of 57-22 the committee was permitted to retire the article.

Ponciano Arriaga then presented a resolution which gave the federal government power to intervene in matters of religious observance and external discipline as provided by law. He urged adoption of this measure on the ground that the federal government could exercise only those powers specifically granted to it by the constitution, and nothing in that document gave the government any control over ecclesiastical affairs. A positive statement was needed to insure the superiority of civil government over ecclesiastical authority, and its omission would make the government powerless in the face of ecclesiastic encroachments. Failure to grant such a power to the government would encourage the reactionaries, since they would deduce from the convention's silence that it did not know what the people really wanted. After a very brief discussion, the Arriaga proposal was adopted by a vote of 82-4 and became Article 123 of the constitution.[26]

Liberals in general shared the belief that their country lagged far behind its potential in economic and social progress because of the stifling influence of the clergy, the military, and the conservatives in general. On the broad questions affecting the church and its role in Mexican life under the new constitution, most of the liberals agreed. They felt that its political and economic power ought to be curbed, its special privileges abolished, and the clergy reformed. The Ley Juárez had already deprived the clergy of some of its special privileges and liberal opinion favored in addition making the clergy ineligible to vote or hold public office. The liberals believed that the clergy was too engrossed in its wealth and privileges to concentrate properly on its religious duties, and therefore favored measures which would limit the clergy's outside interests.

Nor did the liberals argue very much among themselves about depriving the clergy of its lands. The Ley Lerdo, promulgated by

---

26. Zarco, *Congreso.*, I, 771-776, 788-798; II, 93-96, 813-824.

the Comonfort government on June 25, 1856, was intended to disamortize the land held in mortmain by the church. This law did not confiscate church property and it did not deprive the church of its wealth. The property was to be sold and the proceeds turned over to the church, with the purchaser paying a five per cent sales tax to the government. In fact the Ley Lerdo permitted the corporations themselves to make conventional sales of the estates. Church officials felt, however, that they did not have the authority to recognize the right of the civil government to enact such laws, nor to enter into or give assent to any agreement without first obtaining the Pope's approval. But since the three month period given them by the law to sell their property did not allow sufficient time to communicate with Rome, they did nothing about sales, and the sales were made according to the provisions of the law, without the assent of the church.[27]

But here was an apparent paradox, for in the society the liberals were trying to create property was to be sacred. On this point there can be no doubt; they firmly believed in private property and condemned the socialists and the communists for their concept of property.[28] How, then, could they justify forcing the church to dispose of its lands? The answer was easy—by applying the principle of utility (the greatest good for the greatest number). "The right of property is the most sacred of all . . . but the state can modify a right of an individual or individuals when it is to the general interest of the community. All that the individual may ask is indemnification."[29] Obviously, the liberals felt the sale of church lands was in the general interest of the community. The entire country would benefit enormously:

> The country owes Lerdo a vote of thanks. From now on the monopoly of unproductive lands will cease; soon the bankruptcy of the treasury will cease and confidence in its financial operation will resume; labor, from which emanates all that is necessary or gratifying to man, will be stimulated by capital, that powerful lever of production; the law will serve as a point of departure for the reform of the taxation system; it will be conducive to the quick abolition of special

27. F. Hall, *The Laws of Mexico* (San Francisco, 1885), 223.
28. See, for example, the articles on property by Iglesias, *Siglo*, August 18-September 7, 1856.
29. *Constituyente*, Oaxaca, July 13, 1856.

duties; . . . it will increase the number of owners; it will directly help develop agriculture; . . . it will help in a thousand ways industries that today are in a state of complete paralysis; it will permit the government to dedicate itself to introducing improvements, among others the opening of the ways of communication; . . . the pensioners of the treasury will have an old age without privation; our frontiers will be free of devastating invasions of the Indians; . . . and finally it will develop forcibly the spirit of private initiative.[30]

In the liberals' dream of the rosy future, small landholders would develop the country by cultivating unused lands, and the taxes from the sale of each piece of property would fill the treasury. These expectations from the Ley Lerdo were based on a deep respect for property and a belief in the beneficial consequences of small, private ownership. Give each individual a chance to own property and he would produce more than under the system of town and church ownership. The press also stressed the idea of hard work and thrift. The Ley Lerdo did not, of course, produce the anticipated results; it simply transferred the ownership of large landholdings from the church to private individuals and led to a great deal of speculation in land. The lower classes and the Indians could not afford to become owners, and the list of sales[31] included very few small transactions.[32] Although some liberals, as Ignacio Ramírez, opposed the law because it did not confiscate church property, it aroused little debate at the constitutional convention and was incorporated into the constitution as Article 27.

While all the liberals did not believe that religious toleration

30. *Republicano,* July 2, 1856, cited in *Siglo,* July 3, 1856.
31. Lists are in Miguel Lerdo de Tejada, *Cuadro sinóptico de la república mexicana en 1856 formado en vista de los últimos datos oficiales* . . . . (México, 1856).
32. G. M. McBride, *The Land Systems of Mexico* (New York, 1923) and H. Phipps, *Some Aspects of the Agrarian Question in Mexico* (Austin, 1925) have studied the question of the small landholder, but much still needs to be done. For example, what can be discovered by looking into the large number of *señoras* who bought land? How many states in 1856-1857 put the law into effect? Apparently Nuevo León did not. *Siglo,* March 25, 1857, and *Diario de Avisos,* May 21, 1857. In how many places, as in Zacatecas, was the property overvalued by the system where the rent paid was to be capitalized at six per cent, in order to determine the value of the property? In Zacatecas the worst rental housing brought about thirteen pesos per year which, by the six per cent rule, put the value on the property at a little over 200 pesos. Actually such a unit was worth seventy or eighty pesos at most. *Siglo,* July 17, 1856. Property not rented was to be sold at public auction to the highest bidder.

would bring foreigners to Mexico, most of them did think that immigration could be encouraged by proper economic measures. As a step in this direction the constitution abolished most monopolies and allowed individual initiative a clear field. Another objective which they regarded as essential was the improvement of transportation, not just by building roads and railroads but by removing all interference, especially the taxes, on goods passing from one state to another.³³ Some agitation existed for free trade but a substantial number of the liberals disapproved, maintaining that a tariff was necessary. They did agree that articles heretofore excluded should be allowed to enter the country.

To recapitulate: the liberals wanted to establish a federal system of government, to restrict the power of the clergy, to encourage the capitalistic system, to make education free, to establish political and juridical equality, and to develop individual initiative. One can probably say that they felt that enlightened self-interest was the key to social advancement.³⁴ They further recognized that economic rights must be guaranteed by political rights. Freedom to possess property and to follow any profession or trade was of little value without the corresponding freedom of press and speech.

Where did the conservatives stand? By relying on ageless theological points, Aristotle, and on later writers as Joseph de Maistre, they set forth their position. On governmental form the answer was easy. They believed in centralism as the most efficient way to run a government.³⁵ To the question: is it possible for man to govern himself? J. J. Pesado, one of the outstanding conservative thinkers, replied:

> Civil governments are not enough in themselves and an extraneous power is needed that will mark the road for them, give them the vigor they lack and that will win them the love and respect of those who obey. Such a powerful aid can only

33. Newspaper reports in 1856-1857 show that states which repealed such taxes in 1855-1856 had soon reimposed them. The *alcabala* was a vital source of income for the states. Deprived of it they became dependent on the national government.
34. Due to the complete lack of studies of businessmen in Mexico, positive statements on their position cannot be made.
35. This idea may be found in any of the conservative publications of the period, such as *La Cruz, Sociedad* and *Diario de Avisos*.

come from religion because it has the resources that work in the hearts of men.[36]

Moreover:

> Man, degraded in his first day . . . experiences inside himself two forces, two opposing forces, that are the flesh and the spirit, sin and grace. Religion teaches him the true situation, his origin, his fall and his atonement. Political laws are always insufficient because they work on the exterior of man without reaching his heart; it is here that the germs of rebellion die and where individual interests opposed to the common good are born.[37]

Certainly Pesado believed that civil governments were profane and the best to be expected from them was that they would support the Catholic Church. A centralized administration at least made it easier to direct and control the component parts.

The conservatives' concept of sovereignty differed sharply from the liberals'. Sovereignty on earth should be delegated to the proper few; the idea of allowing each state (and individual) to run its own affairs was sheer anarchy. Pesado expressed himself very firmly on this subject:

> The human will is unlimited and if from it is born sovereignty it will also be unlimited. Who does not see in this the principle of despotism? . . . . There is a power to which it must subject itself which is outside of it. Attributing to all men the right and exercise of sovereignty, it is said that man is entirely free. This is false. Collective sovereignty and reasonable liberty are incompatible. Any society that exercises sovereignty upon itself converts itself into a troop of slaves; yes, slaves by common consent, that changes at all hours. To give a people sovereignty is to constitute it as a despot; . . . its legislation lacks not only fixed principles but wisdom and duration. If the people have the right to form their own constitution they will have the equal right to alter it by their whim with reason or without it; if the people have the right to make one constitution a hundred will be made because it is the condition of the people to be unsettled; and if it has the right to unseat one authority it can take away all authority. What guarantee does a society have under these condi-

---

36. *La Cruz*, July 9, 1857. *La Cruz* was undoubtedly the most intelligent conservative publication in the period and Pesado, who did a great deal of writing for it, took extremely intelligent positions.
37. *Ibid.*, August 20, 1857.

tions? . . . . There is no society in which there are not a greater number of ignorant than learned, of inconsiderate than prudent, in short, more bad than good. As such, placing sovereignty in the hands of the people means placing control in the hands of the ignorant. . . . The exercise of sovereignty must rest in the hands of the just and learned who make good use of their power. . . . The idea of sovereignty of the people is the legitimate one of protestantism.[38]

The conservatives could not accept the form of government advocated by the liberals, nor could they accept liberal views on the matter of church-state relations. Pesado again stated the conservative point of view. At one time, he declared, the opponents of religion assailed it openly; they tore down the altars of the true God, proclaimed the cult of reason and publicly worshipped a prostitute. But now the attackers used a different procedure. They pretended to venerate Jesus Christ but did not recognize Him as God. They praised parts of His doctrine and objected to others. They spoke highly of the words of God and at the same time persecuted His Church, its beliefs, ceremonies, discipline, law, and priests. Pesado claimed that revoking the special privileges of the clergy was essentially destructive of the church, for the Ley Juárez implied a rejection of the Pope as head of the church and a denial of the complete jurisdiction of the ministers in church affairs.

Some of the most heated discussions arose over the wealth of the church. The liberals quoted "My reign is not of this world" as support for their view that the clergy should not hold temporal possessions. Pesado replied that the liberals continually used the fact of clerical wealth as justification for expropriation, as if the right of one individual prejudiced the rights of others. The wealth acquired by the church was used for the public welfare, since it served to sustain Catholicism, succor the poor, and alleviate public calamities. Since the church disapproved of usury, the interest and rent which it collected from its holdings had always been small. Every individual had the right to acquire possessions and to keep what he had acquired, for without the right of property there could be no family, no society, no government. Companies or associations had the same rights as individuals. Therefore the state could not

38. *Ibid.*, September 3, 1857. Obviously implied here and found at more depth in other statements is the necessity of historical evolution. The liberals, in general, denied history by denouncing the Spanish background.

deprive the church of its property, which it had obtained legally and which it used for the general good.³⁹

Some of the liberals had joined the issue of religious toleration to the problem of encouraging immigration, but from the conservative viewpoint toleration was not a prerequisite for increasing immigration. Naturally they opposed a policy of toleration and the liberal arguments in its favor, especially since the liberals equated Protestantism with progress and advancement. Pesado, in *La Cruz*, and Morales in *Siglo*, debated at length the proposition that Catholic countries were more backward than Protestant ones.

The conservatives wanted immigrants but wanted them to be Catholics on the grounds that peace and order were necessary for industry and commerce to flourish. Different religious sects would introduce elements of discord and therefore would retard social stability for many years. On this point moderate liberals, as we have noted, supported conservative opinion. Conservatives declared that continual changes in governments and tariffs could not be attributed to lack of toleration but to lack of economic development. Nor was toleration necessary to encourage foreigners to invest capital. Very early in the republic's history mines had been developed with money lent by Europeans.

In spite of many interruptions, including in January performances of *La Cabaña del Tío Tomás—Uncle Tom's Cabin—*that everybody who was anybody went to see, the constitutional convention completed its work early in February, 1857. Although liberal principles had triumphed, many government supporters regarded the constitution with real misgivings.⁴⁰

An unenviable task confronted the president: to put into effect a constitution which few supported ardently and many opposed vociferously. Nor was that the sum of his trouble. In addition he faced the delicate operation of keeping the church in line without giving way on the principles of the reform, and at the same time restraining the radicals who might destroy this balance.⁴¹ The gov-

---

39. *Ibid.*, May 8, 1856; January 29, 1857; October 9, 16, 1856.
40. See, for example, Doblado, February 28, 1857, to Terán. Terán Typescripts, University of Texas. Comonfort himself later said that he had had no great faith in the constitution. Vigil, *Reforma*, 221-222.
41. As early as July, Comonfort felt that one of the disturbing elements among the liberals was the exaggeration of some of the deputies in the constitutional convention. Comonfort, July 24, 1856, to Joaquín Moreno. Comonfort Papers, MSS, University of Texas. Yet a month earlier, June 14, in writing to Moreno

ernment's financial position was, as usual, shaky and revenues had to be found somewhere. Relations with foreign countries, especially Spain, had deteriorated and were demanding attention. Preparations had to be made for the forthcoming presidential elections. And there were always revolts to quell.⁴² Yet in spite of these vexing problems the government looked strong in February, 1857. It had recently suppressed revolts in Puebla and San Luis Potosí; it had obtained complete submission from Vidaurri to its authority; it had settled the outstanding differences with England and was negotiating a loan with the United States.⁴³ Furthermore, Comonfort had survived a cabinet crisis in late December when Lerdo had resigned.

But the constitution posed the main question. Many liberals hoped that the conservatives would accept their defeat and proceed legally by forming a party for the coming elections. To encourage such participation, the government very early in February granted amnesty to political prisoners. On March 11 the government promulgated the constitution and six days later decreed that all government employees, military and civil, must swear allegiance to it or lose their posts.

While the conservative opposition was immediately apparent, the church did not take a formal stand until November 13 when the Archbishop of Mexico issued a circular ordering the clergy not to take an oath to support the constitution.⁴⁴ The archbishop also gave the clergy instructions on how to deal with Catholics who swore to support the new constitution. Such persons were not to receive an ecclesiastical burial, and priests were to say no masses

he admitted that he had to have the support of the radicals in order to carry out his reforms. *Ibid.*
42. Comonfort, writing to Terán on December 15, 1856, expressed his frustration. No sooner had he quashed one rebellion when another began. Terán Typescripts.
43. The United States was to loan Mexico $15,000,000; $3,000,000 was to be used to pay the claims of citizens of the United States against Mexico; $4,000,000 was to pay for the British Convention. Forsyth, February 10, 1857, to Marcy. Manning, *Mexico*, IX, 891-893.
44. A few clergymen refused to carry out the archbishop's orders and were suspended. The group included Plácido Anaya, Rodrigo Victoria, Francisco de Paula Campa, José María Sastra (*Diario de Avisos*, April 28, 1857), Moreno y Jove, Verdugo y Sagasita (*Nación*, October 12, 1857), and Ramón Valenzuela (*Ibid.*, March 16, 1857). One at least, Paula Campa, repented and asked forgiveness (*Eco Nacional*, November 17, 1857). While the number of insurgent clergy was not great, it was at least large enough to make the conservative press work about a possible schism.

for anyone who died without making a retraction, particularly if they had been buried in sacred ground by orders of the civil authorities. Nor were priests to hear the confessions of persons who had taken the oath unless they first repudiated it, and only those who had done their best to prove their repentance should receive absolution. These same restrictions were to apply to anyone who had taken over church property under the provisions of the Ley Lerdo.[45] Thus anyone who had already taken the oath would have to make a public retraction. The church drew the issue clearly; if a man held any government post he was under moral obligation to resign. If he persisted in following the civil authority he was doomed to hell.

Most conservatives believed that Comonfort would never govern a peaceful country, no matter how many troops he had at his disposal, until the constitution was altered.[46] The clergy especially became more convinced of this after the government promulgated laws abolishing parochial obventions and secularizing the cemeteries. The church, of course, repudiated both laws. But, nonetheless, government employees, state and national, proceeded to take the oath, with varying amounts of disturbances.[47] Some employees resigned rather than take the oath, and of course the conservative press made much of these incidents. But, apparently, their numbers were few.[48]

In spite of all these difficulties and of small revolts in various localities, Comonfort did not postpone the elections. Some of the radicals tried to persuade Miguel Lerdo to run for the presidency but they were unsuccessful, and Comonfort faced no real opposition.[49]

45. W. H. Callcott, *Liberalism in Mexico*, 1857-1929 (Stanford, 1931), 9-10.
46. For example, see *Eco Nacional*, December 6, 1857.
47. Local leaders in the state of Mexico described, in their reports to the governor, March to June, 1857, some of the difficulties created by the clergy's open hostility to the constitution. M. Riva Palacio Papers.
48. In March and April, 1857, *Diario de Avisos* indicated that actually disturbances over the oath were more common than other newspapers, such as *Siglo*, would imply.
49. The newspapers *Clamor Progresista* and *Página* were started to support Lerdo's candidacy. With the first issue of *Clamor* its editor, Ignacio Ramírez, was arrested, forced out of his civil judgeship, and fined 300 pesos. *Siglo*, May 14, June 5, 1857. Zarco, in *Siglo*, took Lerdo to task for not condemning the paper for he felt that *Clamor* was a nasty sheet. Lerdo's silence indicated support for the paper's ideas. Although Lerdo finally did denounce the paper, Zarco felt his action came too late. *Siglo*, June 20, 1857.

With Comonfort as president and a new congress[50] which was to convene September 16, 1857, the government was ready to function. But not until October 8 were enough deputies present to constitute a quorum. By this time great apprehension existed over the increasingly disturbed conditions in the country. Shortly after the sessions began and even before he had appointed his new cabinet, Comonfort asked congress for extraordinary powers. The deputies were unwilling to act until after the president had named his cabinet because they wanted to see if he would place conservatives in power. On October 20 the president announced his cabinet: Fuentes, Manuel Ruiz, García Conde, Payno, and Juárez. Reassured by these appointments and especially Juárez' inclusion, congress began considering the president's request in secret session late in October. On November 3 it approved the bill and Comonfort proclaimed it on the same day.

In spite of the federal government's increased power, small revolts continued all over the country, and by late November rumors of an impending coup d'état circulated freely. On December 17, 1857, rumor became fact.[51] The conservatives under the leadership of General Felíz Zuloaga issued the Plan of Tacubaya.[52] The plan revoked the Constitution of 1857 and provided for the election of a new constituent assembly, but it recognized Comonfort as president and conferred extraordinary powers upon him. Two days later Comonfort announced support of the plan, for he felt that by temporarily assuming dictatorial powers he could hold the extremists on both sides in check and pursue a middle course, always his object.

It soon became obvious that such an assumption was mere wishful thinking. He had expected all elements to rally to his support and

50. Francisco Bulnes, *Juárez y las revoluciones de Ayutla y de la Reforma* (México, 1905), 247-249, feels that the country did not approve of the constitution since only twenty-one of those who had served at the constitutional convention were reelected to the national congress. No positive evidence supports this thesis. Nor does any positive evidence support the idea that since many of the delegates lived in Mexico City they were ineligible for election because the new constitution provided that a deputy had to be a resident of the district he represented. Assuming that this election followed the pattern of most Mexican elections in the 19th century, the logical explanation for the change in the make-up of the congress is that Comonfort and the state governors controlled the election.
51. See Manuel Payno, *Memoria sobre la revolución de diciembre de 1857 y enero de 1858* (México, 1860), for an account of the plotting.
52. Text of the plan in Vigil, *Reforma*, 267.

while the first reports from the states were favorable, he soon realized that he could not count on the liberals in the capital. Then came word that Doblado in Guanajuato would not second the plan, nor Parrodi in Jalisco nor Arteaga in Querétaro. When the city of Veracruz on December 31 revoked its approval and several other localities followed, it was apparent that Comonfort's hopes were doomed to failure. Since December 17 men and events had pulled him in so many different directions that he was unable to decide on a definite course of action. His vacillation aroused the suspicions of the conservatives and on January 11 another *pronunciamiento* by Zuloaga removed Comonfort from the presidency. With that, Comonfort swung back to the liberals and in doing so gave the liberals at least one break. The president released Juárez from the prison in which he had been locked up by Zuloaga, but beyond that he could achieve nothing to help the liberal cause. Fighting broke out in the capital between Comonfort's troops and those of Zuloaga, but Comonfort's efforts to get control of the city were futile, and on January 21, he left the capital on his way to exile in the United States. The conservatives then chose Zuloaga as the new president.

It seems strange that Comonfort could have deluded himself into expecting that the liberals would follow him when he supported the Plan of Tacubaya. On the very day of the December revolt the liberals in congress passed a resolution protesting the act and advising the states to defend the legal government.[53] Comonfort's resignation removed the last technical hindrance to the organization of a new liberal government, for it meant that Juárez as chief justice could now succeed legally as temporary president. Thus began a battle of the center of Mexico (conservatives) against the outlying areas (liberals)—a fight to be repeated after the arrival of the French and Maximilian.

53. The statement with its signers is given in *Ibid.*, 282-283.

Chapter II

WAR OF REFORM

The liberal government assembled in Guanajuato with the new president. There were names better known throughout the country than that of Benito Juárez, yet surely no other Mexican believed more doggedly than he in the justice of the liberal cause and in its inevitable triumph. Impassive and slow to act, but standing by his decision once it was made, he was a firm rock in the midst of all the difficulties—the quarrels, the betrayals, the defeats.

Juárez was born in San Paulo Guelatao in the state of Oaxaca, on March 21, 1806, of Indian parents both of whom died before he was four years old.[1] Relatives cared for him until, at the age of twelve, he went to live with his sister in the city of Oaxaca. There he had the good fortune to attract the attention of an old priest who taught him the elements of Spanish grammar and reading. Later he attended the city schools where his grades were excellent. He began the study of law but even before obtaining his degree in 1834 he had begun to participate in politics.

In 1831 he was elected a member of the city council of Oaxaca and in 1832-1834 he served as a member of the state legislature. Juárez was imprisoned for a short time in 1836 on the charge that he was anti-conservative, but in the early forties he associated himself with General León, Governor of Oaxaca, who was anything but liberal. In this period of Juárez' early adventures into politics, liberal and conservative tendencies were mixed, though with the liberal perhaps predominating—a confusion of ideas not at all uncommon among men who are just beginning to find their way up the political ladder. Juárez also taught in Oaxaca and served as a judge, and in 1846 entered national politics as a member of congress. He did nothing to distinguish himself as a legislator, and

1. Most of the available information about Juárez' childhood and youth comes from his *Datos autobiográficos de Dn. Benito Juárez* published in J. M. Puig Casauranc, ed., *Archivos privados de D. Benito Juárez y D. Pedro Santacilia* (México, 1928), which he wrote later in life. Although the autobiographical sketch is generally accepted as being authentic, one must keep in mind that Juárez was writing both as a parent and politician, and on each count he undoubtedly wished to make a good impression.

the evidence suggests that he happily accepted the appointment as governor of his native state. He retained this post and administered it efficiently until 1853 when Santa Anna ordered him into exile. He lived in New Orleans until the Revolution of Ayutla returned him to national politics.

With Juárez in Guanajuato was Melchor Ocampo, one of the truly interesting men of the period, whose death in 1861 was a great loss to the liberal party. During his term of office as Governor of Michoacán, Ocampo carried on a long debate with the clergy which ended when Santa Anna reassumed power and banished him. He and Juárez became good friends during their shared exile in New Orleans and it was apparently at this time that Ocampo, with his fine and inquisitive mind, began to exert his influence over Juárez and to assume the intellectual leadership of the liberals.[2] Juárez now appointed his friend to head the cabinet as Minister of Relations.

The original cabinet also included Prieto, Manuel Ruiz, León Guzmán, and Doblado. Doblado's refusal to second the Plan of Tacubaya had been good news to the liberals, and his acceptance of a cabinet post increased the government's prestige in the interior. On January 19, 1858, while his government (soon to be called the "sick family") was still in Guanajuato, Juárez issued a manifesto to the nation. In it he declared that his was the legal government and he reaffirmed his determination to continue supporting the Constitution of 1857.

From Guanajuato, Juárez and his cabinet moved to Guadalajara where they arrived in mid-February. A month later the liberal government almost came to an abrupt and dramatic end, saved only by Prieto's courage and ever-ready tongue. On the morning of March 13, to the cry of "Viva Religión," a group of conspirators among the troops imprisoned Juárez, Ocampo, Guzmán, Ruiz, and Prieto. A daring but unsuccessful raid by loyal soldiers convinced the rebels that they should shoot the president without further waste of time. Just as the commander of the firing squad ordered

---

2. *Obras de Ocampo*, I. If the volumes in Juárez' personal library accurately reflected his views, then Proudhon must have had a considerable influence on his thinking. In this connection it must be remembered that the substance of Proudhon's economic program, the mutual productive society, was so much a commonplace of the social thought of his period that it received the approval of Napoleon III and John Stuart Mill.

his men to fire, Prieto jumped out in front of Juárez and shouted to the soldiers to raise their guns. So agitated that he later could not remember what he had said, he continued to exhort the men to hold their fire and raise their guns. After some tense moments they finally did so, and the danger was over. Juárez embraced his friend; the others surrounded Prieto and called him the saviour of the Reform.³ An arrangement was finally worked out by which the rebels, who knew *juarista* troops were approaching, agreed for a price to set the president and cabinet free and to leave Guadalajara.

A few days before this incident, on March 9-10, liberal troops under the command of Doblado and Anastasio Parrodi had been routed by a conservative army at Salamanca, Guanajuato. The liberals committed unpardonable errors with expensive results, for this single engagement opened most of the interior to conservative forces. It also cost the liberals one of their strongest supporters for Doblado surrendered at Silao, retaining his freedom on the condition that he would not in the future take any active part in the war. Parrodi retreated to Guadalajara where he and Degollado both arrived on the eighteenth.

At this moment the liberal cause seemed rather forlorn. About all the liberals could really call their own were certain areas in northern Mexico, Veracruz, and some portions south of Mexico City. The government was completely without funds and was expecting the conservatives to attack Guadalajara. Preparations were therefore made to shift the government to Veracruz, but because of the danger from conservative forces, it was decided that Juárez should proceed to the east coast via Panama and New Orleans. The situation was indeed gloomy—the conservatives almost captured Juárez as he made his way to Colima and on March 23 their troops occupied Guadalajara and Parrodi surrendered.

Juárez reached Colima on March 26. He had learned of Parrodi's surrender and now named Santos Degollado (soon to be called by two names—"The Saint of the Reform" and "The Hero of Defeats") to replace Parrodi as Minister of War.⁴ Degollado also received

---

3. The best description of this incident is in Prieto's poem, "Bello y sin par romance del 13 de marzo de 1858 de Guadalajara," *Colección de poesías escogidas* (México, 1897), 164-170.
4. For a sketch of Degollado see F. Ocaranza, ed., *Juárez y sus amigos* (2 vols., México, 1939-1942), I, 65-70. R. Roeder, *Juárez and His Mexico* (2 vols., New York, 1947), 173-174, also has a sketch.

the appointment of Commander of the Army of the North and West with wide powers. From a purely political point of view this was one of Juárez' better appointments, for Degollado's name carried considerable prestige in the interior.

In April Juárez left for Manzanillo, the Pacific coast port where he began his journey. After a long trip the members of the government arrived in Veracruz on May 4, 1858, where Governor Gutiérrez Manuel Zamora greeted the presidential party and arranged a celebration in their honor. Being back on Mexican soil cheered the liberals even though the city, with its malarial climate and its dirty streets and vultures hopping about in open gutters, was not exactly an earthly paradise. News that Degollado had been able to raise fresh troops in southern Jalisco also helped improve their spirits.

They needed encouragement for at this time an impartial estimate would have held the conservatives justified in believing that victory was theirs. In addition to the strategic city of Veracruz and some of the coastal regions, only a few areas in northern and southern Mexico remained in liberal hands. Two of their top generals had surrendered, and for the most part their armies hardly deserved the name. The conservatives held most of the major centers of population and could count on two very capable military leaders, Luis G. Osollos and Miguel Miramón. Very shortly (June 18) the former was killed in action, but Miramón, an uncommonly young man to be a general, carried on throughout the war. Under the circumstances liberal strategy had to be based on holding Veracruz and continuing guerrilla warfare in the center, and, surprisingly enough, the plan worked. In the spring of 1858, however, the conservatives were extremely confident of ultimate victory. Nor did any major changes take place during the remainder of the year which altered the military situation in any important respect. Thus a year after Comonfort's coup the atmosphere was no clearer.

In spite of the apparent strength of the conservative faction, dissension among the leaders was weakening their position. The quarrel came into the open on December 20, 1858, when General Miguel Echeagaray led a revolt against President Zuloaga. Three days later in Mexico City Manuel Robles Pezuela proclaimed himself the leader of the conservative group, and Zuloaga was forced to resign. Some of the conservatives then tried to work out an agreement with

Juárez for ending the war, but a statement issued by Juárez on December 29 indicated plainly that he would not be a party to such maneuvers; either the constitution was accepted or it was rejected. General Miramón's refusal to go along with the revolt against Zuloaga further complicated the situation. In January, 1859, Miramón, who had been with his troops near Guadalajara, returned to Mexico City and reestablished both Zuloaga and the Plan of Tacubaya. It was obvious, however, that President Zuloaga would not hold office much longer, and on January 31 a new decree made Miramón the president.

The liberals as well as the conservatives had internal troubles, the chief headache on their side being the northern leader, Santiago Vidaurri. While the government was in Guanajuato, Juárez had written to Vidaurri on January 29, 1858, asking for his cooperation against the conservatives. From his headquarters in Monterrey, Vidaurri replied, on January 31, that he would fight against the enemy but that he wanted no interference in his frontier area from federal troops.[5] In the absence of any federal authority he would have complete control over the men, money, and territory. Throughout August the central government faced the problem of trying to get Vidaurri's men to obey orders. Degollado finally reached the point where he would not yield to certain of Vidaurri's demands, and as a result the latter issued orders for his troops to leave the federal army. Degollado immediately denounced Vidaurri, and other military leaders supported Degollado. The liberal generals remained united in their opposition to the northern *caudillo*, and finally, in September, 1858, Vidaurri resigned and asked for a passport which the government granted.

As the year 1858 ended the most logical target for the conservatives' military operation seemed to be the liberal capital at Veracruz. Despite certain weaknesses in the center Miramón finally decided on the city as his next objective and in February, 1859, he left Mexico City to take charge of the campaign.[6] The liberal govern-

---

5. S. Roel, ed., *Correspondencia particular de D. Santiago Vidaurri, Tomo Primero, Juárez-Vidaurri* (Monterrey, 1946), 14-19.

6. Juárez, throughout the war, received fairly good information from Matías Acosta (pseudonym for León Guzmán?) in Mexico City. Ocaranza, *Juárez*, I, 11-45. In one of Acosta's letters he suggested the British legation was the best place to clear their letters. He and others kept up as much of an attack as possible in Mexico City through clandestine publications. *Ibid.*, 95-99.

ment made preparations for defense, and its efforts were bolstered by two other factors: the fever which plagued the conservative troops, and the offensive started by Degollado against Mexico City in March. The supplies which Miramón was expecting from the capital were not sent and he consequently abandoned his plan to attack Veracruz, beginning his retreat at the end of March. By this time Degollado was threatening Mexico City, but the conservatives managed to get reinforcements and when the full scale battle took place on April 10 and 11, Degollado's troops were driven back. Although the liberals suffered from the defeat in terms of men and equipment, they gained a mighty propaganda weapon. When the battle was won, the conservative command issued a general order to execute all captured officers. In addition to soldiers, the conservatives had among their prisoners a number of medical students who had come out from Mexico City to attend the wounded of both sides, and these young men were also shot. Several of them were members of prominent Mexican families—Rivera, Portugal, Díaz Covarrubias, and Abad. Although Generals Miramón and Márquez disclaimed responsibility for the crime and each tried to shift the blame to the other, the liberals seized upon these executions as a demonstration of the wanton cruelty which prevailed among the conservatives. For years they commemorated the death of the "martyrs of Tacubaya" with a day of national mourning.

Through the rest of the year conservative victories continued, and by the beginning of 1860 Miramón and his generals still had the military advantage. There had been one slight interruption in the fighting when Degollado made his first attempt to settle the war without further bloodshed. He arranged a meeting on November 12, 1859, near Querétaro, between himself and Miramón. The discussion was frank, but they failed to agree because Degollado insisted on conservative acceptance of the Constitution of 1857. The following day the two generals met again, this time in battle at Estancia de las Vacas, and once more Degollado was defeated. Liberal losses were enormous.[7]

During the two years of fighting both conservative and liberal governments were as concerned with revenues as with armies. Each

---

7. Z. Guerrero wrote Doblado on November 17, 1859, that the defeat would probably postpone the triumph of the liberals by a year. C. E. Castañeda, ed., *La guerra de reforma según el archivo del General D. Manuel Doblado, 1857-1860* (San Antonio, 1930), 173.

side became desperate, and by the beginning of 1860 both had shown themselves willing to negotiate with foreign countries on terms detrimental to the Mexican nation. Because of the financial situation both sides strove for foreign loans and probably devoted too much effort to this end. While they did so, the war went on and ended without either side's receiving any real amount of outside help.

The major military strength of the conservatives was at the same time their chief financial weakness. They did not hold ports, and the customs collected at the ports traditionally furnished the revenue to run a Mexican government.[8] With the regular sources of funds cut off, the conservative government obtained money from some of the local capitalists and the clergy by liens, and by forced loans whenever they were hard put.[9] This financial instability led to negotiations with the United States and Spain. The conservatives indicated their willingness to make great concessions to the former country, although no treaty was ever signed.

In many respects John Forsyth, the American Minister to Mexico, was an acute observer. On February 13, 1858, in reporting to the Department of State on the possibility of obtaining transit rights across the Isthmus of Tehuantepec and changing the northern boundary of Mexico, he stated:

> The Clergy is my main reliance, & there are powerful persons appealing to its interests to lend me its aid & influence. The new Government is wholly dependent upon the Church for support, all the Coasts and Custom Houses being in the hands of the "Coalition." The Church has already loaned its credit to the Government to the amount of a Million and a half of Dollars. It will be very difficult to negotiate these securities, and, at most, not more than fifty per cent can be realized upon them; because Capitalists fear to risk the stability of the Government, and know, that, if the *Puros* come in, the Church property will be declared National. The Church is thus between two fires; in danger, first, of being

---

8. Although the liberals held the ports, the revenues were for the most part pledged to pay off foreign debts.

9. Vigil, *Reforma*, 308-310, has published some of the records of the church *cabildo* in Mexico City showing various amounts contributed by the church to the conservative government. See, also, Miguel Galindo y Galindo, *La gran década nacional, o relación histórica de la guerra de reforma, intervención extranjera y gobierno del Archiduque Maximiliano 1857-1867* (3 vols., Mexico, 1904), I, 435-440.

ruined at a blow from the *Puros,* and equally sure of being ruined by its friends, the present Government. There is no escape but in filling the Treasury from abroad.[10]

As Forsyth suspected when he began negotiations, he found his ideas favorably received and began working through the Archbishop, Bishop Munguía, and conservative agent, Pesado. Forsyth also had a special meeting with Zuloaga in which the latter stated he was willing to go ahead with negotiations. Both realized that the Mexican Minister for Foreign Affairs was the stumbling block to the signing of a treaty. Zuloaga said that Cuevas, the minister, would have to agree to leave the cabinet. At this stage a new element was introduced. The Mexican government attempted to force Americans living in Mexico to pay a special war tax. Forsyth protested and after a nasty exchange of notes with Cuevas, Forsyth asked for his passport and returned to the United States.[11]

Negotiations with Spain were more successful, at least in that an agreement was reached which improved Mexican-Spanish relations.[12] The Mon-Almonte Treaty, signed on November 26, 1859, settled the difficulties existing between the two nations, but Spain received the concessions. Mexico agreed to recognize the claims of certain Spanish citizens against it and also to consider the Mexican-Spanish Treaty of 1853 again in force. By recognizing the Treaty of 1853, Mexico reassumed the obligation to pay claims which many Mexicans had regarded as cancelled, and the liberals, of course, denounced the treaty as an outrage. But neither the treaty with Spain nor the military victories helped fill the empty treasury. Because the financial situation was so bad, Miramón in October, 1859, agreed to the fantastic and infamous Jecker loan. By the terms of the loan Miramón contracted to repay Jecker and his associates $15,000,000 for the approximate $600,000 which the government received in the transaction.[13]

On the other hand, relations with the United States favored the liberals. Dispatches from the American ministers throughout the

10. Manning, *Mexico,* IX, 968-969.
11. *Ibid.,* 969-994.
12. For a complete description see *El Tratado Mon-Almonte,* Vol. 13 of the *Archivo Histórico Diplomático Mexicano.* Hereinafter this set will be cited as AHDM.
13. Manuel Payno, *México y sus cuestiones financieras con la Inglaterra, la España y la Francia* (México, 1862), 254-276.

nineteenth century evince clearly their intense dislike of the conservative-clerical groups and their fear that some European nation would establish a monarchy in Mexico. After the Tacubaya revolt the United States had followed the usual procedure, as had the European powers, of recognizing the government which controlled Mexico City. Although the American Minister, Forsyth, had attempted to negotiate a treaty with the conservatives, relations were broken off, as we have seen, over the question of a forced loan. The Juárez government worked hard for recognition by the United States and sent José María Mata to Washington to try to bring it about. In order to have his own information as a basis for decision, Secretary of State Lewis Cass sent William M. Churchwell as his executive agent to Mexico in December, 1858. Churchwell visited Veracruz, Jalapa, Perote, Puebla, Orizaba, Córdoba, and Mexico City. The Juárez government impressed him, particularly because he sensed that it was prepared to grant concessions, and he therefore recommended recognition.[14] Upon the basis of this report Cass ordered Robert McLane to Mexico and gave him the power to grant recognition if he saw fit. A short time after he arrived at Veracruz, McLane did so, and then began the long drawn out negotiations with Ocampo which led eventually to the signing of an agreement between the two nations.

The liberals had no right to a holier-than-thou attitude with regard to the Mon-Almonte Treaty for on their government fell the onus of having signed the McLane-Ocampo Treaty. One cannot justify on any basis the decision of the Juárez government to sign a treaty that granted to a foreign country the right of transit across Mexico's northern boundary and the Isthmus of Tehuantepec, and, at the same time, guaranteed the foreign government the right to send in troops to protect its citizens in these areas.

Since the treaty was so patently incompatible with Mexico's real interests and cannot be defended, it is all the more interesting to examine its background and the events which led to its signing. Obviously if the liberals were to continue to fight they had to have money. Normally revenues from customs would furnish a good income, but a large proportion of these had been pledged to European countries to pay off debts contracted before the war began.

14. Churchwell, Veracruz, February 9, 1859, to Cass. Manning, *Mexico*, IX, 1024-1030.

At the time the first negotiations for a loan from the United States began, the government had not yet nationalized church property.[15] The liberals hoped to get a loan from the United States with no strings attached, a rather optimistic assumption at any time, and particularly so when the President of the United States was talking about the annexation of northern Mexico. Lacking income and virtually destitute, the government began to sound out the United States.

As has been noted earlier, the United States had sent Churchwell as its special agent to Mexico and he had reported favorably on the Juárez government. McLane then came to Mexico, and agreeing with Churchwell's views, had recognized Juárez. Not altruism but real hopes of territorial aggrandizement at Mexico's expense motivated recognition. These hopes rested on the fact that Churchwell in his talks with the liberal leaders had persuaded them to indicate their "willingness . . . to negotiate affirmatively" upon several points. These included:

1. Cession of Lower California;
2. Transit or right of way from the Rio Grande to the Gulf of California, and perpetual right of way across the Isthmus of Tehuantepec;
3. A portion of the purchase money for the above to be applied to convention bonds;
4. Joint commissioners to adjust claims of the citizens of the United States against Mexico, these claims to be paid out of the purchase money;
5. Reciprocity in trade between the two countries;
6. No transit duties;
7. The United States to receive all commercial rights granted to other countries;
8. Efficient protection to be extended to the citizens of each country;
9. Mexico to reserve the right to make treaties with other nations in relation to the foregoing subjects.

Supplementary suggestions:

1. Free entry permitted to the effects and merchandise belonging to citizens or subjects of the United States or of any other country intended *bona fide* for transit through, and not for consumption within, the territories of Mexico;

15. The Reform Laws will be considered in Chapter III.

2. Mode of protection and defense of said transits to be agreed upon by convention between the two governments;
3. Transit or right of way from some suitable point on the Gulf of California to some point within the southern boundary of the United States.[16]

When McLane began to discuss some of the specific items with Ocampo, he found great reluctance to talk about the cession of Lower California. But on April 21, 1859, he reported the readiness of President Juárez to cede Lower California to the United States, but it was doubtful if the next congress would ratify such a provision. McLane, therefore, suggested separate treaties: one for transits and one for Lower California. He felt that, even if the new congress were elected before Juárez returned to Mexico City, the legislature would not have a quorum for some months. During that time the executive branch of the government would ratify the treaty. By July 10, McLane felt the chance to get Lower California had disappeared, but within two days he notified the Department of State that Lerdo was en route to the United States to negotiate a loan offering church property as security.[17] Lerdo, who had opposed any cession of territory except at an exorbitant price, was changing his views. Earlier he had wanted $30,000,000 for Lower California, but now he proposed to his colleagues that it be ceded for $15,000,000. McLane pointed out to his government that if Lerdo negotiated a loan in the United States it would mean that Mexico need not sell Lower California. If he failed, however, McLane felt that Lerdo would then advocate cession of territory.[18]

16. Manning, *Mexico*, IX, 1038. Mexican, as well as American, sources present evidence to show that the liberal government was willing to sell Lower California. Mata wrote to Ocampo from New York on February 19, 1859, saying that he felt that $20,000,000 was a fair price for Lower California. Paul Murray, *Tres norteamericanos y su participación en el desarrollo del tratado McLane-Ocampo, 1856-1860* (Guadalajara, 1946), 31. On the basis of Churchwell's later appearance in Mexico in 1861 and letters of Mata to Ocampo in March, 1861, Murray suggests the possibility that Churchwell received certain promises in Veracruz and that they were being carried out in 1861. *Ibid.*, 33-34.
17. McLane, Veracruz, April 7, 1859, to Cass. Manning, *Mexico*, IX, 1037-1044; 1050-1056; 1105-1106.
18. *Ibid.*, 1108-1109. Lerdo's opponents claimed that he went beyond his powers while in the United States. He made an agreement with a banker by which the banker would raise and send to Mexico 10,000 armed men. The Juárez cabinet considered the contract and rejected it. Ocampo even went so far as to call Lerdo a traitor, supposedly on the basis of bringing in foreign troops. Francisco Mejía, *Épocas, hechos y acontecimientos de mi vida*. MSS. University of Texas.

Whether the Department of State intervened to prevent the loan or not, the fact was that Lerdo was unable to raise any money in the United States. The negotiations in Mexico continued, but by late August McLane was aware that Juárez would not compromise the government by any cession of territory.[19] Although Ocampo had left the Ministry of Foreign Affairs on August 16 and de la Fuente now held the post, McLane found him no more yielding than Ocampo. McLane left for the United States where in September he held conversations with Lerdo and Mata.[20] What the three men talked about is not known, but on December 7, McLane, back in Veracruz, reported to Cass that Lerdo would not resume his duties as Minister of the Treasury unless Mexico signed a treaty with the United States based on the instructions sent to McLane in August; and that Juárez forced Juan Antonio de la Fuente to retire because of his persistent opposition to those stipulations in the proposed treaty. Consequently Ocampo had returned to the cabinet on December 1, and McLane expected to sign a treaty soon.[21] On December 14, 1859, the treaty was signed.

By the major provisions of the treaty the United States obtained transits and rights of way across the Isthmus of Tehuantepec, and from the Rio Grande and Arizona to the Gulf of California. It also obtained the right to employ military forces for the "security and protection of persons and property" passing over any of the area. For these concessions the Mexican government was to receive "the sum of four millions of dollars, of which, two millions shall be paid immediately upon the exchange of ratification . . . and the remaining two millions shall be retained by the government of the United States, for the payment of the claims of citizens of the United States against the government of . . . Mexico."[22]

Not only the conservatives immediately protested against the treaty, but also many of the liberals felt that the government had gone too far, and even in the government stronghold of Veracruz dissatisfaction was expressed. A newspaper in Ures summed up the liberal reaction: "Doesn't Sr. Juárez know that the liberal party prefers to fall anew under the double despotism of the military

19. Manning, *Mexico*, IX, 1118.
20. Murray, *Tres norteamericanos*, 40.
21. Manning, *Mexico*, IX, 1135-1136.
22. *Ibid.*, 1137-1141.

and the clergy before committing itself to a foreign yoke?"[23]

But the overpowering need for money drove the Juárez government to its decision. Degollado sent instructions to Mata on February 3, 1860, to try to negotiate an immediate loan of $500,000 on the basis of the two million coming from the treaty.[24] Mata of course was unable to get the money but he did his best to exert what pressure he could to get the treaty passed by the Senate of the United States. He employed Edward Dunbar, a correspondent of the *New York Times,* to help him;[25] he also informed his government that it had been indicated to him that if he had about $100,000 or more, he could get the votes needed to pass the bill.[26] McLane was also in Washington doing what he could, but all their efforts failed. Fortunately for Mexico, the Senate refused to accept the treaty.

The amazing part is that some members of the Juárez government continued to hope for ratification by the United States in spite of the furor in Mexico. Efforts continued toward this end as late as May 10, 1860, after Miramón's second attempt to take Veracruz had failed.[27] Certainly the liberals had sufficient information about the conservatives' trouble to know their opponents were getting weaker. Even then the desire for the treaty persisted. On October 4 and 5 the cabinet discussed extending the time limit for ratification. Ocampo, Llave, Emparan, and Mata (then in Veracruz) favored the extension; Fuente opposed it. Juárez sided with Fuente, and the cabinet finally decided against any change.

When the year 1860 began, the conservatives still were in the better military position. In February Miramón left Mexico City to have another try at Veracruz, hoping to give the liberals a crushing blow by driving them from their capital. This time he planned his campaign more carefully. In Havana he had bought two ships whose objective was to blockade the port so that supplies for the liberal forces could not enter while Miramón made his land attack. At the same time, these vessels would be in a position to send supplies to Miramón. The liberal government notified Washington

23. *Estrella de Occidente,* March 30, 1860.
24. Matías Romero, ed., *Correspondencia de la Legación Mexicana en Washington durante la Intervención Extranjera* (10 vols., México, 1870-1892, I, 193. Hereinafter cited as Romero, *Corr. Mex.*
25. *Ibid.*, 173.
26. Murray, *Tres norteamericanos,* 42.
27. Romero, *Corr. Mex.*, I, 216.

that since these two ships could not be considered Mexican they, therefore, constituted a piratical expedition. The ships arrived near Veracruz on March 6, and during the night the American squadron leader, Captain Joseph R. Jarvis, acting in accordance with instructions from his government, ordered an attack. After capturing the vessels he sent them to New Orleans where the district court declared his action illegal. But by that time the protests of the conservatives, the French, and the Spanish made no difference, for the forced change in Miramón's plans had completely disrupted his plan of attack, and he abandoned the campaign against Veracruz.

While Miramón was moving against Veracruz, Cornwallis Aldham, of the English ship *Valorous*, fowarded to the Juárez government a note from the British Minister to Mexico, G. B. Mathew. The message expressed the hope that the two Mexican groups would agree to an armistice, during which time the people would elect a congress to provide a new government. The cabinet discussed this proposal at a meeting on March 13, 1860. Attending were Degollado, Partearroyo, Ruiz, Lerdo, Emparan, Governor Zamora, and Ramón Iglesias. Illness kept Llave away. Lerdo believed that the Constitution of 1857 should be sacrificed, keeping only the reforms (of 1859), and that a triumvirate should be named. Degollado, Emparan, Ruiz, Partearroyo, Zamora, and Iglesias disapproved. Degollado wanted an armistice of six months to a year, during which time both sides could hold elections, a congress be called, and the constitution changed. Lerdo agreed.[28]

Juárez recorded: "I pointed out that a long armistice would be impractical and harmful and that it was a half measure which would result in a reactionary triumph, because a congress thus elected, if it did not approve the reactionary measures, would be broken up by force of arms. Therefore I would never authorize a treaty in which such a measure was included."[29] Ruiz supported the president and the rest of the cabinet then concurred.

On March 14 Juárez assigned Degollado and Emparan to meet with Miramón's commissioners. Degollado and Emparan reported back the proposal approved by the conference that commissioners should be named to meet in Tlálpam to arrange an armistice, after which the permanent peace would be arranged. But Miramón

28. Juárez, *Archivos privados*, 270-274.
29. *Ibid.*, 270-271.

War of Reform

would, under no circumstances, agree to accept the Constitution of 1857. The cabinet met. Lerdo favored ignoring the constitutional issue in carrying on negotiations, but the rest all believed that their government should reject any proposal not based on recognition of the present constitutional order. The delegates received instructions according to the majority sentiment. On this basis, of course, no agreement was possible. But the proposals to arrange a settlement did not stop. On March 25 Aldham again presented an official letter and this time he insisted that an agreement be reached. Juárez summoned his ministers on April 20 to discuss Aldham's note. "Lerdo insisted that we overlook the legal order, and propose any arrangement which would result in peace, because he believed the complete triumph of the constitutional party to be impossible. He was told that if our forces were organized and cooperated efficiently they could carry on the campaign successfully. Lerdo said that even so, he did not believe we could continue." The others believed the contrary. The cabinet, therefore, decided to inform Aldham that the government had made all the concessions possible, but that since Miramón would not agree, no progress could be made.

But Lerdo would not let the matter rest. Juárez recorded in his journal on April 23 that Lerdo asked for a meeting of the ministers. When they had gathered, he proposed, on the basis of a previous suggestion by Llave, that the government determine whether public opinion favored maintaining the present legal order or if it preferred having the government overlook legality. He also wanted to issue a circular to the governors asking them to send commissioners to Veracruz to discuss with the cabinet what might be done. Emparan and Llave considered this a good idea. Ruiz was against it. Juárez recorded: ". . . the convening of the commissioners was unnecessary and impractical and, furthermore, harmful to the public exchequer. We decided not to accept the proposal of Lerdo."[30]

With the collapse of the efforts at peaceful settlement, the fighting was once more resumed. Miramón returned to the campaign in the interior, but the failure at Veracruz was to prove fatal and the fortunes of the conservatives declined rapidly thereafter. Miramón retired to Mexico City[31] after his defeat at Silao on August

---

30. *Ibid.*, 271-273.
31. Led by Francisco Zarco the liberals in Mexico City attempted a coup

10, and the liberals occupied Guanajuato. Within another month their troops occupied most of the interior. But the government's troubles did not end with the coming of a brighter day. In the summer and fall of 1860 some of the military chiefs, particularly Degollado, displayed little confidence in their cause. Despairing letters sent to Juárez, and exchanged among the military themselves, reflected their pessimism.[32] Difficulties with Lerdo, Doblado, and González Ortega plagued the government; confusion increased with the rumor that Comonfort might return to Mexico.

The break with Lerdo, a minor affair compared to the others, came over his proposals to suspend payments on the foreign debts for a brief time. Juárez had agreed but then reversed his decision after public announcement of the suspension. Lerdo naturally felt that he had been completely rebuffed.[33]

The rumors concerning Comonfort involved Doblado since the feeling prevailed that the two of them were working together to arrange Comonfort's return.[34] Doblado had been in New Orleans in January and February, 1860, and Comonfort was there in the same period. Even Prieto was a little dubious about Doblado.[35] Actually, the rumors had basis in fact since the followers of the ex-president tried actively to get him back into the country. They realized that if their plans were to succeed they would need the help of Governor Zamora of Veracruz. Ezequiel Montes on July 23, wrote him suggesting, for all practical purposes, that Comonfort be brought back to replace Juárez.[36] While Zamora disapproved of the plan and refused his support, the possibility remained that its advocates might later find a way to carry it through.

against the conservative government in July, 1860. It failed when the government learned in advance about the plans. P. Mariano Cuevas, ed., *Diario de sucesos notables de Don José Ramón Malo, 1832-1864* (2 vols., México, 1948), II, 565; Ocaranza, *Juárez*, II, 33-37.
32. See, for example: General José López Uraga, Guadalajara, July 29, 1860, to Juárez. Ocaranza, *Juárez*, II, 116-117; Degollado, León, September 13, 1860, to Juárez. *Ibid.*, 55-56; Degollado, Guanajuato, August 29, 1860, to Ortega. José G. Ortega, *El golpe de estado de Juárez* (Mexico, 1941), 43.
33. Lerdo, Veracruz, July 23, 1863, to Ortega. Ortega Typescripts, University of Texas. Juárez accepted the resignation May 31, 1860. Ocaranza, *Juárez*, II, 107-108.
34. Doblado had returned to active participation in the war for he claimed that the conservatives had not kept their word, and he thus felt free to break the agreement made earlier at Silao. Castañeda, *Guerra*, 73-77.
35. Prieto, San Luis Potosí, June 26, 1860, to Doblado. *Ibid.*, 188-190.
36. Ortega Typescripts.

War of Reform 41

In planning the final step of the campaign, the liberal leaders decided to attack Guadalajara rather than proceed directly against Mexico City. But this operation would take money, and to get it Doblado was desperate enough to order Ignacio Echeagaray in early September to seize a consignment of silver. Degollado, whom Doblado had consulted, later took full responsibility for the action, defending it as necessary.[37] Juárez, of course, reprimanded those involved and ordered the return of the money.

González Ortega was selected to command the operations against Guadalajara. Since the liberals hoped that the surrender of the city might be arranged (perhaps by bribery) without a battle, Ortega invited Severo Castillo, the conservative commander, to a conference. During their meeting, Castillo suggested that Juárez resign and that the constitution be changed, and while Ortega added some qualifying provisos, he agreed with these ideas.[38] The liberal government could not, of course, accept such a plan, and Guadalajara had to be taken by force. Later Degollado twitted Ortega, saying he thought Ortega had gone a bit too far, but the latter, showing no humor, replied that he felt he had not gone beyond his instructions and powers. Ortega went on to criticize Degollado for his dealings with the English Minister, George B. Mathew.[39]

The Mathew incident was one of the most critical of the period. Degollado was so sure the liberals had no real chance of winning that in late September, during the siege at Guadalajara in which he was participating, he contacted Mathew in the hope of ending the war. Degollado proposed to the British Minister that a group composed of several members of the diplomatic corps in Mexico City, plus a representative from both governments, choose a provisional president. The liberal generals, as well as Juárez, refused to support Degollado. Juárez wrote to him pointing out that his plan involved nothing less than the surrender of gains made in three years of war and the solution of Mexico's internal problems by

37. Ortega, *Golpe*, 43. Doblado had first written to Degollado on September 10 telling him it was necessary to take the consignment if the armies were to be kept going. García, *Raros*, XI, 124-127. Degollado, two days later, supported the move. *Ibid.*, 127-129.
38. Ortega, San Pedro, September 26, 1860, to Degollado. Ocaranza, *Juárez*, II, 69-73. Juárez wrote on the back of his copy of this letter: "Degollado and González Ortega urge the president to give up his office." *Ibid.*, 74.
39. Ortega, Belem, October 2, 1860, to Degollado. Ortega Typescripts.

foreign representatives who had supported the conservatives.[40] Such a display of defeatism left Juárez no choice but to dismiss the general and appoint González Ortega as Commander in Chief. Under his leadership Mexico City fell on December 25, 1860; on the first day of the new year Ortega made his formal entry into the city. Doblado wrote to him on December 24, 1860, "Remember that a learned French Minister once said that the battle is not really difficult until the day after victory."[41]

40. Juárez, Veracruz, October 4, 1860, to Degollado. Ocaranza, *Juárez*, II, 76-78.
41. Ortega Typescripts.

Chapter III

THE GOVERNMENT'S PROGRAM
AND THE REFORM LAWS

On July 7, 1859, the Juárez government in Veracruz issued a manifesto outlining in broad terms its program of aims and objectives.[1] It summarized the government's thinking not only on military aspects of the war but also on the administrative changes to be carried through when peace was restored. In view of the revolt it had originally been intended to postpone publication of the program, but the war had lasted longer than had been anticipated and the fighting had become extremely bitter. Under the circumstances, the government finally concluded that it would be shirking a duty which the situation demanded were it to withhold any longer its plans for correcting the basic defects of Mexican society. The affairs of the nation had reached a crisis, declared the manifesto, for on the outcome of the bloody struggle which the conservatives were waging against the principles of liberty and social progress depended the future of the nation. The government felt itself bound to make known to the people their rights and interests, not only to unify public opinion but also that the people could then better understand the reasons for their great sacrifices and that the civilized world would know the true objective of the struggle in Mexico.

Since the government derived from the Constitution of 1857, it naturally subscribed to the doctrines of that charter; equal rights and guarantees for all citizens, administration within the clearly defined limits of the law, and the principle of state autonomy as long as the states did not interfere with the rights and general interests of the republic. Although these basic ideas had formed a part of almost every liberal code written since independence, they had not yet been able to take root in the nation. Nor would they do so as long as social and administrative institutions retained various elements of despotism, hypocrisy, immorality, and disorder

---

1. *Archivo Mexicano. Colección de leyes, decretos, circulares y otros documentos* (6 vols., México, 1856-1862), IV, 54-81. Hereinafter cited as *Archivo Mexicano*.

which all worked together to prevent the establishment of good principles of government. The Juárez administration pledged itself to eliminate these vicious elements, for it believed that as long as they persisted order and liberty would be impossible.

To achieve its twin aims of stability and freedom the government intended to unify opinion on the question of social reform through a series of measures which would produce a complete and durable triumph of desirable principles. Specifically the program listed the following: separation of church and state; suppression of monasteries and secularization of clergy living in those institutions; abolition of brotherhoods and other organizations of a similar nature; abolition of novitiates in convents; nationalization of all the wealth administered by the secular and regular clergy; and elimination of the civil authority in the matter of payment of church fees.

The government believed that only by enacting these measures could the clergy be made to submit to the civil authority in temporal matters and still be left free to carry on their sacred calling. In addition the government also considered it indispensable to protect religious liberty throughout the nation, for freedom of choice in this regard was essential to the country's prosperity and growth.

The general statement of the government's program thus included an outline of the Reform Laws which were to be issued shortly, but that was only the beginning of what its liberal rulers envisioned doing for the improvement of Mexico. They also intended to overhaul the administration of justice; and their plans included the formulation of civil and criminal codes, the introduction of the jury system, and the elimination of court fees. The country would have more free primary schools, and a new plan of studies for secondary schools and colleges would be drawn up. Attention would be given to aiding the states in order to strengthen the ties which should exist between the states and the federal government. The government believed that one of the best ways to attain this unity was through establishing better internal security, not only because the highwaymen were a plague to the inhabitants but also because it felt that the insecurity kept out of the country much capital and many industrious people who would otherwise come. The constitutional provision eliminating passports would be implemented as part of the government's program to clear away all obstacles to free movement within the country. A free press and a civil register would be established.

The Government's Program and the Reform Laws 45

The last half of the program was devoted primarily to fiscal and financial matters. In the field of public finances the government believed radical changes were needed, and leading the list was reform of the national treasury. The government planned to abolish all domestic taxes collected on the movement of money and persons.[2] Similarly, although its effects were not quite as injurious to the nation's economic health, the tax on the transfer of rural and urban property was also slated for repeal. In the same category came the removal of restricting and unfair taxes on mining. The government promised to do its best to stimulate foreign commerce by simplifying the commercial regulations established under existing laws and by reducing taxes.

In the government's opinion, the various laws promulgated to regulate the division of revenues between the national and state governments had failed to establish a clear distinction in sources of income. To clarify the situation the government proposed that revenues from direct taxes on persons, properties, commercial and industrial establishments, and professions be kept by the states; revenues from indirect taxes would go to the national government.[3]

One of the great burdens on the government, a problem inherited from Spain, was the many pensioners classified variously as retired officers and government officials, old age pensioners, widows, and others. The situation called for prompt attention, and the government felt that the only solution was to capitalize these claims once and for all. Whether they were acquired justly or unjustly, the government believed that in all fairness they could not be disavowed if they had been granted in accordance with the laws and by competent authorities. The revenue to settle these claims would be raised by a special series of so-called capitalization bonds which would be issued upon the basis and under the circumstances to be fixed by law.

The plan to clear up pension payments would have an added advantage. As the system had functioned, the government took deductions from the salaries of government employees and men in the army with the view to providing them with a pension, but the promised security had almost always proved illusory. In the future no deduction would be made, and the individual could invest

2. These taxes were the *alcabala* and *peaje*.
3. Note that this places customs in the hands of the national government.

the extra money to provide for his old age. He could put it in savings banks and in mutual assistance societies whose establishment the government favored and which it assumed would spring up in all parts of the country. Mutual assistance societies, in addition to being a very effective means of insuring the savings of government employees as well as those of all people with scanty resources, would also produce immense advantages for society in other ways, because their regular accumulations of capital would serve to carry out many undertakings both useful and profitable for the whole country.[4]

The government also intended to reduce the public debt. One method of achieving this objective would be provided in the law, soon to be issued, nationalizing church holdings. The law would require new owners to pay part of the purchase price in currency and the remainder in government bonds. A similar arrangement applied to the sale of public lands would also help reduce the debt. The government expressed confidence that if these two methods of amortization were used to pay off the outstanding government indebtedness, a great part of both the capitalization bonds and the foreign debt would be retired. If these revenues were not sufficient to pay off foreign commitments, the government pledged itself to continue to respect the agreements it had made regarding payments.

The government was anxious to encourage immigration, but before any success could be expected two things were essential. Jobs had to be available when the immigrants arrived, and to help meet this need the government envisioned projects such as roads and canals. In addition, the newcomers must feel secure in their person and property. The latter objective would be only one of several advantages anticipated from the improvement of the army and the creation of a national militia, proposed elsewhere in the program. To give impetus to immigration, large landholders in the interior would be urged, in their own interest and that of the country, to make arrangements to sell or rent lands on reasonable terms to the newcomers. Disposition of public lands would also be linked to plans for colonization.

---

4. In addition to the creation of mutual aid societies, the liberals must also have been thinking about a substitute for the abolished brotherhoods which had served as a type of mutual aid society.

In considering the problem of improving transportation facilities, the program declared that the government ought to abandon the custom of building roads itself. Instead contracts should be given to private enterprises with government inspection to see that the work was properly done. A new law regulating railroad construction would be passed which would contain ample and generous concessions in order to stimulate both domestic and foreign capital to enter this field of investment.

But important as the program was in indicating the government's stand on various matters, it was completely overshadowed by specific laws affecting the status of the church. The effect of this body of decrees, generally known as the Reform Laws, would be felt for many years. Obviously the Reform Laws were only one part of the general program, but it was natural that attention, both at that time and ever since, should be focused on them.[5]

While subsequent decrees were of significance in their effect upon the church, the law promulgated on July 12, 1859, was the real bombshell. The first article provided for the confiscation of all the wealth administered by the regular and secular clergy. To prevent a repetition of mortmain holdings the law stipulated that while the clergy would be free in the future to accept offerings for the religious services which they performed, under no circumstances could such gifts take the form of real property. The law also decreed the separation of church and state and promised state protection of public worship to all religions, whether Catholic or any other denomination.

The articles dealing with the regular clergy abolished all the brotherhoods and regular orders and prohibited the establishment of new monasteries. The regulars were to join the secular clergy and as such would thereafter be subject to the proper ecclesiastical authority. Every regular who accepted the government's decree was to receive a gift of 1,500 pesos, but any monks who reassembled in an effort to continue their communal way of life would be expelled from the country. Upon petition from the archbishop and bishop of the diocese, the civil authorities would designate the churches of the suppressed orders which would continue to serve as houses of worship, and the sacred objects from all others would

---

5. The Reform Laws may be found in D y L, *Legislación,* VIII, 680-683; 688-695; 696-705; 762-766.

be turned over to the bishop. The books, antiques, and works of art would be transferred to public libraries and museums.

Convents which were in existence when the decree appeared were to continue without interference, but no novices were ever to be admitted in the future. In addition, nuns were encouraged to leave their convents by the promise of financial assistance.

Another decree issued the following day established the procedure for an inventory of the nationalized property by civilian authorities, and outlined the procedure by which individuals could acquire ownership.[6] The groups of buildings formerly occupied by the regular orders were to be subdivided and a price put on each piece of property by an official appraiser. These properties were then to be offered at public auction, but they would be sold only if the bid were equivalent to two-thirds of the appraised value. Of this amount, one-third had to be in cash and another one-third was to be paid in securities of the national debt. If more than one bid were received the property would go to the individual offering the largest amount in government securities.

All the mortgages held by the clergy, whether they resulted from property sales consummated before the law of June 25, 1856, or from sales carried out in accordance with that law, could be paid off by the mortgagors under the following terms: three-fifths of the sum owed to be paid in government bonds and two-fifths in money payable in forty monthly installments. A mortgagor who wished to take advantage of this opportunity had to appear within thirty days at the office of the proper official to make his intention known, and at the same time pay the amount due in government securities and present his promissory notes for the cash payments. Lack of action within the thirty-day period meant that the mortgagor renounced his right to redeem his mortgage, and the right of redemption was to be transferred to the first person who solicited it within the next ten days. Any person who acquired the mortgagor's claim would have to pay off the mortgage on the same terms as the original debtor. In each district the officials would publish a list of all the mortgages which were subject to redemption, and each week they would make public a list of those which had been redeemed. After the ten days had expired, unredeemed property would be sold at public auction on the same terms of two-fifths in money and

6. Ibid., 683-688.

The Government's Program and the Reform Laws 49

three-fifths in securities, with bidding only on the amount to be paid in securities.

All the estates under the clergy's management which had not yet been disamortized under the law of June 25, 1856, were to be sold at public auction. The same general rules and regulations governing the redemption of mortgages would apply to the transfer of the estates, except that in auctions of estates the appraised value would be calculated on the amount of taxes the property had paid.

Any person who brought to the attention of treasury officials church property of whose existence that department was unaware would have the right to acquire title to it. In such cases the buyer would have to pay seventy per cent of the property's value in government bonds and the remainder in forty monthly cash installments. If such a person did not take up his option to buy within twenty days, the government would sell the property at public auction.

Twenty per cent of the money, both cash and time payments, collected as a result of this law was to remain in the states. They were to use this money for the improvement of roads and other means of communication and for the projects which promoted the general welfare.

Other decrees followed in 1859 and 1860 which secularized cemeteries, made marriage a civil contract, and recognized legal separation, although absolute divorce was prohibited. Additional laws reduced the number of religious feast days and spelled out the regulations governing religious toleration.

The law nationalizing church property did not embody an idea that was completely novel to Mexican thinking; as far back as the 1830's, and particularly during the time Gómez Farías was in power, demands were made that such a decree be issued. The same situation repeated itself in 1846-1847 during the war with the United States and in 1856-1857 at the time of the constitutional convention. As a matter of fact, before the national government issued the Reform decree of July 12, some of the states on their own initiative had already taken rather drastic action against the church. In the north, Vidaurri had confiscated church property, as had Ortega in Zacatecas. In Michoacán a beginning had been made toward the eventual suppression of all monasteries. In a sense, therefore, the national government was legalizing actions which some states had already undertaken.

Not much doubt can exist that the concept of nationalization of church lands had considerable support from the liberals; but which man was responsible above all others for changing theory into law? Prieto, says Roeder; Miguel Lerdo, say Knapp and many others; Degollado, says Justo Sierra. While certainly a number of men contributed in urging the government to issue the decrees, on the basis of facts given by Manuel Ruiz,[7] a cabinet member, Sierra would appear to be correct in assigning to Degollado the role of agent of the Reform.

According to Ruiz, when the liberal government was in Guadalajara in 1858 the cabinet, of which Lerdo was not yet a member, considered for the first time confiscating the clergy's wealth. The cabinet had met to consider what steps it could take to raise money, and one of the ministers proposed that the government seize without delay the money in all the mints, using as its authority the law of November 15, 1857. Those who owned the money would be repaid their capital and the legal interest due them with the clergy's wealth. The cabinet rejected this plan insofar as it related to taking the money from the mints and decided instead to impose a forced loan. But the ministers agreed to make a start on the reform, beginning with the seizure of mortmain property.

Having determined to take advantage of the first opportunity to expropriate such holdings, they agreed, in addition, to send José María Mata to the United States as minister plenipotentiary with special instructions to negotiate a loan guaranteed by revenues from the sale of confiscated lands. Ruiz emphasized that since Lerdo was not a member of the cabinet which gave Mata these orders, it could hardly be claimed that Lerdo was the man who first introduced the idea to its members. He added that his version could be confirmed by Degollado, Ocampo, León Guzmán, and Prieto. Ruiz' statement that work on the Reform Laws had begun some time before their publication was corroborated by Ocampo, who wrote that once the formation and promulgation of the Reform Laws had been decided upon, the cabinet met and read over most

---

7. Published in Mexico, February 18, 1861, and quoted in Jorge F. Iturribarría, *Historia de Oaxaca*, 1821-1854 (3 vols., Oaxaca, 1935-1939), II, 188-194. Early in 1861 a battle was raging in Mexico City over Lerdo, a battle in which Ruiz did not support Lerdo. While this fact must be remembered in using Ruiz' account it does not invalidate the evidence.

of the material which he, Juárez, and Ruiz had written on the subject since June of 1858.⁸

As to specific laws of reform, Ruiz personally claimed the responsibility for the one issued on July 12, nationalizing the wealth of the clergy and ordering the exclaustration of the regulars. Lerdo, Minister of the Treasury, drew up the regulations of July 13 for acquiring ownership of property which had been nationalized. The law of July 23 on civil matrimony was also the work of Ruiz, and Ocampo wrote the law of July 28 on the civil register, that of July 31 on cemeteries, and that of August 11 on suppression of fiesta days.

Ruiz also denied that Lerdo was responsible for the program published by the government on July 7. Lerdo, so the story went, had drawn up the program while he was in Zacatecas and had later come to Veracruz to present it to Juárez and the cabinet. When asked to become Minister of the Treasury, Lerdo made the acceptance of his program the condition for joining the cabinet, and his demand was met. He took over the treasury post and the manifesto was issued.

Ruiz claimed, on the other hand, that upon arriving in Veracruz, Lerdo went to see the president and volunteered his services. Juárez received the offer with pleasure and appointed Lerdo to the double task of Secretary of the Treasury and Fomento. After joining the cabinet, Lerdo told the president he had some ideas on various matters of interest which he would like to present to the cabinet. Juárez called the ministers together and Lerdo set forth his views, after which everyone discussed frankly the points he had raised. In general, the cabinet agreed with Lerdo's ideas but the objections to two of his proposals caused a lengthy discussion. Lerdo advocated the financial support of the church and clergy by the state, and the intervention of civil authority in ecclesiastical affairs.⁹ The president and the other members had previously held long conferences on both these points, and they had reached the opposite conclusions. They wanted nothing less than complete separa-

---

8. Ocampo, *Obras*, II, 168.
9. Lerdo's position was similar to that of many Mexican liberals of the 1820's and 1830's. Gradually they came to favor the complete separation of church and state.

tion of church and state[10] and a clergy financially independent of the civil administration. After the ministers explained to Lerdo the reasons for adopting such a position, the conference continued with the discussion of other matters.

Lerdo had taken notes during the cabinet meeting and from them he then drew up a circular which he sent to the printers without consulting the president or the other ministers. When Juárez learned that the press was busy printing this document, he sent for Lerdo and talked to him in private. Ruiz did not know what was said at this meeting, but as a result the circular was not issued.

Degollado, who knew that the ministers were sympathetic to projects for reform, wrote from the interior that he felt the cabinet ought to take some positive action. He then appeared in Veracruz to plead in person for his ideas, and after a long consultation with the president convinced him that the government should act. As a result Juárez called the cabinet together to consider issuing the laws.

After a discussion the cabinet agreed to issue a manifesto to the nation and to promulgate immediately afterward, in the form of laws, the various measures affecting the church which the cabinet had been considering. At this point Lerdo brought out the notes he had taken during the earlier discussion which included Juárez' ideas on the absolute independence of church and state and the nonintervention of the civil authority in clerical affairs. The cabinet went over the notes, and with some modifications they served as the basis for the July 7 manifesto, which Lerdo was assigned to draw up.

The next day Ruiz, as Minister of Justice, presented to the cabinet his bill for the decree later issued on July 12. He proposed giving the regular clergy who accepted the law the lump sum of 3,000 pesos. Much discussion followed on this point because Lerdo asserted that they should not receive anything, while Ruiz argued for the grant. After a day of debating the two opinions, the cabinet finally decided to give each regular half of what Ruiz suggested. It approved the remaining articles with slight modifications. On the following day, Lerdo presented a draft of the rules and regulations

---

10. Juárez made his views clear in a letter to Vidaurri, July 14, 1859, in which he stated that he felt the most important part of the law nationalizing church property was the provision for separation of church and state. Roel, *Vidaurri*, 20-21.

The Government's Program and the Reform Laws   53

for carrying out the law. The government then published the law and the accompanying regulations on July 12 and 13.

Lerdo believed strongly that the government should try to raise money in the United States and he was convinced that he could get a loan on the basis of the law confiscating church property. He was so anxious to undertake this mission that once the president had approved his trip he left immediately without waiting for the remainder of the Reform Laws to be promulgated.

From the Ruiz account it is apparent that with regard to the role of the church in a secular state, liberals in general shared similar views, but that it took the impetus given by Degollado to embody these opinions into law.[11] When the cabinet did decide to act it was relatively easy to incorporate as law ideas that practically all of them agreed upon. In a sense the situation was somewhat comparable to Jefferson's writing the Declaration of Independence; he did not have to consult books; the ideas were well known and accepted.

But while the laws were the expression of the general theories which the cabinet held in common, the discussions revealed many differences on particulars among the individual members. Ocampo and Lerdo especially had difficulty in getting along together, their quarrel stemming partly from differences of opinion and partly from personalities. The fact that Lerdo made slight effort to conceal his feeling of superiority did little to ease the difficult situation.[12] Because of these disagreements Lerdo on June 27 and July 5 asked permission to resign. After the second request Juárez wrote his minister:

> Your letter of today [July 5] in which you insist on resigning because we do not agree on the principles of reform which we have been discussing lately, comes as a great sur-

---

11. The belief that Degollado influenced the government in its decision to publish the Reform Laws is reinforced by his letter of July 4, 1859, from Tampico, to Doblado, in which he stated: "You already know what the reasons were which caused me to leave Colima in order to confer with the President and his cabinet upon what was needed, in my opinion, in order to cut short the terrible fight that is destroying the country. I now have the satisfaction of telling you that my journey had good results and that we can all hope for a quick end to the civil war and the triumph of good principles. The Government has promised to send me [copies of] all the decrees which deal with the nationalization of the wealth of the clergy, abolition of monasteries . . . and other major points. . . ." Castañeda, *Guerra*, 71.
12. Ocampo, *Obras*, II, 170.

prise to me. If it [the disagreement] were true, your desire to resign would not seem strange; but when we have already finished the program, when we have designated eleven o'clock today as the time to continue discussing the laws we have agreed to issue, when we concur on the major points of the reform, and when in order to expedite our work we have agreed to increase the length of our sessions, I do not understand how you can advance our disagreement as the reason for your resignation. The only question is whether or not the program will be published simultaneously with the decree; certainly the settlement of this point should not be a motive for abandoning our labors. . . .[13]

Lerdo withdrew his resignation and since he left for the United States almost immediately after the first law was promulgated, the dissension did not break out into open warfare.

In Sierra's opinion,[14] Ocampo wanted the nationalization of church lands to result, as it had in France, in the creation of a landholding middle class loyal to the Reform. For this reason he wanted to defer promulgation of the Reform Laws until after the government was reestablished in Mexico City so that they could be carried through in orderly fashion for the benefit of the many. Ocampo felt certain that if the church lands were distributed while the government was still in Veracruz the benefits would accrue to only a relatively small number. Lerdo considered his colleague's ideas too visionary and was himself in favor of publishing the laws immediately. For one thing, he believed that putting control of nationalization into the hands of the central government would be a brake on those revolutionary leaders who were expropriating the clergy's wealth entirely on their own initiative.

But Lerdo's chief reason for pushing immediate nationalization was that the government would then have church lands as a guarantee for the loan he wanted to negotiate in the United States. Actually Lerdo could not, and did not intend to, use the lands themselves as the guarantee. According to his plan the security backing up the loan would be the promissory notes given to the government by those who purchased property formerly held by the clergy. In this scheme Ocampo had little faith, since he felt the entire operation was being calculated on a grossly inflated estimate of the value of

13. Juárez, July 5, 1859, to Lerdo. Ocaranza, *Juárez*, I, 183-184.
14. Justo Sierra, *Juárez, su obra y su tiempo* (México, 1948), 159-160.

The Government's Program and the Reform Laws 55

mortmain property. But the fact that Juárez published the laws immediately and Lerdo went to the United States indicates that the president shared the latter's views rather than Ocampo's on this subject.

Did the central government obtain as much revenue as it had anticipated from the law nationalizing church lands? The answer certainly must be no. In the first place Ocampo was probably correct in his opinion that the value of the church holdings was greatly overestimated. In addition, state governors and military chiefs received extraordinary powers enabling them to sell property and to dispose of the income. State governors were also authorized to allow the new owners to pay off their indebtedness at a high discount rate, on condition that the balance be paid in cash. The central government also permitted the governors to use this money for war expenses in the states. Not until the fighting ended in 1861 did the government change its policy of permitting the states great discretion in the disposition of nationalized property.

As a source of income, as a lever for getting a loan from the United States, and as the instrument for creating many small property holders, the nationalization of church property was a disappointing measure. But the program undoubtedly had positive effects in the attempt to reduce the public debt, to establish the capitalistic system, and to deprive the clergy of its economic influence.

Chapter IV

1861-1863

For those who had spent the years fighting or directing the liberal movement, the return to Mexico City was a great relief. But victory did not mean peace, much less prosperity, and the liberals discovered the truth of Doblado's reminder to Ortega. The military triumph over the conservatives was indeed just the beginning. In the next six years the liberals needed all their wits and recuperative powers to hold Mexico together against internal strife and foreign invasion. The domestic problems alone were staggering; the government had to wrestle with the destruction wrought by the war, the division in the social classes, and the lack of money. Another difficult task was that of reestablishing the authority of the central government over the various local political and military chieftains. During the war the government had of necessity delegated to these men wide powers over civil, judicial, and military affairs; at other times local leaders merely appropriated the authority on their own initiative. After independently exercising wide powers, such leaders were not anxious to follow again the dictates of a government in Mexico City.

A question which arose immediately and caused much dissension within the liberal party itself was what to do with those who had supported the reactionary regime. The radicals were determined to inflict severe penalties, while the moderate element of the party felt that a conciliatory policy would be the best way to heal the wounds caused by the war.

Melchor Ocampo, who had preceded Juárez to the capital, issued two decrees on January 3, 1861, designed to punish supporters of the late rebellion.[1] The first provided that all government employees who had served the Tacubaya rebellion were to lose their posts. The other declared that since the clergy had been the principal instigators and supporters of the revolt and of the disastrous war which followed, they were consequently to be held responsible for the damages resulting from the conflict. Another decree stipu-

1. D y L, *Legislación*, IX, 3-4.

lated that in accordance with the Reform Laws the viaticum could only be taken through the streets without display and no special mark was to distinguish the priest carrying it. The government appointed architects to divide the nationalized convents into lots, appraise them, and lay out the streets which should be opened.[2] Even these measures, however, did not satisfy some of the liberal press, and *El Monitor Republicano* on January 6 called for more drastic action against the conservatives.[3]

On January 10 at Guadalupe, where he spent the night before making his entrance into the capital, Juárez issued a proclamation to the people. In it he took no definite position on the issue, merely stating that amnesty would be as complete as sound policy would permit.[4] Following his entrance into Mexico City the next day, the president lost no time in decreeing the expulsion of the foreign representatives of Spain, the Vatican, Guatemala, and Ecuador. He justified his action on the ground that they had shown themselves hostile to the liberal government by the aid they had given to the reactionaries. The government later revoked its order on the Ecuadorian representative when it became convinced that he had not been involved with the conservatives. Almost at the same time came the decree expelling the archbishop, Lázaro de la Garza y Ballesteros, and bishops Joaquín Madrid, Clemente de Jesús Munguía, Pedro Espinosa, and Pedro Barajas from Mexico.

The more radical sections of the press and some of the politicians censured the president's order with regard to the bishops as being beyond his powers. They wanted the clergymen tried by the courts which, it was assumed, would punish them more severely. From within the cabinet itself came disapproval of the president's action, for when the ministers first discussed the matter at a cabinet meeting, Juan Antonio de la Fuente spoke out against the exile of the bishops and the suspension of several members of the supreme court.[5] This disagreement led to his resignation in mid-January,

2. Vigil, *Reforma*, 446.
3. As early as January 2, 1861, Prieto wrote to Doblado from Mexico City that various liberals were making war on Ocampo, but the latter was remaining firm and carrying out his program. Prieto also reported that Lerdo was in partial eclipse and remained in his home. His followers, however, were working hard for his presidential candidacy. Castañeda, *Guerra*, 269.
4. *Archivo Mexicano*, V, 25. As late as January 20, Juárez asked Doblado for his opinion regarding punishment of the reactionaries. Doblado Typescripts, University of Texas.
5. Juárez, *Archivos privados*, 276.

and in his letter to the president he pointed out that the government had no right to deprive the courts of their legal powers. He believed the executive branch had exceeded its authority.[6]

The question of the clerics and the court created a popular outcry, but the real furor arose over the case of Isidro Díaz. Soon after the president reached Mexico City the cabinet received word that Miramón's former minister had been captured by liberal forces. The government issued orders for his execution, but apparently through the intercession of Señora Miramón and Benito Gómez Farías, the sentence was later commuted to five years' exile.[7] When the radicals heard the news there was much complaining and many demonstrations. Fear that the president was going to issue a general amnesty added greatly to the agitation.[8]

Leadership against the government's stand on Díaz came from the clubs.[9] In considering the clubs it is important to remember that their membership included some of the most articulate and intelligent men in the country, making these organizations an extremely important factor in politics. They served various functions: they were debating societies, pressure groups, and centers of support for political candidates. The clubs that proved to be the loudest were those of the radicals. Their members wanted to assume control of the government and to take drastic measures against those whom they considered enemies of the Reform, particularly the clergy. Had they been able to get into power, the result probably would have been a mild form of the horrors of the French Revolution. Certainly Juárez and his supporters deserve much credit for evading the demands of the radicals and keeping power in their own hands.

On the night of January 17, several clubs sponsored an open meeting at the University, and some reports estimated that 5,000 citizens attended the session. At the meeting the clubs appointed a committee to visit the president and plead with him for a strict law on amnesty and no pardon for Díaz. After talking with Juárez

6. *Archivo Mexicano*, V, 60-62.
7. Señora Miramón came to plead with Juárez accompanied by Gómez Farías who told Juárez that when he and Degollado had been captured in Toluca, Díaz prevented their executions. Juárez, *Archivos privados*, 277.
8. Baigén to Doblado, January 15, 1861; Prieto to Doblado, January 15. In a postscript to Prieto's letter Ignacio Ramírez accused the Juárez government of being a parody of the earlier Comonfort regime. Doblado Typescripts.
9. The word is used in English in the Mexican press.

the committee reported back that the president had said he could carry out his program and that he would punish those guilty of common crimes in accordance with the law. In view of this response, which the clubs believed evasive, and convinced that Díaz' pardon was a certainty, they ordered the committee to draw up an indictment against the president and his cabinet for having circumvented the constitution. The accusation would first be presented to the nation through the press, and then to congress when it convened. They also approved a resolution asking the president to change his cabinet.[10]

When the clubs met again on the following night, García Munive, president of the Club de la Reforma, explained that no indictment had been formulated. The committee decided not to act after receiving a letter from General Valle stating in substance that the president had rescinded the order sending Díaz into exile and had ordered him to stand trial. Valle therefore recommended that the accusation be dropped, and García Munive offered a resolution to this effect. But the membership refused to accept the committee's decision and insisted that the accusation be made. Valle, who was present at the meeting, then arose to announce that he was authorized to speak for the president, whom he and Romero Rubio had seen in the morning. After they had described the state of public opinion, they said the president informed them that the cabinet had resigned[11] and that Ignacio Ramírez would replace de la Fuente as head of Justice in the new ministry. The president added that he had given orders for Díaz to be returned to Mexico City to be tried. After a long discussion the members finally agreed to drop the accusation.[12]

Even before Juárez reached Mexico City the clubs had tried to pressure him into changing his cabinet. While he was in Guadalupe, reports reached him that some liberal circles in the capital wanted new faces in the cabinet, but he had refused to consider the resignations offered by his cabinet.[13] Now, however, the clubs had achieved their objective of forcing the president to choose new

10. *Boletín de Noticias,* January 18, 1861. In its issue of the same date *Siglo* reported the resignation of the cabinet.
11. On January 17, Ocampo, de la Llave, Ortega, and Emparan resigned from the cabinet. De la Fuente had resigned the day before. *Archivo Mexicano,* V, 60-62; 74-75.
12. *Boletín de Noticias,* January 19, 1861.
13. Juárez, *Archivos privados,* 276.

ministers. He privately conceded that the Díaz pardon had been a mistake and that it was responsible for the cabinet crisis. But he believed he had corrected the error with the change in orders regarding Díaz and the formation of a new ministry.[14] In the cabinet announced on January 21 were Zarco, Ramírez, Prieto, González Ortega, Miguel Auza of Zacatecas, and Pedro Ogazón of Jalisco. Auza and Ogazón[15] were governors of their respective states and until they arrived in the capital their posts would be held temporarily by other members of the cabinet.

Of all the cabinets Juárez would have, this one was without any doubt by far the most radical. The presence of Ignacio Ramírez was the decisive factor in determining the color of the ministry for he was one of the most radical men of the period. His belief in materialism put him among the few confessed atheists of his time. "Since nature sustains itself . . . there is no God," he had said in his younger days at a learned meeting. With these words a "tumultuous scene occurred," but the audience finally allowed him to finish reading his paper.[16] His conviction of man's goodness made him willing to give the individual citizen greater responsibility; for example, he favored direct popular suffrage, a measure which had little support from most liberals. So firm was his belief in equality before the law that on one occasion he went to Puebla from Mexico City to defend a clergyman because he felt justice must be done. Yet he grasped the fact, which eluded most of his contemporaries, that juridical equality would not improve living conditions for the mass of people. Although he was not a learned man, he possessed a tremendous amount of scattered knowledge which made him effective in the press and in congress. His wit and sarcasm were always most stinging against any tendency which he thought smacked of his *bete noire*—dictatorship. At all times he was willing to stand up and be counted on an issue, even if it meant losing a job or landing in jail.

Of the other prominent men in the cabinet, Zarco, the editor of *Siglo,* tended more toward the moderate position while Prieto leaned to the left. González Ortega was more difficult to classify

14. Juárez to Doblado, January 20, 1861. Doblado Typescripts.
15. These two men were probably appointed at the insistence of Ortega who felt that the states should have some voice in shaping administration policy. Ortega, January 17, to Doblado. *Ibid.*
16. G. Prieto, *Memorias de mis tiempos* (2 vols., México, 1948), I, 136-137.

since he was indecisive and opportunistic. These tendencies inclined him to follow the lead of the political clubs, usually the radical organizations, rather than giving careful study to the work he was responsible for as a cabinet member. Yet for several reasons he was absolutely essential to the liberals. He was governor of Zacatecas, he had a brilliant military record, and his ability to get along with people gave him a large following.

With the formation of the new cabinet, the government issued its program on January 20. Again the emphasis was on judicial equality and capitalism rather than on the church-state question. In this program the administration outlined its objectives:

1. To restore constitutional order;
2. To put into effect the Reform Laws of Veracruz;
3. To reduce the public debt and balance the budget;
4. To hear and deal justly with complaints of foreigners;
5. To treat fairly those who had fought against the government;
6. To reform the judicial system and abolish judicial costs;
7. To make freedom of teaching effective and entrust it to the family, municipalities, the states, and religious associations; the government doing everything possible to extend primary education and provide education for women;
8. To permit a free press;
9. To increase the number of property holders, thereby emancipating the Indians from quasi-slavery;
10. To abolish the sales tax as soon as possible;
11. To aid colonization;
12. "To provide commerce, industry, agriculture, and mining the best possible protection, which is the freedom to grow, to develop, and to join together for mutual help.... The Government intends to protect all useful undertakings, to stimulate the spirit of association, and to carry through improvements even though slowly. It considers as an obstacle to industry and to the opening of avenues of communication the profusion of privileges which earlier administrations granted with a lack of foresight and which have had only illusory value."[17]

With a new cabinet and a program the government did not, however, find even temporary quiet. As usual lack of money was the most pressing problem. This chronic difficulty had been ag-

17. *Archivo Mexicano,* V, 77-79.

gravated by the fact that during the war centralized collection of revenue had been completely disrupted. The government had necessarily conferred wide administrative powers on the states, and in addition many governors had simply taken over such powers. Shortly after Prieto became Minister of the Treasury, he attempted to correct the situation by an appeal to the governors' patriotism, and in a circular describing the serious financial plight of the administration, he exhorted them to greater cooperation with the executive.[18] He pressed the state governors to relinquish the extra powers they had assumed during the war, especially in regard to fiscal affairs, and to do so voluntarily, in the knowledge that to continue in the present fashion would lead to anarchy. Although Prieto agreed that the national government should not have many powers, he wanted it free to exercise energetically those it had. He also warned the governors that public credit was in a state of chaos and that it was urgent to reestablish it on a sound basis: "we ought not to forget that our international obligations can make a farce out of our national independence." But public credit involved much more than international relations; unless the country's credit was sound, it would be unable to develop its rich resources and make the material progress everyone anticipated. Cooperation from all quarters was needed if the country were to enjoy the benefits of the revolution.

But the minister's good intentions and earnest entreaties did not improve matters. The treasury continued under fire and finally attacks in the press and the clubs became so violent that Prieto again wrote the state governors to give them the real picture of the treasury situation.[19] He pointed out first that the interests, which had so bitterly fought each other during the past war, had now carried their struggles to the treasury. It was one of the busiest government offices, but when he took it over treasury administration was totally disorganized. Ocampo's circular of January 3 dismissed the employees of the treasury, and with their departure the ministry lost even the simplest traditions of routine.[20]

18. *Ibid.*, 208-220. The circular is undated but it must have been written in late January or early February.
19. *Ibid.*, 601-609. As Prieto noted in his circular the government, due to lack of funds, did not at this time have an official paper in which to defend its policies.
20. Prieto assumes little responsibility for the disorganization of his department, but Roeder asserts he was not an efficient administrator. Roeder says that

Prieto discussed the traditional sources of revenue and demonstrated in each case how it no longer brought income into the treasury. The customhouse at Veracruz had eighty-five per cent of its income pledged to pay foreign debts.[21] The cabinet did not have power to decrease this amount and yet no order was possible without some adjustment. From the remaining fifteen per cent, the national government received practically nothing. The customhouses of Tampico and Matamoros had smaller incomes and proportionately greater debts. The customhouses of the Pacific were carrying obligations which took up all their income. So the chief source of federal revenue was eliminated. The income from other taxes had been taken over by the states and could no longer be considered as contributing anything to the national government. In short, the government could not count on any of its regular sources of income except the taxes in the Federal District. The monthly deficit, excluding international commitments, was about 400,000 pesos.[22]

Prieto considered it futile to try to eliminate the deficit by increasing income from existing tax sources or by creating new taxes since in either case the government controlled revenues only in the Federal District. To attempt a loan, either foreign or national, he regarded as equally useless. The only plan he could offer to put the nation on its financial feet was the consummation of the Reform, the establishment of peace, and the reduction of the military budget to not more than three million pesos.

In both his circulars Prieto discussed the disappointing results, social and financial, of the laws nationalizing church lands. The government hoped by the land laws of 1856 and 1859 to put property holding on a broad base, making land available even to those of small means and thus emancipating rural workers and tenants. It hoped to rescue the needy, glorify work, and eliminate social

---

when Prieto produced his accounts just before his resignation, they showed disorder and carelessness. Obsolete debts were being paid when there was not enough money to run the government. Roeder, *Juárez*, 291.

21. Prieto wrote to Doblado on January 20 that "everything is pledged; we do not have a peso." Doblado Typescripts.

22. Corwin, the American Minister, wrote to Seward from Mexico on August 28, 1861, that the Mexican government was often compelled to borrow from individuals sums varying from $20,000 to $100,000 at enormous rates of interest. U. S. National Archives, Mexican Dispatches, Vol. 28. The situation described by Corwin had been chronic almost since the government's return.

afflictions. But the legislation was badly drawn with the result that the land in fact made its way into the hands of speculators and of business interests who only wanted the poor to change masters. Prieto felt that it was not yet too late to make the Reform Laws achieve their original aims. In his opinion two changes in administration would help achieve the desired effect: the treasury must compile records of all the transactions made with regard to lands, and the governors must cease using the powers granted them to dispose of lands under the Reform Laws. In addition, until the treasury resolved the ambiguity and conflicts in the various laws, the circulars issued by Ocampo, and the procedures in the states, the government could hope for no revenue from lands. In his efforts to bring some sort of order out of the prevailing chaos, Prieto promised to protect those who had genuine titles to their lands and to punish illegal speculators.

Prieto's major attempt to clarify titles to land ownership came in a decree issued on February 5, 1861, and his accompanying circular of February 12.[23] Part of the difficulty over titles stemmed from the fact that the disamortization law of June 25, 1856, had recognized the clergy as proprietors of the land they held. With the law of July 12, 1859, the government reversed its point of view and held the clergy merely to be the managers of such property. In accordance with this position, the July 12 law stated that any sale by the clergy, or by an unauthorized government official, of property included within the scope of the law was null and void. It also placed penalties on the buyer and the official who authorized the contract. Prieto vigorously maintained that the law of July 12 was retroactive: in other words, the nation had owned this wealth before the law was enacted.

Since the clergy, according to Prieto, were only the administrators of the national wealth and therefore had no right to sell the properties under their charge, all such sales were illegal. Some purchasers, among them accomplices of the clergy, had sought to arrange matters so that their titles would be secure no matter who won the war. This involved a double purchase—one dated either before December 17, 1857, or authorized later by a constitutional authority, and a second title to the same property obtained by purchase from the clergy. To punish such doubledealing the

---

23. D y L, *Legislación*, IX, 54-62; 71-74.

February law declared every sale, whether of land or other effects, made by the clergy without express authorization from the government, null and void. Persons who had secured double titles to property lost their rights to legitimate acquisition; and they could claim no indemnification for money paid to the clergy or any unauthorized government official. However, any person who lost title to his property through the operation of the law could recover his right to repurchase by the payment of what amounted to a fine. Those who decided to take advantage of this provision were allowed thirty days after publication of the decree to make known their intention. Proprietors who had bought their land only from the clergy retained no rights at all, and their land was to go to the persons who had applied to the civil authorities for purchase.

A surge of protests followed the publication of the decree, but more important than the outcry was the wave of speculation in lands. Apparently some of Mexico's wealthier families of later periods built up at least a part of their fortunes by speculating in this period. The invalidation of titles dumped a great deal of land on the market all at once, sending the price down to around one-third of its value. Moreover, the law stipulated that sixty per cent of the sale price of land was to be paid in government bonds, which the seller had to accept at face value. Since these bonds had almost no market value, a double speculation in bonds and land could, and did, take place. It became notorious that a few persons were becoming extremely wealthy.[24] The bonds seldom circulated outside of Mexico City and since many foreigners were bondholders they too became involved in the speculation.

Actually speculation in clerical lands had occurred even before 1861. For example, a number of properties in the Federal District were denounced in Veracruz during the years 1859-1860. Most of them involved large sums and companies did the denouncing— Limantour y Ca., F. F. Rodríguez y Ca., Balbontín y Ca., José Lelong y Ca.[25] Press reports[26] and statements in congress[27] in-

24. See, for example, the protests of Suárez Navarro in the congressional session of May 30, 1861. Felipe Buenrostro, *Historia del segundo congreso constitucional de la República Mexicana, que funcionó en los años de 1861, 62 y 63* (México, 1874), 80-81. Hereinafter cited as Buenrostro, *Congreso*, 1861-63.
25. *Boletín de Noticias*, February, 1861.
26. See *Siglo*, January 21, 1861, and *Amigo del Pueblo*, April 26, 1861, as examples.
27. Buenrostro, *Congreso, 1861-63*, 31-32.

dicated that many Mexicans were becoming worried over this new monopoly of land and also over the fact that foreigners were acquiring large holdings. In an effort to check the trend Aguascalientes tried unsuccessfully to limit to 17,356 acres the amount of land an individual could own.

Prieto demonstrated conclusively that government revenues from the sale of land were disappointing. But the only real record of land transactions available is one drawn up for the first eleven months of 1861 which shows sales totaling approximately $16,584,477. However, over $14,000,000 of that sum was paid for land in the Federal District so the report sheds little light on what happened in the states.[28] While the government did not profit much in cold cash from nationalization, it did benefit financially in that it was able to reduce somewhat the amount of government indebtedness.

In addition to the fact that few little people profited in a positive way from nationalization, some of them actually suffered from the changes in ownership. Many of the new proprietors were not as considerate of their tenants as had been the church, and some of them thought up the scheme of getting their tenants to pay rents for the period 1858-1860. Although these owners had not actually been in possession of their land during the reaction, by law it was legally theirs during that period. They had not, of course, received income from it and now demanded that the tenants pay up their back rent.[29] The new landlords were also increasing rents. A congressional committee, which had considered a bill to moderate rents by law, admitted in its report to congress that proprietors were charging exorbitant rents. The committee, however, refused to approve restraining legislation, declaring that any action to limit rents would be interfering with private property and contracts. Such a position was not strange in view of the widespread acceptance of the laissez-faire doctrine, and Vicente Riva Palacio, a liberal and a property owner, supported the committee's position.[30] Some gestures were made in an attempt to relieve the con-

28. Phipps, *Agrarian*, 82; 88.
29. *Boletín de Noticias*, January 1, 1861.
30. Felipe Buenrostro, *Historia del primero y segundo congresos constitucionales de la República Mexicana* (México, 1874-1882), III, 78-79; 146. This is really a seven volume set but it is listed as volumes III-IX. It is a continuation of his work on the congresses of 1856-1857 and 1861-1863 but

dition of the agricultural populace but with no success. In Colima, for example, there was an effort to have all debts of the workers cancelled and to have their wages paid them in money.[31]

The government had anticipated that the nationalization of land would be a great stimulus to Mexico's economic life; it would bring greater mobility of capital, more incentive, and higher production which would, in turn, result in increased activity in other areas. Disappointed in these expectations, the government kept trying in other ways to revive and expand the national economy.[32] To stimulate trade the government removed two stifling restrictions, the age-old sales tax and the toll charges, and repealed the law against usury. In an effort to facilitate the transportation of goods, a new tax on property was levied to provide money to improve roads.[33] On April 5, 1861, Antonio Escandón received a concession, which included a large government subsidy, to construct a railroad from Veracruz to the Pacific. Four units of rural militia were created in order to improve safety of travel. Revenues from a new tax on the sale of tobacco were assigned to improve the telegraph system.

Still clinging to the belief that the country needed colonists, the government took steps to encourage foreign immigration. Foreigners, whether individuals or members of colonies, who purchased and worked land did not have to pay property assessments for five years, and they received a ten-year exemption from all other taxes. In addition all imported goods consumed directly by the immigrants were free from customs and tariffs for two years. The government recognized that concessions such as these had proved ineffectual in the past, due chiefly to two factors: the almost constant state of revolution and the lack of records showing precisely what lands were available for distribution to settlers. To eliminate one of these drawbacks the government ordered a general land census of both public and private property.

While Juárez the executive was trying to bring some order to the administration of the country's affairs, Juárez the politician was

it carries a different title. Hereinafter this set, covering volumes III-IX, will be cited as Buenrostro, *Congresos*.
31. *Siglo*, March 23, 1861.
32. Laws may be found in D y L, *Legislación*, IX, 113-207.
33. This tax was a substitution for the toll charge but it proved to be unfair for it fell most heavily on those owning land nearest the road. *Siglo*, May 7, 1861.

busy parrying attacks against his power from within the liberal ranks. From Veracruz on November 6, 1860, the government had issued a decree calling for special elections in January, 1861, to choose a new congress and president. Although, in fact, the elections would not be completed until several months later, immediately upon the government's return to Mexico City the contest among the major presidential candidates, Miguel Lerdo, González Ortega, and Juárez, turned into a bitter fight. In the course of the campaign, Lerdo became involved in a press debate with Ocampo who was supporting Juárez. Ocampo charged that Lerdo lacked the insight and sound judgment required of a capable executive. To demonstrate his point he cited Lerdo's opinion during the late war that the liberals could not triumph except with the aid of armed Americans, and that the war could not be ended by force of arms alone. Ocampo again repeated his belief that the laws bearing Lerdo's name were unjust and that neither his laws nor his ideas would contribute to the country's progress. In reply, Lerdo challenged Ocampo to prove his charges,[34] to which the latter obliged with what he considered ample evidence. He published a statement based on his memorandum to Juárez on October 22, 1859, complaining that Lerdo did not grasp the land question.

Prieto joined the attack on Lerdo and tried to make the candidate commit himself on the Reform Laws. In a letter dated January 22, he asked Lerdo's opinion with respect to the easiest method of putting the laws into practice.[35] But Lerdo was not to be trapped into an open exchange of this type, and instead his supporters kept up a steady stream of criticism against the government's policy of allowing the conservatives to return to their positions in the treasury. Prieto's reply was that they were the only competent bureaucrats available.

By March the press was again stridently complaining about the government's inertia and was demanding a new cabinet. Many of the clubs joined in the cry, among them the powerful Club Reforma. On March 14 an eminent member of the Juárez cabinet, González Ortega, accepted the post of honorary president of the Club Reforma, when he certainly must have known that the club was one of the government's bitterest critics. To add to an already

---

34. Ocampo, *Obras,* II, 144-146.
35. *Boletín de Noticias,* January 26, 1861.

anomalous situation, the club on March 29 sent the president a letter asking for the resignation of the entire cabinet.³⁶ In addition, Lerdo's death on March 22 had strengthened Ortega's presidential hopes for it meant that he could naturally expect the support of many of Lerdo's followers, especially if he could show that he was critical enough of the government.

On April 6 Ortega gave up his post as Minister of War, precipitating a real crisis. In his letter of resignation he said that although the president had not seen fit to accept his proposal that the entire cabinet resign, he felt that he personally should leave. No other action was possible, Ortega stated, since the attitude of the press and the tone of political circulars made it clear that public opinion was hostile to the cabinet. The resignation concluded with protestations of his respect for legality and the assertion that he would remain at the head of the Division of Zacatecas to sustain democratic institutions.³⁷ The president immediately accepted the resignation. In answering for the government, Zarco told Ortega that he had confused public opinion with the noise of a club which possessed no political significance and that he had been moved to act by a minority which had no real political principles. In conclusion Zarco informed Ortega that he should await a decision by the national government on the question of command of the Division of Zacatecas.³⁸

As the honorary president of the Club Reforma, Ortega could hardly ignore Zarco's charges that it was a politically insignificant organization composed of irresponsibles. The next day he wrote to Zarco attacking the administration. Public opinion—not just a club but the people—he maintained, opposed the cabinet for any number of reasons. The government had issued a large number of laws and decrees without careful thought, it had showed favoritism, and it had failed to restore peace. Finally, the cabinet was unpopular because it had refused to listen to public opinion. As for his right to retain his military command, Ortega replied that the Zacatecas Division was made up entirely of troops from the

---

36. *Siglo,* April 8, 1861.
37. Ortega, April 6, 1861, to Secretary of Relations. Ortega Typescripts. Ortega was especially opposed to Zarco and Ramírez. *Siglo,* April 7, 1861. The whole question is summarized in I. E. Cadenhead, "González Ortega and Mexican National Politics," unpublished doctoral dissertation, University of Missouri, 70-73.
38. Zarco, April 6, 1861, to Ortega. Ortega Typescripts.

state national guard and that it was under his exclusive control.[39]

The resignation caused an uproar in the capital, and for a time the Juárez government seemed to be in real trouble. Great crowds of people went to the palace to petition the president to dismiss the rest of the cabinet and bring Ortega back. Juárez, however, was not to be found. The next day, April 7, throngs again gathered to repeat their demands, but the president was still not available.[40] For two days feelings were at a peak over what was, in a sense, the question of a civilian president against a popular military hero. It also involved the question whether a well organized opposition could force the president to yield to its demands. The police had difficulty in maintaining order, and the newspaper *Constitucional* did nothing to ease the situation when it urged on April 8 that the only solution was to invade the palace and throw the ministers out.[41]

But while some of his followers advocated strong measures, fortunately Ortega himself had no intention of trying to overthrow the government. On May 1 he issued a proclamation to the people urging them to have faith in their public officials. He declared that the rumor which had him preparing a revolt was the work of people who wanted to split the liberal party. He assured the nation that he would never lead a revolution nor lend his name to such a cause for the time of the sword had passed. Mexico must now begin to solve her problems through peaceful, legal channels.[42]

Even before Ortega's statement renouncing any appeal to arms, changes in the cabinet had cooled the public fever. Prieto had resigned on April 6 in despair over the country's financial situation, and on April 21 Mata agreed to take over the Ministry of the Treasury. Since he had been elected to congress, he consented to stay on only until the session convened when he would submit his resignation.[43] Ignacio Zaragoza replaced Ortega as Minister of War. But the lull was only temporary and even before congress held its first regular session on May 10 some radical newspapers, among

39. Ortega, April 7, to Zarco. *Ibid.*
40. Ortega, April 8, to Doblado. Doblado Typescripts. Ortega reported in this letter that people had besieged him all day with requests that he return to the cabinet but that he was determined to accept no post until Zarco and Ramírez resigned.
41. *Siglo,* April 9, 1861.
42. Ortega Typescripts.
43. *Archivo Mexicano,* V, 629-636; 798-799.

them *Heraldo* and *Movimiento,* were suggesting a coup d'etat."
The new session was the first meeting of congress since the days of Comonfort in 1857. On May 9, 1861, Juárez addressed congress and surrendered his extraordinary powers. The event so many Mexicans had anticipated with hope and eagerness was now a fact: the constitutional regime was reestablished. All the ministers resigned on May 11 on the theory that Juárez should be allowed to pick his new cabinet in the light of the elections, although the outcome of the presidential voting was not yet known. The new congress would provide Juárez with the opportunity, if he wished, to pick his cabinet from the parliamentary majority. Juárez felt, however, that under the constitution he had complete freedom to choose anyone he wanted for the cabinet, and he appointed León Guzmán in the important post of Relations, Joaquín Ruiz in Justice, while Zaragoza continued in War. The Treasury post was not filled until May 20 when an unknown, José María Castaños, took the portfolio. The cabinet changes did little to soothe the opposition; anti-administration clubs and newspapers continued their attacks. By late May many of the clubs had begun to arm, and one paper, *Movimiento,* was calling upon congress to turn itself into a convention.⁴⁵

Shortly after the first of June the bitter political dispute was interrupted temporarily when word reached the capital that Melchor Ocampo had been shot by the conservatives. He had gone to his estate in Michoacán and, although warned that conservative guerrilla bands were in the area, he refused to leave. On May 4 he had written to Juárez that he was coming to take his seat in congress now that the harvests were over,⁴⁶ but for some reason he delayed his departure. On June 1 the conservatives captured him and he was executed two days later. When the news reached Mexico City, public reaction was violent; from all sides came demands that the government act swiftly and harshly to punish the guilty. Public indignation was so great the government had to take precautions to prevent the populace from rising against the conservatives. Although some violence occurred and a mob destroyed the presses of the conservative paper, *Pájaro Verde,* Juárez kept matters quite well in hand. And Ocampo's death was to have a tragic sequel,

44. *Siglo,* May 3, 1861.
45. *Ibid.,* May 25, 1861.
46. Archivo Juárez, MSS. Biblioteca Nacional, Mexico City.

In a very dramatic session of congress, Degollado, previously dismissed from the army and discredited, unable even to get a trial, asked permission to go out and destroy the conservatives who had shot Ocampo. The chamber granted his request and on June 15 he set out for what was to be his last defeat; the conservatives ambushed the government troops and killed Degollado. Leandro Valle, one of the most promising young liberals, then took over the task of avenging Ocampo, but on June 23 he, too, fell into the conservative hands and was executed. After these reverses, Ortega undertook the job of routing out the guerrillas.

While the military situation and the deaths of three outstanding Mexicans occupied popular attention, events were also moving forward in politics. Tabulation of the presidential electoral vote showed 5,289 for Juárez, 1,989 for Lerdo, and 1,846 for Ortega, and in its report the committee on elections declared Juárez president. The minority report protested that Juárez did not get enough votes to be elected and moved that congress choose between him and Ortega. On a vote, the majority report received congressional approval, but only by the small margin of six votes, 61-55.

Although Juárez controlled enough deputies to win the election, a hard core of oppositionists in the chamber sought persistently to undermine his power. In the session of May 24 several deputies had introduced a bill to create a Committee of Public Safety which would suggest to congress appropriate measures to end the guerrilla warfare carried on by the reactionaries. In the debate, government supporters attacked the measure as an underhanded device to set up a dictatorial machine to take over the most important executive powers. Congress, however, approved the formation of the committee by a close vote, but then denied it any power to conduct investigations. It had the authority to recommend legislation, and, in addition, congress assigned it the task of drawing up a bill to suspend certain guarantees. After the chamber accepted the committee's bill on June 5, the extremists tried to get congress to stipulate that the executive should exercise these powers in consultation with the committee. When the deputies voted down this proposal Riva Palacio asked congress to suspend the committee, since it had no power anyway, and on June 12 a large majority voted the committee out of existence.[47]

47. Buenrostro, *Congreso, 1861-63,* 73ff; 121-123.

Not only did the opposition toy with the idea of a Committee of Public Safety in its attempt to find some way of getting rid of the president, but it also considered having congress declare that the president's term would end in December of 1861; the procedure was so obviously unconstitutional that it did not receive much attention. They then advanced a scheme to create a triumvirate replacing the president, the members being Doblado, Ortega, and Uraga. Apparently the determent to carrying out this plan was the great opposition expected from the states.[48]

On June 27 congress elected Ortega Chief Justice of the Supreme Court although legally it had no power to do so. Ortega, in the field with the army during all these maneuvers, believed that Juárez had done everything in his power to prevent the election because he was afraid of losing the presidency once Ortega ascended to the Supreme Court.[49]

The United States Minister, T. Corwin, judged Juárez to be in a critical position. He reported to Seward on June 29 that congress had elected Ortega as Chief Justice and suggested that, in view of the pressure being put on Juárez to resign, Ortega's elevation to the court was in preparation for his taking over the top post. Corwin felt the plan would succeed.[50]

The president was indeed in a difficult position. Not only was the opposition devising schemes to curtail his power and even to remove him from the presidency, but the conservatives were continuing their guerrilla tactics, keeping the countryside in turmoil. In addition, large numbers of bandits, owing loyalty to nothing except their own gain, raided unrestrained all over the country. Even in the area immediately outside of Mexico City travel was unsafe for any but the well protected. In an attempt to eliminate such lawlessness, congress had voted the suspension of guarantees on June 5, and after a raid on Mexico City itself, on June 25 it declared the Federal District in a state of siege.[51]

Although Juárez had just formed a new ministry in May, he faced another cabinet crisis the next month when Castaños and Guzmán resigned on June 17. Juárez then did his best to get the

48. José Linares, June 14, 1861, to Doblado; Careaga to Doblado, June 12, 1861. Doblado Typescripts.
49. Ortega, *Golpe*, 64-65, in a letter to his wife, July 1.
50. U. S. *37th Congress*, Document No. 100, 12.
51. Buenrostro, *Congreso, 1861-63*, 155.

strong man Doblado to accept a post, but on June 19 Doblado refused on the ground that the problems the government faced were so overwhelming that he felt incapable of mastering them.[52] Needless to say, Doblado was not entirely frank with the president. He was aware that to accept a cabinet post would be a bad move for him politically, for his friends sent detailed reports on the difficulties of the government.[53] Juárez also attempted to get Olaguíbel and Sebastián Lerdo de Tejada to form the cabinet but with no better luck. Not until July 13 was the president finally able to put together a new cabinet composed of Zamacona in Relations, Blas Balcárcel in Fomento, Ruiz in Justice, and Zaragoza in War. On the sixteenth José H. Núñez took over in Treasury. The new ministry was definitely moderate in outlook.

On the very day the new ministers took over their posts, they assembled for a long meeting and then went into secret session with congress. Although the next day was a fiesta, congress met again with the ministry in secret session, a procedure repeated on the following three days.[54] The subject of their discussion was the possible suspension of payments on the debt conventions. The cabinet had first considered such action while Guzmán was still its chief, and at that time had rejected Juárez' proposal to ask congress for appropriate legislation. According to Guzmán,[55] Juárez had received suggestions that he initiate and congress pass a law suspending indefinitely the payments on the national debt. Juárez presented the idea to the cabinet members who agreed to study it, although they considered it a rather dangerous idea. After discussions with the diplomatic corps and with its approval, the government decided to suspend payments for two years on the interior debt but not on the conventions. Foreign countries were little concerned with changes affecting the retirement of the domestic debt, but suspension of payments on the conventions would mean that they would no longer receive the money pledged from the customs receipts for that purpose. Yet a few days after the cabinet's decision, Juárez returned to the idea of suspending pay-

52. Archivo Juárez.
53. Letters to Doblado in June, 1861. Doblado Typescripts.
54. *Siglo,* July 14-18, 1861.
55. Guzmán, El partido constitucional la, 2a y 3a época del President D. Benito Juárez. Typescript, University of Texas. Series of five articles he intended to publish. As far as the author knows he never did so.

ments on the conventions.[56]

In the meantime a new cabinet had been formed and it was more receptive to the measure and decided to go forward with the suspension. Zamacona later claimed in a letter published in *Globo*, June 26, 1866, that the decision had not been unanimous since he had voted against it. Before entering the cabinet he had had several conferences with the president, and when they discussed the government's financial plight, the president had told him that a solution was in prospect and that the treasury would present the plan in the first cabinet meeting. On July 13 Núñez, although he did not officially take office until three days later, laid the measure to suspend payments before the cabinet. Since all the ministers favored it except Zamacona, he felt he ought to resign, but the others managed to talk him out of it. Zamacona felt that these facts, plus his early resignation, absolved him from any responsibility for the suspension law. According to Juárez, however, Zamacona argued merely to postpone taking action and then eventually agreed with the others to send the proposal to congress,[57] which was done two days later.

Congress agreed with the executive point of view and on July 17 passed the law which suspended payment on the foreign and domestic debt for two years.[58] Undoubtedly the manner in which the government proceeded was inept, for technically the European diplomats knew nothing about the action until they learned of it from the newspapers. Consequently they felt doubly insulted. As a result diplomatic relations were broken off on July 25.

Long before the debt suspension was to provide an excuse for intervention, individuals interested in the project had been working to bring European influence to bear on the Mexican political situation. Some elements, among them the reactionaries and clergy, felt that only under the rule of a European monarch would order be restored in their chaotic country. José M. Gutiérrez de Estrada,

---

56. This was apparently on May 28, 1861. Juárez, *Archivos privados*, 285. Guzmán in his *Partido* . . . claimed that he checked with the diplomatic corps once again. He was informed that if Mexico suspended payments on the conventions, the European nations would break diplomatic relations and intervention would follow. However, Wyke's dispatches to England do not support Guzmán's statement. And if Guzmán had made such a suggestion to Wyke he would certainly have reported it to Russell. I am indebted to Prof. David Pletcher for checking the British Foreign Office on this point.
57. *Ibid.*, 299.
58. D y L, *Legislación*, IX, 243-245.

a Mexican conservative, had been in Europe for some time trying to sell this idea, but it was not until 1854 that his proposal received any substantial support. On July 1 of that year, Santa Anna, still in office but losing his hold, authorized him to approach the courts of London, Madrid, Paris, and Vienna with the object of setting up a monarchy in Mexico under a prince of one of the European dynasties. Gutiérrez then carried the credentials he formerly had lacked, and he was also able to obtain an assistant, José Manuel Hidalgo, to help him in his task. In 1854 the long negotiations with Napoleon III began.

European bondholders, too, were interested in intervention. Foreigners who held bonds of the interior Mexican debt, selling at three to five per cent of their face value, expected the value of their securities to rise with the creation of a monarchy.[59] In France the group which stood to profit from repayment of the Jecker loan urged intervention, and their interests had a powerful advocate at court in Napoleon's brother, the Duc de Morny. Comte de Saligny, the French Minister in Mexico, was a strong and helpful ally of the interventionists, for his reports, which greatly distorted the situation, had considerable influence on French action. Without doubt the Minister—always pictured in Mexican cartoons with a tremendous red nose, unshaven, and bottle in hand—shared the financial interest of the Jecker group in advocating intervention.

A considerable number of Mexicans felt that the only way to stop the expansion of the United States was for Mexico to have either a European ruler or a European alliance. As early as 1853 Foreign Minister Alamán had sounded out the French Minister in Mexico to see if his country would offer Mexico a guarantee against American encroachment. Something might have come of the inquiry but for the outbreak of the Crimean War. Mexicans were apprehensive with good cause, for throughout the nineteenth century men holding responsible positions in the United States government had considered publicly the possible annexation of Mexico. The Texas question, the Mexican War, a post-war movement for annexation of the entire country, and finally the Gadsden Purchase, all increased Mexican fears. Buchanan, in his message of 1858, actually recommended to congress the partial occupation of Mexican terri-

---

59. Francisco Bulnes, *El verdadero Juárez y la verdad sobre la intervención y el imperio* (México, 1904), 33.

tory, especially Sonora and Chihuahua. Had it not been for the issue of slavery, the United States might well have annexed northern Mexico and Lower California.

The events leading up to intervention by England, France, and Spain, and their culmination in the French attempt to put Maximilian on a throne, are well known and will not be considered here in any detail. In joining the scheme for intervention England had no ulterior motives; her aim was the announced one of collecting lawful debts.[60] The Mexicans, strangely enough, considered the real threat to be from Spain, since they felt that she wanted to reconquer her former colony. They remembered that in 1846 Spain had intrigued for monarchy in Mexico, an attempt which had collapsed with the coming of the war with the United States. Napoleon III, apparently misled about conditions in Mexico, believed a strong monarchial group existed which could be easily helped into power. With the United States involved in civil war, a wonderful opportunity for intervention presented itself for one of the principal objectives of French policy was to checkmate the United States. The three nations, England, France, and Spain, signed the tripartite agreement on October 30, 1861, by which they agreed to intervene in Mexico for the collection of debts.[61]

Through de la Fuente, its representative in Paris, the Mexican government made an effort to forestall intervention by trying to justify its action on the debt. On August 31 in a note to Foreign Minister Thouvenel, de la Fuente explained that his government had decided on suspension as a temporary expedient only after deliberate consideration. He described the measure as a "terrible necessity," essential for the preservation of both government and society from attacks by the reactionaries. Mexico had hoped to secure a measure of financial stability with the income from the sale of church property, but nationalization of lands had brought into the treasury only a relatively small amount of revenue. The disappointing results were due to a variety of causes, an important

---

60. During the War of Reform, however, some of the conservatives had asked for British intervention and Otway, the British Minister, favored it. Daniel Dawson, *The Mexican Adventure* (London, 1935), 6-11.
61. The published correspondence of the interventionists, including a number of the clergy, shows quite clearly that much disagreement existed among the conservatives; they were fearful that moderates such as Doblado would succeed in restoring diplomatic relations, and they were afraid that Prim and Wyke might botch the whole undertaking. García, *Raros*, I.

one being speculation. Since foreigners living in Mexico were among those who had profited most, they joined Mexicans in deploring the conduct of Saligny who was protecting, although perhaps unintentionally, the faction rebelling against the government. De la Fuente, therefore, requested Thouvenel to delay any contemplated action until the French government was completely informed of the facts, but the appeal proved unsuccessful. Thouvenel on September 4 curtly informed de la Fuente that his government approved of Saligny.[62]

In the event intervention became a reality, Mexico's hope for foreign aid lay with the United States. Seward's first effort in dealing with the Mexican situation was to suggest to Corwin that the United States assume the interest charges on the Mexican debt for three years, taking a lien on the public lands in the northern states of Mexico—Lower California, Chihuahua, Sonora, and Sinaloa. In advance of the actual treaty negotiation, the administration decided to try to get a resolution of approval from the Senate, a project on which Seward worked hard. The capable Mexican representative, Matías Romero, did his best to promote the resolution through his contacts with some of the most influential men in the government. His relations with Charles Sumner were cordial, and he was well acquainted with Postmaster General Blair. But contacts were to no avail and the Senate rejected Seward's proposal.[63]

Corwin did negotiate a treaty, however. It provided that if Europe would forbear resorting to hostilities, the United States would agree to pay the interest on the funded debt for five years. In return, Mexico gave a lien on the public lands and mineral rights in Lower California, Chihuahua, Sonora, and Sinaloa, which would become the property of the United States at the end of six years in default of reimbursement. Sentiment both in the United States and abroad was hostile to these terms, and although the treaty was submitted to the Senate it never had a chance of ratification. Mexico also hoped for loans from private sources in the United States, but these expectations were never fulfilled.

When France, England, and Spain invited the United States to join the tripartite agreement Seward refused but did not try actively

62. *AHDM*, X, 24-28.
63. Dexter Perkins, *The Monroe Doctrine, 1826-1867* (Baltimore, 1933), 420-424.

to interfere. In a circular memorandum of December 4, 1861, he restated the Monroe Doctrine, without using the term, and indicated that the United States would not sanction a change of government in Mexico by means of intervention. Under the circumstances it was the strongest statement he could make. The Mexicans, of course, hoped for a more belligerent policy, but the Civil War prevented any overt support.

On October 30 Juárez recorded that the three European nations had decided on intervention. At the same time came word that Spain's warships and troops were in Havana ready to sail for Veracruz. After studying the dispatch, the Minister of Foreign Relations reported to the cabinet that Spain particularly was determined to undertake the intervention, so an order went out to check the defenses at Veracruz.[64] But for weeks after the news of European intervention was known in Mexico, the British Minister, Sir Charles Wyke, continued to negotiate with the government for a peaceful solution of the debt question. In all this time, due to delays and probably to loss of correspondence, Wyke never received definite instructions on policy from his government, and apparently he did not have official notice of the allied expedition until it had actually arrived at Veracruz.[65] In his negotiations with Zamacona, he got the latter to promise immediate repayment of money stolen the previous autumn from the British Legation and from the silver shipment. He also persuaded Zamacona to promise to resume payments on the interest due bondholders of the Mexican foreign debt. Zamacona refused to concede that British commissioners be installed at the Mexican ports to supervise the allotment of customs duties; but, even on this point, he yielded the substance of the request by consenting that British consuls at the ports should be empowered to examine the books and accounts of the customhouses. Zamacona promised, in addition, that his government would do all in its power to secure the passage in congress of a bill providing for a fifty per cent reduction of duties on English manufactured goods.[66]

The final draft of the treaty based on the above features recognized all previous agreements for hypothecating portions of

64. Juárez, *Archivos privados*, 310-311.
65. Dawson, *Mexican Adventure*, 70.
66. Peña y Reyes, *La labor diplomática de D. Manuel María de Zamacona como Secretario de Relaciones Exteriores in AHDM*, Ser. 2, 97-100.

the customs revenues to meet payments on the British-held debt of Mexico. To meet payments on claims arising from the civil war, not only against the Juárez government but against the conservative regime as well, Mexico agreed to increase the percentage of the total customs returns allocated to payment of claims. British consuls or agents of the bondholders were to be permitted to inspect the books and records in the customs administration. Finally, British agents were to have the exclusive right to sell special Mexican treasury certificates for satisfying tariff charges to foreign importers.[67]

Zamacona had difficulty in getting Juárez to agree to these terms, and the treaty was not signed until November 21. Apparently Zamacona had checked ahead of time to be sure of congressional approval. The deputies' consent seemed tacitly implied when congress, in secret session on November 15, granted the executive the power to reform tariffs. But when the real test came Zamacona suffered a complete rebuff for in the secret sessions of November 22-23, 1861, congress revoked the law of July 17 as it related to the diplomatic conventions and the English debt. It also voted by a large majority to reject the Wyke-Zamacona Treaty, a rejection due primarily to the efforts of Sebastián Lerdo de Tejada.[68] In reply to this action Wyke delivered a note on November 24 in which he stated that either Mexico must ratify the treaty or he would leave. The reply had to be negative; Wyke, therefore, applied for his passport on December 13 and left Mexico City three days later.[69] In the meantime, on November 26, the government had published the law which repealed certain provisions of the law of July 17 and which provided for immediate resumption of payments on the conventions and on the British debt.[70] Thus the British had gained their objective through diplomatic channels and had little to gain from intervention.

Not until November did the press begin to reflect any real fear that intervention might actually occur.[71] The politicians showed scarcely more concern, for the threat from abroad did not unite

67. Frank A. Knapp, *The Life of Sebastián Lerdo de Tejada, 1823-1889* (Austin, 1951), 72.
68. Buenrostro, *Congreso, 1861-63*, 55, 63.
69. Dawson, *Mexican Adventure*, 72-73.
70. D y L, *Legislación*, IX, 327-328.
71. See *Siglo* as an example.

the liberal party but rather gave anti-administration elements more ammunition to use against the government. In August and September Deputy Ignacio Altamirano, later to become an outstanding author and critic, wrote two letters which summed up the views of the radical liberals.[72] Altamirano could not understand how Juárez remained in power. Not only did the hopes of great accomplishments under his administration remain unfulfilled; he had lost liberal support by committing every conceivable error and blunder. The worst mistake, in Altamirano's opinion, was the conciliatory policy toward the late enemy, for Juárez had pardoned reactionary leaders when he should have punished them severely and had given many of them government positions. Such toleration and indulgence would lead only to another reactionary revolt. And not only were the conservatives a political threat; they were a military menace as well, for reactionary bands pillaged at will. Even within a league of the capital travel was unsafe, and between Mexico City and many sections of the country communication was almost completely disrupted. Altamirano did not expect the cabinet to bring about much improvement in the situation since, with the exception of Balcárcel, he regarded the ministers as incompetents. Due to inept diplomacy Mexico's ports would soon be blockaded. Comonfort was again in the picture, but the government viewed his appearance with indifference. The clergy were becoming more insolent every day. To Altamirano the scene was unrelievedly gloomy.

While Altamirano's description of prevailing lawlessness was true, the government was, however, making some effort to wipe out conservative forces. In the interior Ortega continued his pursuit of the conservative guerrillas who had killed Ocampo, Degollado, and Valle. But the general was constantly demanding more provisions and money; without additional resources he said he could not carry out his assignment.[73] Ortega evidently feared the government had deliberately put him in an awkward situation in the hope

---

72. Diego Alvarez, *El ciudadano General Diego Alvarez a sus conciudadanos* (Acapulco, 1868), 33-38. Alvarez published these letters after he had quarreled with Altamirano. A fine Altamirano gem was written into his personal notes, May 22, 1869: "I am no longer young. I am thirty five years, six months, nineteen days old. I am spent!" C. Sierra Casasús, "Altamirano íntimo," *Historia Mexicana*, I, 97.
73. Ortega, Cuernavaca, July 17, 1861, to Minister of War, as an example. Ortega Typescripts.

that he too would be defeated and discredited. In its turn, the government apparently never completely trusted Ortega. Yet there are indications that the government did send him a good deal of money, at times more that it really could afford.[74]

Ortega's prestige was considerably increased, however, when on August 13, 1861, he defeated Márquez at Jalatlaco. Although the battle did not put an end to conservative activity it did mean temporary relief, and the news was received with great jubilation in Mexico City. Shortly after his victory Ortega returned to Mexico City and on August 20 he went before congress to be sworn in as head of the Supreme Court. After the ceremony he made a speech[75] in which he praised the people for their courage and patriotism and then went on to deplore the fact that the government had not been able to turn the people's military victories into real peace throughout the nation. He intimated that part of the government's failure was due to its preoccupation with punishing the few reactionaries who remained. He warned that it was not enough to win the fight for principles; they must be put into practice. Many people felt the speech was very critical of the government, but some of the press[76] expressed the opinion that it was simply composed of fine generalities with no hidden meaning.

By this time liberals of all shades of opinion were greatly dissatisfied with the president's inaction in the face of so many pressing problems, and the radical liberals were calling for a dictatorship.[77] The anti-juaristas continued, with or without Ortega's consent, to associate his name with their activities, and they maintained pressure on Juárez in the hope of getting him to follow their advice. On September 3 the president refused the request of several deputies that he dismiss his cabinet in order to quiet the opposition in congress. On September 7 a petition signed by fifty-one deputies was sent to Juárez asking his resignation. While the petition contained no reference to Ortega, it was generally understood that should Juárez agree to relinquish his office, Ortega would become the acting president because of his position on the court. On the same day, however, fifty-two members of congress

74. Anto. Aguado, Mexico, September 8, 1861, to Doblado. Doblado Typescripts.
75. Ortega, *Golpe*, 72-73.
76. *Siglo*, August 23, 29 as examples.
77. Reports from *Constitucional* and *Movimiento*.

signed a second petition voicing confidence in the administration.

Another event indicative of the relations between Juárez and Ortega took place at this time. On August 23 Ortega had been ordered into the field against the conservative general Mejía. Ortega asked permission from congress to absent himself from the court for this purpose, and after some debate the leave was granted. During this interval Ortega had been arguing with the administration about the money and supplies needed for the campaign, and on September 2 he and the president discussed the subject. Juárez expressed the opinion that hard work, rather than a huge army, was the essential element needed to defeat Mejía. With the administration so unsympathetic to his needs, Ortega a week later advised the government that under the circumstances he could neither accept the field command nor be responsible for the outcome of the campaign as Commander in Chief.[78] On the tenth of September the government accepted Ortega's resignation and two days later named Doblado Commander in Chief.[79]

At the same time the government instructed Ortega to turn the command of the Zacatecas National Guard over to General Francisco Alatorre. Ortega protested the order on the grounds that he had not resigned his command of the state troops and that under the state and national constitutions he had the right and duty, as governor of Zacatecas, to continue at the head of the state forces. Ortega informed the Minister of War, however, that under his command the Zacatecas troops were at the government's disposal for as long as it desired their services.[80]

Ortega's offer evidently did not mollify the president. Juárez had been dissatisfied with Ortega's leisurely and elaborate preparations for taking the field against Mejía since he had felt the situation called for a light force striking quickly. Ortega's assertion that the Zacatecan forces would not fight willingly except under his command because they had no confidence in the central government led the president to believe that such troops would impair the army's morale. Consequently, after informing Ortega that his

---

78. Juárez, *Archivos privados*, 303-304; Ortega, *Golpe*, 75-76.
79. Juárez, September 13, 1861, to Doblado; Zaragoza, September 13, 1861, to Doblado. Doblado Typescripts.
80. Ortega, September 21, 1861, to Zaragoza. *Ibid*. Ortega had been named governor in January and, in spite of his election to the Supreme Court, he was still recognized as governor.

troops were no longer a unit of the national army, Juárez ordered it to return to Zacatecas where its services could be used in whatever manner the state government deemed advisable.[81]

Ortega evidently hoped for some support from Doblado in this controversy,[82] but Doblado's response was hardly sympathetic. He told Ortega that with a little more tact and consideration on his part, the affair would have blown over without a fuss. Bad friends and bad advice had put him in his present anomalous position. But Doblado was willing to do what he could to smooth matters over if Ortega wished it.[83] Seemingly Doblado's efforts at reconciliation were successful, for on October 2, Ortega was named second in command of the army under Doblado.[84] Thus was settled another threat to the civilian government, and very fortunately for Mexico Ortega, by not making an attempt to seize the presidency, proved himself to be a great patriot.

On October 10 anti-administration elements in congress again tried to force Juárez into a cabinet change. This time the opposition agreed that Zamacona and Blas Balcárcel could remain but insisted that the others must go. Juárez refused on the ground that such a concession would make him only the docile instrument of congress. Any time the minority opposition demanded it, the president would have to make changes in his cabinet. But on November 26, after congress refused to accept the treaty he had negotiated with Wyke, Zamacona insisted on resigning. His departure forced Juárez to make other changes. The president tried to get Olaguíbel to head the cabinet, but the latter suggested offering the job to Lerdo in order to quiet congressional opposition. Emissaries approached Lerdo but no agreement could be reached, and again Juárez called upon Olaguíbel. Olaguíbel had not changed his mind and repeated his refusal, this time proposing that someone like Doblado be asked to serve.[85] After first trying to get Mariano Riva Palacio with no success, on December 5 Juárez wrote to Doblado asking him to become Minister of Relations.[86]

In an interview a few days later, Doblado replied that he would

81. Juárez, September 28, 1861, to Doblado. *Ibid.*
82. Ortega, two letters dated September 23, 1861, to Doblado. *Ibid.*
83. Doblado, September 29, 1861, to Ortega. Archivo Juárez. Copy sent to Juárez.
84. *Siglo,* October 2, 1861.
85. Juárez, *Archivos privados,* 306-307, 312-31; *Siglo,* November 27, 1861.
86. Doblado Typescripts.

accept only if the president would agree to two conditions. He wanted complete freedom in selecting a cabinet and, in addition, he demanded a free hand to manage affairs as he saw fit, with no interference from the president. Doblado argued that since sole responsibility would rest on him and the other members of his cabinet, he ought to be able to choose the men with whom he would be working. Such an arrangement would be advantageous for the president, too, since by giving Doblado responsibility for selecting the cabinet, he would avoid the unpleasantness of displeasing those people to whom he felt obligated through gratitude or commitments. Doblado's reason for stipulating that the cabinet have the power of independent action was that the government ought to adopt an energetic policy and to work dictatorially, doing whatever seemed best to promote the Reform. Juárez replied that since assuming the presidency he had been careful to uphold the constitution and the Reform, as well as the powers and prerogatives granted to him by law. The president explained to his prospective appointee the difference between the Mexican and European cabinet systems. In Mexico the ministers did not have sole responsibility for the conduct of the government, as was the case in Europe, because the constitution made the president also responsible by virtue of his power to name and remove cabinet members.

The next day the conversations continued with both men more or less repeating their positions. Doblado at first did not even want to tell the president the names of the men he intended to invite into the cabinet, but finally he produced his list of candidates—Pedro Hinojosa in War, Jesús Terán in Justice, and González Echeverría in Treasury.[87] Juárez was able to agree to the selections so Doblado immediately took over as head of the cabinet, and the others were in their posts by December 25.[88]

On December 11 congress, which was to end its session on the fifteenth, granted the executive extraordinary powers to deal with the crisis.[89] The new law continued the suspension of many individual guarantees in accordance with the law of June 7. In addition, it conferred upon the executive the power to take whatever measures he considered advisable during the emergency, the only

---

87. Juárez, *Archivos privados,* 313-314.
88. H. H. Bancroft, *History of Mexico* (6 vols., San Francisco, 1883-1888), VI, 26.
89. D y L, *Legislación,* IX, 334.

restrictions being that he must maintain the nation's independence and territorial integrity, the form of government established by the constitution, and the principles of the laws of Reform. Even these limitations almost caused Doblado to resign on December 12, but he reconsidered.

At the same time cabinet negotiations were underway, the threatened intervention became a fact with the arrival of a Spanish squadron at Veracruz. The troops landed immediately, and in January, 1862, French and British forces joined them. Statements issued by the English and Spanish indicated that they had come only to collect their debts, but the French were obviously intent on more than money. The difference in objectives soon caused disagreement among the allies, and their first attempt to negotiate with the Mexican government failed completely. The Europeans then sought permission to move their men from the coast to higher land since Veracruz was notoriously unhealthy. Juárez chose Doblado to carry on the conversations and he gave his minister very specific instructions: unless the allied powers recognized the constitutional government and offered to respect Mexico's independence and sovereignty in all matters, the administration would not allow them to move their troops to Jalapa and Tehuacán. Two days later, on February 14, Doblado left to open the negotiations.

In his conversations with General Juan Prim at La Soledad near Veracruz, Doblado received the assurances his government had demanded. The European powers declared it was not their aim to attack the independence and sovereignty of Mexico, nor the integrity of its soil. In return, the Mexican government gave the allies permission to move their forces to Córdoba, Orizaba, and Tehuacán. The allied powers agreed to withdraw the troops to the lines in front of the Mexican defenses near Veracruz if a peaceful settlement of the dispute proved impossible. The Soledad Convention, signed on February 19 and ratified by the European powers on the same day, also provided that the formal treaty negotiations should be held at Orizaba among Doblado and representatives of the three powers.

Before the Orizaba conference convened, the representatives of France, England, and Spain met to discuss the situation among themselves. The upshot was that Prim and Wyke could not go along with the French position. On April 11 the allied powers notified Juárez that the London Convention was dissolved and that the Spanish and English forces would reembark, leaving the French to choose their own course of action. When the Mexican government replied that it was prepared to negotiate, Wyke and Prim accepted and asked that Doblado be sent to carry on the discussions.[90] On April 24 Juárez instructed Doblado to renegotiate, in substance, the Zamacona Treaty. He was, however, to insist on several changes, one being not to permit foreign overseers in the customhouses.[91] Doblado, in spite of the president's orders, signed an agreement on even more onerous terms than the Wyke-Zamacona Treaty.[92] It had absolutely no chance of ratification.

With the breakdown in tripartite negotiations, the French troops began to withdraw according to the La Soledad Convention. But French officials accused the Mexicans of breaking the agreement on a technicality, and their troops never returned to the position agreed upon by the Soledad preliminaries. Full scale war now began between Mexico and France.

During all this time the Juárez government was actively making preparations for defense. In an effort to raise funds, it levied special contributions in Mexico City, reestablished the sales tax, and laid a one per cent tax on buildings. The states of San Luis Potosí, Puebla, Veracruz, Tamaulipas, and others were declared in a state of siege. On April 14 a call went out for volunteers, and state governors were asked to supply troops. On January 25 Juárez had issued a law which declared that all persons who in any way encouraged or assisted the intervention would be subject to capital punishment. With the breakdown of negotiations, the government decreed on April 12 that all places occupied by the French would be automatically in a state of siege and any Mexicans who remained in those areas during the occupation would be considered guilty of treason and their property confiscated.[93]

The first big battle occurred at Puebla where General Ignacio Zaragoza had concentrated his troops and where on May 5 the Mexicans repulsed the French attack in a day-long battle. Judging from the accounts now available, the French commander, General

90. Juárez, *Archivos privados*, 316-317, 323.
91. Archivo Juárez.
92. Juárez, *Archivos privados*, 323.
93. D y L, *Legislación*, IX, 350-352; 355-358; 364; 367-371; 423; 434-436.

Laurencez, evidently chose the worst possible place to attack and never was able to overcome his initial disadvantage. Probably no one was more surprised than the Mexicans over the outcome, and the country received the news with great rejoicing and, in certain areas such as in Zacatecas, with some anti-French rioting. Unfortunately the Mexicans were in no position to follow up their victory and could only wait for the attack to be repeated, but it was not until the following year that the French were able to capture the city.

Ortega, feeling that Mexico was now in a stronger position to negotiate with the invader, wrote on June 10 to Saligny. He explained to the French Minister that Mexico was genuinely republican and would not tolerate a monarchy. Then appealing to Saligny as a diplomat and as one who would be concerned with history's verdict, he asked if it would not be better to settle the issues by diplomacy rather than by war. If Saligny agreed, Ortega promised an immediate armistice. Ortega forwarded a copy of the letter to Juárez and gave his reasons for approaching the French. Juárez' reply was restrained but firm. He recognized, he said, Ortega's good intentions, but henceforth the general should confine himself strictly to military activities and refrain from entering the field of diplomacy. On June 17, having heard not a word from Saligny, Ortega wrote to Juárez that his proposal had been made in the strictest confidence and that there would be no embarrassment to the government because of his letter.[94]

As the war progressed and it became obvious that the hierarchy of the church was participating in the French intervention, the cries increased for drastic action against the clergy. Following the end of the civil war in 1861 anti-clericalism had led to some excesses: priests had been mistreated in the streets, government interventors had desecrated holy places, and churches had been robbed.[95] Although the government tried to prevent such manifestations,[96] it had not been completely successful and it took certain steps which violated the concept of religious toleration. A law issued on Feb-

---

94. Archivo Juárez.
95. See, for example, *Amigo del Pueblo*, March and April, 1861. It might be pointed out for this period that reports were coming in from various places that the clergy were continuing to stir up disobedience. For the Puebla area see the reports of Fco. de Lamadrid in the Ortega Typescripts.
96. *Archivo Mexicano*, V, 287.

ruary 1, 1861, reduced the number of convents, and on the next day the government assumed control of all hospitals and benevolent establishments of the church. But demands continued during the following year for greater restrictions on the clergy, especially when the foreign crisis threatened.

The government moved in this direction by issuing on August 30 a law which made it a crime for any clergyman to preach against the government or the laws. In addition, the same decree forbade the clergy to appear in public in ministerial garb and suspended the operation of all ecclesiastical chapters, except that of Guadalajara, for the duration of the emergency. On September 6 came another decree prohibiting religious demonstrations outside of the churches.[97] But as usual the radicals remained unsatisfied. They insisted that the government suppress all convents, as it had monasteries, under the law of July 12, 1859. Groups ran through the streets of Mexico City at night shouting "Death to the French, the Pope, and the Clergy." Even Prieto, apparently somewhat influenced by beer, got into the act.[98] The pressure continued on through the fall and into the next year,[99] when, finally, the government on February 26, 1863, succumbed to the demands and ordered all convents disbanded except the Sisters of Charity.[100]

Juárez was also having his troubles with Santiago Vidaurri. Vidaurri had agreed to help in fighting the intervention, but to the administration's repeated pleas for the promised aid he always replied that he had no money.[101] Actually he had more ready cash than any other governor and probably more than the national government for he controlled Tamaulipas and its very important port, Matamoros. By opening Matamoros to trade for the Confederates, Vidaurri made a profit from the movement of goods flowing through the city.[102] In typical Vidaurri fashion, however, he refused to cooperate with Juárez.

In August another cabinet crisis confronted the president. On the thirteenth Doblado told Juárez he wished to resign because of the

---

97. D y L, *Legislación*, IX, 32-33; 69-70; 524; 527.
98. Pedro Carbaja, Mexico, September 24, 1862, to Doblado. Doblado Typescripts.
99. See *Palo de Ciego* for January, 1863, as an example.
100. D y L, *Legislación*, IX, 594-595.
101. Roel, *Vidaurri*, 120-184.
102. F. L. Owsley, *King Cotton Diplomacy. Foreign Relations of the Confederate States of America* (Chicago, 1931), 118-139.

outcry against him. Although the complaint that he was attacking the principal liberal leaders was unfounded, Doblado believed the misconception was spreading and might eventually culminate in a revolt against the government. Doblado felt it better that he resign before this happened, and Juárez agreed.[103] Zarco maintained that no real opposition to Doblado existed, noting that the press had not attacked him even though he was invested with great authority.[104] But Zarco did not speak for all the liberals, many of whom feared Doblado and what he might do.

Within ten days the president had reorganized his cabinet. Juan Antonio de la Fuente took over Doblado's post in Relations; the other ministers were Terán in Justice, Núñez in Treasury, and Blanco in War. These changes did not satisfy many of the liberals, and the retention of Terán was the subject of bitter press attacks which charged that he was not moving fast enough against the known conservative leaders in Mexico City.

The liberals suffered a great loss when General Zaragoza, the hero of Puebla, died on September 8 of typhoid fever. In his place Juárez chose Ortega as head of the army in Puebla.[105] Very soon after his appointment Ortega had the opportunity to show that he had learned from his previous letter writing experience. Forey, recently appointed as French Commander in Chief, wrote to Ortega in November to thank him for returning some wounded French soldiers. He went on to say that he hoped in the future that Ortega would be fighting for a better cause and added some offensive remarks about the Mexican president. Ortega immediately forwarded the letter to Juárez, who advised him to tell Forey that his letter was not an insult to Juárez himself, but rather to the government and to the dignity and sovereignty of the nation.[106] Ortega followed the president's instructions and at the same time he returned Forey's letter, stating that it had no place among his records.[107]

After taking over the Puebla command, Ortega spent his time fortifying the city. He asked the government to unify the command

103. Juárez, *Archivos privados*, 324.
104. *Siglo*, August 17, 1862.
105. At this time the liberal forces consisted of three armies: the East under Ortega, Interior under Doblado, and Center under Comonfort. The latter had been allowed to reenter the services of the Mexican government.
106. Archivo Juárez.
107. Romero, *Corr. Mex.*, III, 96-97.

of the eastern and central armies under either himself or Comonfort, depending on whether the attack was made on Puebla or Mexico City. The request apparently was a maneuver to get the command into his own hands for, judging from French activity, the attack was certain to come against Puebla. The Minister of War was unsympathetic to the plan and decided to continue the independent armies.[108]

In February, 1863, Juárez visited Puebla to review the troops, inspect fortifications, and, in general, strengthen soldier morale. Later in the month Forey began his march toward the city. The actual fighting did not begin until March 21 and soon developed into a siege. Lack of coordination between the besieged troops and Comonfort's army eventually put Puebla's defenders in an impossible position, and on May 17 Ortega surrendered the city. The French took a large number of prisoners of war as a result of the defeat, among them Ortega himself, Patoni, and Porfirio Díaz. Fortunately for Mexico many of those captured, including Ortega, managed to escape while being transferred to Veracruz.

With the surrender of Puebla and the loss of one of his armies, Juárez began making preparations for the defense of Mexico City. But the government soon realized that the city could not be saved, especially after the state governors informed the administration that they needed their troops at home. It therefore decided to abandon the capital and move north. Juárez asked congress for an extension of his extraordinary powers, which the chamber granted after a lengthy debate.[109] On May 31 congress closed its session and that evening Juárez, his ministers, a small group of advisers, and a few deputies left Mexico City for San Luis Potosí.

108. The decision probably reflected some mistrust of Comonfort, for Juárez was receiving reports that Comonfort's agents were in the Puebla area suggesting that Comonfort would be the next president. Archivo Juárez.
109. *Siglo*, May 29, 1863.

Chapter V

INTERVENTION

As in the period of the War of Reform, Mexico again had two governments. The Juárez group represented the liberal, republican concept of democracy. The French, and later Maximilian, were the hope of the conservative-church faction which had encouraged the Intervention in the hope of recovering the ground lost to the Reform. In the war which ensued the liberals were decidedly the underdogs. The conservatives had the troops, and only a few large scale battles occurred after the early days of the war for the very good reason that the *juaristas* had practically no army. So precarious was the liberal government's position that it was almost constantly on the move and often threatened with capture by enemy forces. Yet all these advantages did not, in the end, add up to a conservative victory.

After leaving Mexico City the *juaristas* arrived in June, 1863, in San Luis Potosí where they set up their government. Here, because the French halted in Mexico City, Juárez had a breathing spell. But while for the moment San Luis offered a haven from the enemy, it did not offer the president any respite from the maneuverings of his associates. The cabinet carried over from Mexico City was discredited, and various factions sought to influence the choice of a new ministry, hoping thereby to control government policy. Practically everybody who was anybody turned up to see the president. Military leaders wanted men selected for cabinet posts who would be sure to give them complete cooperation. Radicals and moderates continued with unabated fury their old struggle for power. A deadly feud raged between the followers of Zarco and Zamacona and the more conservative moderate elements who regarded Doblado as the logical choice to lead the cabinet. Some of the former worried about Juárez' swinging over completely toward the more conservative position, and certainly he had been moving in that direction for some time.[1] Complicating the situation still further was the bitter personal antagonism between the supporters of

1. León Guzmán voiced this complaint in his El partido constitucional. . . .

Zarco and those of Doblado. Even before the government reached San Luis, Doblado's adherents were writing him about the lack of cohesion in the cabinet and complaining that Zarco seemed to be Juárez' top adviser, although he was not even in the cabinet.[2] Certain elements in both camps were not above trying to stir up trouble between the president and the general, but Doblado received warnings against these evildoers and assurances that Juárez had said he wanted to reach an understanding with Doblado.[3]

By mid-July Juárez was under tremendous pressure to change the make-up of his cabinet and to give Doblado a post. Those agitating for the change harped on the fact that nothing was being done to cope with the many problems facing the government; inactivity and paralysis seemed to them the outstanding characteristics of the cabinet.[4] On July 19 Vicente Riva Palacio and Joaquín M. Alcalde had a conference with the president. Riva Palacio did most of the talking and stressed the fact that a cabinet change was imperative for the ministers were unpopular and lacked prestige. Juárez, however, defended his cabinet against their attacks, saying it was a good cabinet and motivated by the greatest patriotism. Riva Palacio did not deny that the president's view might be correct but he insisted that a ministry so lacking in prestige and popularity ought to be dismissed. The president refused to commit himself but said he would think the matter over.[5]

Although Juárez almost invariably resisted outside demands for a cabinet change, seemingly as a matter of principle, two other factors probably added to his reluctance in this case. When Doblado had served earlier, he and the president had differed widely in their concepts of what the cabinet's power should be. In addition, the radicals would oppose the appointment for they distrusted Doblado. Therefore, Juárez moved slowly, as usual, but with the arrival on August 8 of General José López Uraga, a trusted friend and representative of Doblado, pressure on the president increased. In a two hour meeting with the cabinet, Uraga spoke his mind plainly and sharply for he felt the situation so perilous

2. José Linares, Querétaro, June 7, 1863, to Doblado. Doblado Typescripts.
3. Prieto, San Luis, July 19, to Doblado; José M. Núñez, San Luis, July 19, to Doblado. *Ibid.*
4. Letters to Doblado from Alcalde, San Luis, August 9; Riva Palacio and Alcalde, San Luis, July 15; Prieto, San Luis, August 9. *Ibid.*
5. Alcalde, San Luis, July 19, to Doblado. *Ibid.*

that all would be lost unless the president took quick action.⁶ Uraga insisted on the necessity of a cabinet change, and although Juárez again postponed his decision, obviously the feeling against the cabinet was running very high.⁷

Alcalde, also convinced that the government's inertia was leading to its political suicide, decided to apply pressure from another quarter. He planned to offer to the Permanent Deputation of Congress a resolution calling for the dismissal of the cabinet because of lack of public confidence,⁸ but Uraga and Prieto used their influence to prevent his introducing at that moment what amounted to a vote of censure. They suggested instead that he go to Juárez and explain the idea, pointing out that if the motion were presented the ministers would patriotically resign and Juárez would not have to suffer the embarrassment of asking them to leave. The fact that the president was being notified of the move beforehand should indicate to him that the action did not reflect any lack of respect or confidence in him personally. When Alcalde presented his arguments, Juárez replied that he felt the resolution was unnecessary; he counseled prudence in order to avoid a scandal since, if Alcalde persevered in his plan, the enemy would use the affair to play up the disagreements within the liberal camp. Juárez added that for the past five years he had been exhorted continually to change his cabinet and if he had given in each time he would have had a new cabinet every month.⁹

But the president soon yielded to the clamor for a new ministry. On August 14 Terán submitted his resignation and the others followed, but even before this time Juárez had begun to look for replacements. He sent Uraga to see if Doblado would be willing to accept the Ministry of War. Whom Juárez had in mind for the top post in the cabinet is not clear. But to offer Doblado the War Ministry was a fine political maneuver for it would keep him in a relatively minor position, perhaps meet the demands of his supporters, and at the same time might satisfy the radical faction. Doblado's mere presence in the cabinet would also increase its stature and prestige.

6. Uraga, San Luis, August 9, to Doblado. *Ibid.*
7. Prieto, San Luis, August 9, to Doblado. *Ibid.*
8. Alcalde, San Luis, August 9, to Doblado. *Ibid.*
9. Same to same, August 10. *Ibid.*

Doblado refused the bait, telling Juárez that the reorganization plans would leave intact all the existing difficulties and add new ones.[10] Uraga, after meeting with Doblado, gave the president more detailed reasons for Doblado's refusal. Although he had repeated to Doblado all the Juárez arguments and had even added some ideas of his own, Doblado would not agree to accept the post. Doblado had told Uraga that one could not have confidence in a cabinet unless it was composed of men who were perfectly united on the ends they were seeking. Moreover, the post of Minister of War had always been occupied by nonentities and he, too, would eventually become an unknown, thus losing whatever influence he might bring to the government.[11]

In response to another plea from Juárez[12] that he serve as Minister of War, Doblado on August 21 stated his terms plainly: "If you will allow me to take the cabinet post I want and to place in the other positions those who merit my confidence, then I will come and serve you." He added that under no other conditions would he agree to enter the government.[13] On the twenty-second Juárez wrote the reluctant general that he was willing to have him as chief of the cabinet along with Uraga as Minister of War, Sebastián Lerdo de Tejada in Justice, and Núñez in Treasury.[14] In short, Juárez realized he had to give the major post to Doblado in order to get him to serve, and the bargaining between the two men was now over who would name the remainder of the cabinet. Doblado did not concur in the president's selections; he replied only that he was coming to talk to Juárez about the men he wanted in the cabinet.[15]

On September 1 Doblado arrived in San Luis, and conversations between the two men began that night. Doblado said he approved of Lerdo as Minister of Justice, but he rejected the president's choice of Uraga for War and Núñez for Treasury. Juárez also had planned to send de la Fuente as Minister to Washington, and again Doblado announced his opposition. Juárez strongly defended the qualifications of the men he had selected, but finally he gave in and

10. Doblado, León, August 14, to Juárez. Archivo Juárez.
11. Uraga, León, August 14, to Juárez. *Ibid.*
12. Juárez wrote on August 15 and then, fearing his letter had been lost, on August 20 he sent a copy to Doblado. Doblado Typescripts.
13. Archivo Juárez.
14. Doblado Typescripts.
15. August 23, 1863. Archivo Juárez.

agreed to appoint Doblado's candidates: Comonfort in War, Careaga in Treasury, and Romero as the envoy to Washington. The next day Doblado returned to tell Juárez that after reconsidering he felt Núñez should remain in Treasury. The final arrangement having been made that afternoon, the cabinet was announced— Doblado, Lerdo, Comonfort, and Núñez.

The composition of the cabinet offered hope for a strong and stable administration, but within two days Doblado had precipitated a new crisis. He cut off the money paid to Zarco and Zamacona for their work in publishing newspapers for the government and ordered both of them to leave San Luis within two weeks and to be out of the country within a month.

On the afternoon of the fourth Zarco and Zamacona called on the president to discuss the order. Juárez told them he knew nothing about it but would talk to Doblado. Later that afternoon he summoned Doblado and told him that the order had to be revoked. Not only did the president deem it unjustifiable, but he pointed out that even if the two men had committed a crime punishable by exile, such a penalty could not be applied to them. The law granting the government extraordinary powers specifically exempted from its provisions high government officials, and Zarco and Zamacona enjoyed this immunity as members of congress. Doblado replied that he would revoke the order, but if Zarco remained in San Luis he (Doblado) would find it impossible to carry on because of Zarco's continual opposition. The president answered that if such a day should ever come, he and Doblado could agree then on the proper remedy, but for the moment they must avoid the storm which his order was certain to arouse. Doblado again said he would rescind his instructions, but he added that, in view of the way the government was organized, he did not feel he would be of much use and wanted the president to accept his resignation. Juárez urged him to consider the matter carefully since he did not think the episode sufficiently important, especially in the present circumstances when the government needed all its resources to cope with the great problems facing it. During the night and the following morning Lerdo and Comonfort pressed Doblado to stay on, and he did not persist in his idea of resigning.[16]

16. Juárez, *Archivos privados*, 325-327.

Unfortunately Doblado would not let the matter drop. When he saw Zarco he told him: "I have revoked the order because I found that the president respects what he calls the law; but nevertheless . . . if you do not leave San Luis within a week, I will use force to put you out."[17] When Zarco appealed to the president for protection, Juárez called in Lerdo and told him to get in touch with Doblado for the issue was creating a scandal and must be settled.[18] The next day Doblado saw the president and informed him that he simply could not work effectively if Zarco and his supporters remained and used their congressional immunity as a shield for their opposition; therefore he had to submit his resignation.[19] This time Juárez did not object, and on the same day Doblado left San Luis.[20] Juárez put his finger on the difficulty when he explained that Doblado and he had disagreed over the interpretation of the extraordinary powers granted to the president by congress. Doblado would not respect the immunities protecting the deputies and other high government officials while Juárez felt they must be upheld.[21] At this stage some hope still remained that Zarco would resolve the problem by leaving voluntarily, thus enabling Doblado to reenter the government. When it became evident that Zarco intended to remain, many of Doblado's followers felt increasingly bitter toward Zarco.[22]

The next day, September 8, both Comonfort and Lerdo submitted their resignations in order, so they said, to allow Juárez complete freedom in picking his new cabinet. Juárez felt there was no reason for them to leave the cabinet since they had disapproved of Doblado's order and were, therefore, in no way responsible for his resignation.[23] After three more days of discussion, Juárez was able to announce the formation of a new ministry in which Lerdo held the post of Minister of Relations and Comonfort that of War. José María Iglesias took over the Ministry of Justice and Núñez the Treasury. Of these men, Lerdo and Iglesias stayed in the cabinet throughout the Intervention.

17. Zarco, San Luis, September 6, to Juárez. Archivo Juárez.
18. Juárez, *Archivos privados*, 327.
19. Vicente Riva Palacio claimed that Doblado could not govern with a tutor. His letter to Doblado, September 8. Doblado Typescripts.
20. Juárez, *Archivos privados*, 328.
21. Juárez to Plácido Vega. Vega Papers, MSS, Vol. I, University of California.
22. For example: Prieto, San Luis, September 8 and 10, to Doblado; Alcalde, September 10, to Doblado. Doblado Typescripts.
23. Juárez, *Archivos privados*, 329.

Lerdo, perhaps trying to play both sides, assured Doblado that the whole situation was very distasteful to him, but that under the circumstances he and Comonfort had no other choice. The president had been greatly disturbed over their desire to resign and was sure that a great deal of turmoil would result, in which case he declared that he, himself, would leave the government. Finally, after several days of repeating their excuses and vainly suggesting other names, Lerdo and Comonfort accepted the inevitable and agreed to stay, but Lerdo repeated he was not happy over his situation.[24]

Iglesias sent a plea to Doblado for cooperation, assuring him that one of his chief aims was to preserve complete harmony between the government and Doblado. Perhaps in the hope that trust would bring reliability, Iglesias remarked that he was sure Doblado, working in cooperation with the cabinet, would patriotically use the powerful military force at his disposal to help preserve the national independence. No one in the cabinet, Iglesias asserted, was in the least hostile to Doblado; on the contrary, all the ministers held him in high esteem and felt he would be of great service in the present crisis.[25]

Although the new cabinet headed by Lerdo probably suffered from Doblado's absence, at least an administration existed which could now set to work. The military situation was particularly urgent for the government needed a competent general to take charge of the army of the center which, at the moment, was split into three sections. Uraga seemed to be the best choice, and Juárez dispatched Lerdo and Comonfort to persuade him to assume the command. After a conference also attended by Doblado, Lerdo reported that it would be difficult to bring Uraga into line since he kept stating conditions for his acceptance. Having finally exhausted all indirect methods of getting his point across, Uraga admitted candidly that the command would damage his reputation for he knew he would never receive sufficient men and matériel to be successful. Lerdo and Comonfort tried appealing to his sense of duty as an officer and patriot, but none of their arguments moved him.[26]

24. Lerdo, San Luis, September 12, to Doblado. Doblado Typescripts.
25. Iglesias, San Luis, September 13, to Doblado. *Ibid.*
26. Lerdo, Celaya, October 2, to Juárez. Archivo Juárez.

After failing to persuade Uraga to take command even by consenting to certain conditions, Juárez apparently then tried to make him do so by issuing an order giving him the top post without the concessions. In his reply Uraga expressed his complete distrust of the government: "I do not now have confidence in any post in which you place me. . . ."[27] There was nothing that could be done immediately and the division of the command among Uraga, Doblado, and Comonfort continued.

While internal crises were not conducive to positive accomplishments, the government did give its attention to the important problem of keeping the recognition of foreign nations. In identical notes sent on July 22 to the governments of the friendly powers, de la Fuente emphasized that Juárez represented the legal government of Mexico; he had been and was still the legally elected president. In addition, the constitutional government which he headed retained the loyalty of the great majority of Mexicans and controlled most of the national territory. The conservative success in capturing Mexico City did not necessarily indicate ultimate victory for, although their enemy had held the capital during the War of Reform, the liberals had won. De la Fuente concluded with a warning that the Intervention was not just a threat to Mexico but a menace to all nations.[28] His note had little effect, however, for the important European nations had already decided to recognize the Empire, while the United States very early indicated its disapproval of the scheme.

To give a concrete demonstration that a bona fide government did indeed exist, Juárez attempted to assemble congress. A less dedicated man would scarcely have considered such a move, but not until December, 1863, did Juárez abandon the idea. The permanent deputation of congress, however, continued to meet.

In October the French Commander, General F. A. Bazaine, undertook his own diplomatic negotiations in an effort to get the Juárez government to come to terms. Manuel Siliceo, serving as Bazaine's intermediary, wrote to Comonfort informing him that the French were sending an agent to San Luis to confer with the liberals. The emissary failed to make any headway for Lerdo notified him that before any negotiations could be undertaken the

27. Uraga, Querétaro, October, to Juárez. *Ibid.*
28. D y L, *Legislación*, IX, 642-646.

French must agree to respect Mexican independence and to leave the Mexicans free to choose their own form of government. Bazaine could not, of course, accept such conditions.[29]

Without awaiting the outcome of their peace feelers, the French had opened their campaign against the interior late in October. The troops which started out from Mexico City were divided into two sections: one under Castagny and Márquez had Morelia as its objective; the aim of the second under Douay was to capture Guadalajara by way of Querétaro and Lagos. Their first important conquest was Querétaro on November 17. On the last day of November, Berriozábal surrendered Morelia, and since the fall of the city meant in effect the loss of the whole state of Michoacán, Uraga attempted its recapture on December 17 but was repulsed with great losses. Earlier, on December 8, Doblado gave up Guanajuato, and French forces moved north to San Luis which they occupied on the twenty-fifth, the government having left three days earlier. Negrete's assault in an effort to recapture the city on December 27 was unsuccessful. When the French took Guadalajara on January 5, 1864, it meant they were in possession of a considerable part of the interior and held some of its most important cities.[30]

As the French troops under General Tomás Mejía advanced toward San Luis, the government decided to leave the city and move farther north to Saltillo. On the eve of its departure another cabinet shuffle had occurred: Iglesias took over from Núñez in the Treasury and Uraga, in spite of the previous disagreements, filled the vacancy in War created by Comonfort's death in November.

But even en route to Saltillo, where he and his followers arrived on January 9, 1864, Juárez got no relief from his political problems. The series of reverses had been discouraging and the idea occurred to some liberals that the solution to their problem was a change in the presidency. Doblado and Ortega were the spokesmen for this faction, and after the two had conferred, Doblado wrote to Juárez from Zacatecas on January 3. In his letter Doblado said he had learned that before Juárez left San Luis, he had stated he would resign from the presidency if this would help put an end to the disastrous situation in which the republic found itself. Doblado enthusiastically endorsed the idea, assuring the president that this

---

29. Knapp, *Lerdo*, 83-84, has an excellent summary of the whole affair.
30. Bancroft, *Mexico*, VI, 115-121; Vigil, *Reforma*, 621-622.

was the only way to save the country from the imminent ruin which threatened it. The French had said repeatedly that, although they would not deal with Juárez, they would respect the independence of the country. Such talk was sheer pretense, but the only way to prove the French insincere was to go through with the resignation. Such a move would unmask them and demonstrate their bad faith to the whole world. On the other hand, if the French actually meant what they said Juárez would truly be the saviour of his country.[31] Not satisfied with merely writing letters, Ortega and Doblado each sent representatives to Saltillo to confer with Juárez and to urge him to resign. At the meeting which took place on January 14, the commissioners repeated the arguments, but without effect.

In letters to Doblado and Ortega,[32] Juárez announced firmly that he had no intention of leaving the presidency because, at such a critical time for the nation, neither honor nor duty would permit him to abandon the office to which his countrymen had called him. His resignation, he pointed out, was exactly what the French wanted, for it would make the government look ridiculous and would plunge the country into disagreement and anarchy. Since the enemy had already demonstrated that they were not interested in individuals and that their object was to destroy the legal government, Juárez did not share Doblado's faith that the French would deal with Ortega. Nor would they, in his opinion, negotiate with anyone else who did not first accept the Intervention. Juárez reminded Doblado that the Mexicans themselves might not approve of his resignation. They might also refuse to recognize the legality of Ortega's succession, basing their stand on the fact that after he had been elected to two public offices he had selected the governorship of Zacatecas. Should even one state take such a position, Ortega would be compelled either to bring it into line by force or lose prestige, and in either case the French would profit.

Ortega was always harping on the theme that the French would never deal with Juárez but would come to terms with some other liberal leader, yet Bazaine's letters concerning generals who might desert to the French do not support Ortega's contention. In all cases Bazaine was very clear: no bargaining would be allowed;

31. Archivo Juárez.
32. Dated January 20, 1864. *Ibid.*

new adherents must submit completely to the government in Mexico City. Bazaine's position, taken earlier in the previously mentioned conversations at San Luis, was restated plainly in the negotiations with Doblado in late 1863 and early 1864, at the very time Doblado was pressing Juárez to resign. General Mejía had written Bazaine that Doblado wanted to suspend the fighting temporarily in order to conduct negotiations. Bazaine replied that this was not the first time Doblado had suggested talks; but, before any conference could take place, Doblado had to submit completely to the Intervention. On this point no compromise would be permitted.[33] In reporting the incident to the French Minister of War, Bazaine explained that as usual Doblado was laying down certain conditions for submission: he demanded the acceptance of the London Convention and the establishment of an independent Mexican government under the protection of the three powers who signed the convention.[34] In view of Bazaine's adamant stand that negotiations must be preceded by acceptance of the Intervention, it was sheer illusion to think that a liberal government would survive any arrangement with the French.

Fortunately for the Juárez government neither Doblado nor Ortega regarded Juárez' refusal to resign as an excuse to withdraw their support. And at this time their help was essential, for Juárez was again having trouble with Vidaurri.

On leaving San Luis in December the government had considered moving to Monterrey to establish its permanent residence. But since Monterrey was Vidaurri's headquarters and therefore a refuge of questionable safety, the government finally decided to make Saltillo its temporary headquarters until it could break Vidaurri's power. For Juárez realized, even before leaving San Luis, that this time he could not afford to compromise with Vidaurri since control of northeastern Mexico and its ports was at stake.[35] Two factors made it imperative. In the first place, Vidaurri insisted on administering the states under his control in whatever way he pleased, with no interference from the central government. Not only was such a situation bad in itself, but Vidaurri thus became a constant

33. January 9, 1864. García, *Raros*, XVII, 174-176.
34. March 9, 1864. *Ibid.*, XVIII, 55-56. There is the possibility that Doblado was negotiating simply to gain time so that he could secure his fortune before leaving Mexico for the United States. *Ibid.*
35. Juárez, *Archivos privados*, 17.

Intervention. 103

incitement to other would-be potentates. In addition, the traffic in goods, especially through the port of Matamoros, gave him a handsome revenue which he guarded jealously and refused to share with the national government. Two compelling reasons then, one political and the other financial, convinced Juárez that the time had come to attempt a showdown with the *caudillo* from Monterrey.

In January, Iglesias, Minister of the Treasury, notified Vidaurri that the federal government needed money badly and ordered him to send to the national treasury all the revenue collected in the states of Nuevo León and Coahuila which belonged to the federal government. Vidaurri, being loathe to part with any of his income, replied that to carry out the order would ruin his state. Iglesias answered that the instructions could not be revoked.

The administrator of the customhouse at Piedras Negras, on receiving notice from Iglesias to turn over his receipts to the federal treasury, informed the Minister that Vidaurri had repeatedly instructed him never to obey instructions from the federal government to turn funds over to it. Consequently, he could not send any money to Iglesias. Further correspondence with Vidaurri on the matter of revenue brought no results, and finally Iglesias bluntly asked the governor whether or not he proposed to obey the national government.[36] Vidaurri's reaction to this query was defiant, whereupon the government determined to move to Monterrey[37] so that it could deal directly with the governor and decide what action to take. Fortunately Doblado had arrived with his troops, and on February 10 he and his troops preceded the government out of Saltillo. That evening Juárez and his party came upon Doblado camped four leagues outside of Monterrey and learned that the cannon which Doblado had set up in the city to salute the president on his arrival had been seized by Vidaurri. But the president was not to be deterred and on the morning of the twelfth he entered the city. No welcoming demonstrations greeted him and the atmosphere was generally hostile. Vidaurri remained in his headquarters surrounded by troops and in spite of much urging, he refused to meet with Juárez. The stalemate continued until Vidaurri

36. Niceto de Zamacois, *Historia de Méjico desde sus tiempos mas remotos hasta nuestros días* (22 vols., Barcelona, 1878-1903), XVII, 47-63. The last four volumes in this set were written by Francisco Cosmes.
37. A circular of February 5 announced the change in capital. Bancroft, *Mexico*, VI, 129.

received reinforcements; then he notified the government that if Doblado's forces were not out of the city on the fourteenth, he would attack. Since Doblado was now without artillery he could not risk a battle and agreed to withdraw. Vidaurri had told the government it could stay on and make its headquarters in Monterrey, an invitation which was not accepted.[38]

Just before Juárez was to leave he and Vidaurri finally got together and, while accounts of their meeting differ, all versions agree on one point—it was very short, lasting about ten minutes. Although Prieto did not attend the conference and awaited the results in the street below, his description is probably as accurate as any since he was very close to the members of the government and must have received a full report. Lerdo, Iglesias, and Suárez Navarro accompanied the president. The interview was cool and came to an abrupt end when Vidaurri's son drew a pistol and declared for revolt. Lerdo, having anticipated some such denouement, had the foresight to station a coach in the street, and Juárez and his companions, leaving the room "with great haste," hurried down to the carriage where Prieto joined them. As they drove off, a mob followed shouting insults, but a few loyal soldiers held off the infuriated crowd and the party made its escape.[39] Even granting that Prieto exaggerated somewhat, the retreat could hardly be called dignified.

Once back in Saltillo the president undertook a series of moves designed to break Vidaurri's power.[40] He sent secret agents into the state to undermine the governor and concentrated additional federal forces in the area. On February 26 the government issued three decrees which dissolved the union of the states of Nuevo León and Coahuila and declared both of them in a state of siege. When Juárez ordered Vidaurri to Saltillo to stand trial for his defiance of the central government, Vidaurri replied by publishing a letter Bazaine had written him on February 15, inviting him to join the Intervention. Vidaurri did not commit himself; instead he announced a plebiscite in which the people of Nuevo León and Coahuila could vote whether they wanted peace or war—peace, of course, meaning recognition of the Intervention. On March 5 the

---
38. Vigil, *Reforma*, 628-630.
39. G. Prieto, *Lecciones de historia patria escritas para los alumnos del colegio militar* (México, 1893), 503.
40. Zamacois, *Mexico*, XVII, 67-91; Vigil, *Reforma*, 630.

Intervention 105

government issued a decree which declared Vidaurri a traitor and defined as a treasonable act any participation in the scheduled elections.[41] By this time Juárez had some 7,000 men with which to threaten the governor, and Vidaurri realized his position was critical. Within twenty days he sent commissioners to Juárez to offer terms for settling the differences between them. But the president now held the power and did not need to be conciliatory, so word went back to Vidaurri that he must submit without reservation. Refusing to yield, Vidaurri decided to retreat to Piedras Negras but, this course proving impossible, he finally took refuge in Texas.[42] Later he went over to the French but by that time he was no longer of any value to them. On April 2 Juárez moved to Monterrey;[43] a few days later Maximilian entered Mexico City.

Even before the Vidaurri episode ended, more trouble was brewing with another general. Because distances were great and communications poor, Juárez found it necessary to delegate extensive powers to military chiefs.[44] Thus on March 31, Uraga was appointed General in Chief of the Army of the Center with complete authority to decide the civil, fiscal, and military policies necessary for the defense of the states of Jalisco, Colima, Michoacán, Guanajuato, Querétaro, and two districts in the state of México.[45] Unknown to the government was the fact that in March, Uraga had started negotiations with the French.[46] But the liberals had begun to suspect his intentions when on March 28 he had issued a manifesto critical of the president. He had rejected the label of *juarista,* and although he solemnly promised to defend Mexico and her independence, he had made no reference to the constitution or the Reform Laws.

When General Corona, who had signed the manifesto, became aware of the liberal reaction he felt compelled to issue a statement in which he said that he interpreted the manifesto as a pledge to defend the constitution and the Reform. When Uraga learned of Corona's explanation, he wrote his subordinate an angry letter,

41. D y L, *Legislación,* IX, 673-679.
42. Zamacois, *Mexico,* XVII, 67-91.
43. When Juárez took over control of northeastern Mexico the Confederate government was afraid that he might put a stop to its shipping. But he needed money and the trade continued. Owsley, *King Cotton,* 143-144.
44. José M. Iglesias, *Revistas históricas sobre la intervención francesa en México* (3 vols., México, 1867-1869), II, 330.
45. D y L, *Legislación,* IX, 679-680.
46. García, *Raros,* XX, 120-126.

telling him that any time he wished to ask for a leave it would be granted. Corona now became convinced that Uraga was up to no good and tried to persuade Governor Arteaga to take action quickly before Uraga could do any damage. Arteaga, having complete faith in Uraga, tried instead to make peace between the two men, but Corona would not change his mind and asked to be transferred.⁴⁷ But the distrust continued, and finally Arteaga accused Uraga of having treasonable correspondence with the enemy. Uraga, realizing his position was now completely exposed, resigned and went over to the enemy. In doing so, however, he was able to take a number of his officers with him.⁴⁸ On July 1 Arteaga was made General in Chief of the Army of the Center and granted all the powers previously held by Uraga.⁴⁹

During the months the government remained in Monterrey, Juárez and his cabinet devoted most of their energies to keeping armies in the field for survival hinged on the military. In southern Mexico, Díaz was doing a good job, but in the north prospects were gloomy. The French had continued the successes of their campaign launched in the autumn of 1863. After capturing Guadalajara in January, they went on to take Aguascalientes and Zacatecas to the north and Colima to the south. In mid-May the republican cause suffered a severe blow when Doblado encountered the interventionists at Matehuala and was routed with a loss of about 1,200 men and all his artillery. By the end of June the top generals in the north, Negrete, Ortega, and Patoni, with Cortina and Garza in Tamaulipas, commanded about 12,000 men scattered over a wide area.⁵⁰

As the French moved northward toward Monterrey the government tried to strengthen its forces by bringing Colonel Julián Quiroga back into the fold. Quiroga, who had supported Vidaurri, kept insisting that the government make a number of concessions to which the president would not agree. Juárez maintained that any compromise meant the loss of dignity and he demanded that Quiroga pledge himself to obey the national government. After much negotiating through intermediaries, of whom Ortega was one,

---

47. Vigil, *Reforma*, II, 644-645.
48. García, *Raros*, XX, 197.
49. D y L, *Legislación*, IX, 686-687.
50. Bancroft, *Mexico*, VI, 125, 162. A short time later Doblado applied for and received permission to reside in the United States. There he died not long afterward.

Quiroga finally agreed to the president's terms. In return, the government on August 2 granted him amnesty for his part in the Vidaurri revolt. After the Quiroga affair had been settled, Ortega was ordered to Saltillo to prepare for battle against the advancing French; Juárez sent his family to Matamoros from whence they could proceed to the United States.[51] On August 15 the government left Monterrey. Quiroga betrayed Juárez' trust by attacking the government party after it left Monterrey, but the presidential escort was able to beat him off.[52]

From Monterrey the government traveled westward to the state of Durango. At the hacienda of Santa Rosa a conference was held with Ortega and José María Patoni to determine what the military strategy should be. The decision was taken to make Durango, capital of the state, the object of the campaign, and Ortega was put in charge of the troops with Patoni as second in command. The president and his entourage awaited the results of the battle, for on its outcome depended the future location of their headquarters. On September 21 news arrived of the complete defeat of the liberal forces at Majoma and the disintegration of the last sizeable army in the north.[53] Many people complained, even Juárez himself, that Ortega had botched the command.[54] Five days later the *juarista* forces surrendered Matamoros; the French had already occupied Monterrey on August 26.

With the news of the army's defeat, the presidential party and its military escort started out for the city of Chihuahua. After a difficult journey through the desert, during which provisions were scarce and desertions frequent, the small group finally reached its destination on October 12, 1864. For over two years, until December, 1866, the sparsely populated state of Chihuahua was the home of the republican leaders.

From the time of the government's departure from Monterrey until well into 1865 when the French intention of withdrawing became apparent, the liberals continued to experience dark days. Although the Civil War in the United States ended in April, 1865, and the American government made it plain both to France and to Maximilian that it would not tolerate continuance of the empire

51. Juárez, *Archivos privados*, 344-348.
52. Zamacois, *Mexico*, XVII, 460-461.
53. Vigil, *Reforma*, 654-656.
54. Juárez, *Archivos privados*, 30.

in Mexico, some time elapsed before this sterner attitude could have its effect. In the meantime, although the imperial troops continued to defeat the liberals and to gain more territory, they could hardly claim to have pacified the country. Not having sufficient strength to attack in force, the republicans made guerrilla warfare the basis of their operations, and they continued to fight even though at times their cause seemed so futile as to be ridiculous. During this period, the French twice captured the city of Chihuahua and forced the Mexican government to Paso del Norte, but not once did Juárez cross over into the United States.[55]

From time to time the burden was lightened by a celebration, perhaps of a national holiday or the president's birthday, and then a few corks could be popped. But these occasions were rare, and the daily routine of the members of the government was one of waiting, waiting, waiting: waiting for the mail to come from Romero in Washington so they could find out what was happening in the world and in southern Mexico, for he was their main source of information; waiting (and hoping) for money; waiting for letters from friends and family. Juárez never forgot his family in the United States and kept up an active correspondence with them and his son-in-law. In most of the letters to his family Juárez is stiff, but when news arrived that Pepe, his favorite child, was ill, his emotions showed plainly in a letter to Santacilia:

> I write to you under the most profound grief that breaks my heart, for Romero in his letter of November 14, which I received last night, told me that my dear son Pepe was gravely ill and that there was fear for his life. I know it was only because Romero did not want to tell me the sad news of the little one's death that he said he was gravely ill; but really my little Pepe now is no longer alive, no longer alive, isn't that so? You know how much I suffer from this irreparable loss of my boy who was my delight, my pride, my hope. Poor Margarita. She will be unconsolable.[56]

By January 12, however, hope for Pepe's life had returned and

---

55. In a conference with the president in Monterrey on July 28 Ortega had told him there was much discouragement because many people felt that the government was about to disappear and that Juárez himself intended to leave the country. Juárez answered that it was not true he was leaving the country; he intended to die in Mexico. *Ibid.*, 344.

56. Chihuahua, January 6, 1865. *Ibid.*, 35.

he could imagine him going to school. So he wrote to Santacilia telling him that the children should not be instructed by any Jesuit nor any religious group; that they should understand philosophy in that they should learn to search for the truth by reason.[57] But a month later the sad news arrived of the death of Pepe and Juárez again wrote to Santacilia telling him of his grief and asking him to watch over his wife.[58] He soon heard from his wife and her courage made him feel better.[59]

The Juárez government continued its efforts, though with little success, to get help from abroad. Terán had been sent to Europe, but from the beginning his mission was destined to fail. He was appointed Envoy Extraordinary and Minister Plenipotentiary to Spain and England until 1865, when he became simply an agent of the government.[60]

The United States offered more hope. In the instructions drawn up and sent to Romero by Lerdo in December, 1864, the Foreign Minister expressed the government's confidence in its envoy in Washington. Romero was instructed not to sign any agreement which would deprive Mexico of its independence or territorial integrity but, within those limitations, he was allowed a great deal of freedom in his negotiations for loans, military supplies, and troops.[61] Although Romero constantly pressed Secretary of State Seward to take positive action, as long as the Civil War continued the United States could do little. In spite of the American refusal to enter into any formal agreement with Mexico, Juárez personally appreciated the value of American moral support. He wrote to Santacilia on July 12, 1865: "I believe I have already told you that even though the United States does not give us any direct aid, its attitude and its refusal to recognize Maximilian are enough. . . ."[62]

Romero's frustrations often made him very bitter toward Seward, but he was nonetheless a very capable propagandist who did a good job for his country. By lobbying and by maintaining and extending his contacts with those who might be of help, he carried on a very effective campaign to gain sympathy and support for the

---

57. *Ibid.*, 36.
58. February 23. *Ibid.*, 39.
59. March 23. *Ibid.*, 48-49.
60. *La misión confidencial de Don Jesús Terán en Europa, 1863-1866*, in AHDM, 2nd Series, Vol. I.
61. Romero, *Corr. Mex.*, IV, 565-567; Knapp, *Lerdo*, 105-106.
62. Juárez, *Archivos privados*, 73.

Mexicans. By the time the Civil War ended many men, both in military and government circles, favored unrestricted aid to Mexico.[63]

Besides Romero many other Mexican representatives were at work in the United States, one of the most active being Plácido Vega in San Francisco. He found a good deal of sympathy for the Mexican cause and was able to play upon it in a Mexican newspaper published in the city. Vega hoped to get clearance for goods and materials to be shipped to Mexico but he encountered all kinds of legal trouble.[64]

While the United States never did agree formally to send aid, the liberal government was receiving arms from that country even during the Civil War, with the supply increasing after the war in the United States ended. For example, W. W. Mills, Collector of Customs at El Paso during the period Juárez was just across the river in Paso del Norte, stated that he furnished arms to the republican government by devious means.[65] General Sheridan wrote in his memoirs: "During the winter and spring of 1866 we continued covertly supplying arms and ammunition to the Liberals —sending as many as 30,000 muskets from Baton Rouge alone."[66]

Although the military situation was hardly favorable to the liberal cause, the government throughout these dreary months did not lose hope in ultimate victory. The official newspaper, the *Periódico Oficial,* reflected the administration's attitude. Its European news stressed the dissensions abroad which might worry the French sufficiently to cause them to withdraw their troops from Mexico. Since the government never relinquished its hope that real aid would come from the United States, the *Periódico* repeatedly mentioned the vindication of the Monroe Doctrine. Also the subject of frequent discussion was the dissension among the followers of Maximilian and the controversies between church and state which still flourished under the empire. Omitting no possible means of salvation, the paper also considered the effect Napoleon's death would have on French foreign policy. After concluding that

63. Dexter Perkins, *Hands Off. A History of the Monroe Doctrine* (Boston, 1942), 123-130.
64. Vega Papers. Robert B. Brown, "Guns over the border: American aid to the Juárez government during the French Intervention," unpublished doctoral dissertation, University of Michigan, sums up the various attempts to obtain aid.
65. W. W. Mills, *Forty Years at El Paso, 1858-1898* (El Paso?, 1901), 85-87.
66. P. H. Sheridan, *Personal Memoirs* (2 vols., New York, 1888), II, 224-226.

the result would be an end to French support for Maximilian, the *Periódico* callously observed that the present would be a most judicious time for Napoleon III to die, since it had to happen sometime.

Not all this speculation was idle dreaming for the *Periódico's* visions had some substance to them. With the end of the Civil War in the United States, Seward was adopting a stiffer attitude toward the French. Events in Europe were an additional lever, for Napoleon watched uneasily the increase of Prussian power, and the French people complained over the cost of the Mexican expedition. Disunity among the Mexican conservatives was also a fact, the disaffection being especially pronounced among the clergy. At no time, either before or after accepting the crown, had Maximilian made clear his position regarding the church. The French had decided, before the emperor reached Mexico, to keep the land laws of the liberals, a decision which gave little immediate encouragement to the clergy. The hierarchy must have expected better things from Maximilian, but the emperor had no desire to decrease his power by accepting the clerical position. Ultimately his attitude toward church-state relations came to be practically identical with that of the *juaristas,* and the attempt to settle the church question by friendly negotiations with a papal nuncio ended in an utter fiasco.

Disagreements between Maximilian and Bazaine over matters of policy and authority weakened the empire still further, and Maximilian's tendency to blame his difficulties on the French commander did not improve the situation. Actually Maximilian, whom the French nicknamed "el archidupe" and the Mexicans "el empeorador," was proving something less than the ideal sovereign. Published documents and Corti's account of the empire demonstrate the complete lack of realism with which he so frequently approached any problem.

While the military situation had not favored the liberals in the months following the government's retreat to Chihuahua, Juárez had at least enjoyed some relief from the squabbles within the liberal ranks for cabinet posts and power. By the end of 1865, however, the president was again defending his position, this time against Ortega's claims that the presidency legally belonged to him. Under the provisions of the constitution the president's term of office began on December 1 and lasted for four years. In the absence of an elected president, the president of the supreme court served as chief executive until elections were held. Juárez had assumed office in May of 1861 and, consequently, the question arose whether his term should expire in December, 1864, at the end of three and one-half years in office, or whether he could legally continue until December, 1865, which would make his term six months longer than that prescribed by the constitution.

On November 30, 1864, Ortega had asked Lerdo for an interpretation of the constitution fixing the date of Juárez' retirement from office.[67] Lerdo replied that under the constitution the president could serve until the last day of November of the fourth year following his election, which meant that Juárez' term did not expire until 1865, an interpretation which Ortega accepted.

In this same exchange of letters Ortega inquired about his own legal position. Was it possible, he wanted to know, for him to hold his post on the supreme court and the governorship of Zacatecas at the same time? Article 118 of the constitution provided that no person could hold simultaneously two elective positions in the government, but the person concerned might select the position which he preferred. Lerdo answered that, as the government had said many times, Ortega would have to make a choice, adding that he probably preferred the governorship. Had Lerdo stopped right there Ortega would have been put on the defensive and would have been forced to declare himself. But Lerdo went on to say that under the circumstances and in view of the impossibility of providing for a successor to the presidency, the government still considered Ortega as first in line of succession in the event the presidency were left vacant.

Although this answer could be interpreted two ways, apparently the matter was not pursued further. Shortly afterward Ortega asked permission to leave Chihuahua to fight the enemy, and he also requested that he be allowed to take the most convenient route to the interior, even if that might mean crossing through a foreign country. The government complied with Ortega's wishes and granted him an indefinite leave which would expire only when he returned to

67. This whole question of Ortega's bid for the presidency is well summarized in I. E. Cadenhead, "González Ortega and the Presidency of Mexico," *HAHR*, XXXII, No. 3, 331-346.

Intervention

government headquarters or the administration recalled him or gave him a specific commission. He was given complete freedom to operate against the French with whatever armies he might raise, the only restriction being that he must coordinate his efforts with whatever republican forces were already in the field.[68] Ortega then proceeded to the United States where he remained during the year 1865.[69]

Juárez had considered for some months the possibility that Ortega might claim the right to assume the presidency in the fall of 1865.[70] By October the question was being discussed openly, and finally on November 8 Juárez issued two decrees designed to take the initiative away from Ortega and answer his claims before they were made. The first extended the terms of the president and of the president of the supreme court until such time as new elections became possible.[71] Juárez based his authority for this action on the extraordinary powers granted to him by congress which empowered him to take any steps necessary to save the independence of Mexico, the constitutional form of government, and the principles of the Reform.

The second decree[72] declared that since Ortega had remained in a foreign country without the permission or commission of the government, upon his return he would be subject to judicial proceedings on two counts. He would have to face charges to determine if he were guilty of the political crime of voluntarily abandoning his post as president of the supreme court. In his capacity as general of the army he would be arrested and tried for the crime of deserting his men and the cause of the Republic. To fill the vacancy created by Ortega's withdrawal, the decree empowered the government to name a substitute president of the supreme court, who would be next in line of succession. As we have seen, Ortega had received permission from the government to remain out of the country indefinitely, but Juárez denied to Prieto

68. Ortega, *Golpe*, 223-225.
69. Juárez had expected Ortega to go to Sonora, Sinaloa, or Coahuila since the routes there were not threatened by the enemy. He chose instead to go to New York because he was tired and discouraged and needed to get far away from the enemy to revive his sagging spirits. Juárez to Santacilia, Chihuahua, May 18, 1865. Juárez, *Archivos privados*, 63.
70. See his letters to Santacilia from May, 1865, ff. *Ibid.*, 63-87.
71. D y L, *Legislación*, IX, 718-719.
72. *Ibid.*, 719-721.

that this had been his intention and claimed he had so written Ortega.⁷³ There does not, however, seem to be any evidence to support the president on this point. Although at least as early as September Juárez had considered the question of presidential succession, he claimed he had not at that time made up his mind as to what course he would follow. He believed he had the power to extend his term but feared that some liberals, considering his action illegal, might use it to foment a civil war which would mean Mexico's ruin.⁷⁴ Eventually he became convinced that the nation would approve his continuing in office and that there would be no danger of a rebellion, and the fact that no real disturbances occurred justified the step in his own mind.⁷⁵ Lerdo had a great deal to do with the procedure the government finally adopted to extend the president's term.⁷⁶

On December 26 Ortega issued a statement protesting the legality of the president's action and arguing his own case.⁷⁷ He dealt first with his retention of both the supreme court position and the governorship of Zacatecas. Under Article 95 of the constitution a magistrate might resign his office only for a grave reason, and the resignation had to be approved by congress or the permanent delegation of that body. Ortega noted at this point that at various times after 1861 he had held two or more positions simultaneously and no one had complained. He also brought to his defense Title IV of the constitution which stated that congress, acting as a grand jury, was to decide whether there was cause for proceeding against the president of the court when he was accused of a crime of the common order, such as the charge of desertion brought against him in the second decree of November 8. Juárez, therefore, did not have any power under the constitution to order Ortega's arrest and trial, nor did his extraordinary powers give him that authority. The congressional decrees granting the president those

---

73. The two old friends broke over the succession issue. Although they continued to address one another in the familiar in their letters, obviously the relationship had become strained. Correspondence in Archivo Juárez.
74. Juárez, September 27, to Santacilia. Juárez, *Archivos privados*, 90-91.
75. Paso del Norte, November 10, 1865; Chihuahua, November 24, December 1, December 8, 1865. *Ibid.*, 101; 104-107.
76. Knapp, *Lerdo*, 103-104.
77. Cadenhead, "González Ortega and the Presidency." Ortega was not the only claimant. Manuel Ruiz was also insisting on his rights to the presidency. His position is made clear in his *Ministro constitucional de la suprema corte de justicia de la nación* (México, 1868).

wide powers specifically prohibited the executive from contravening in any way the provisions of Title IV of the constitution.

In defending his absence from the country Ortega published the letter granting him permission to leave the country for an indefinite period, with the understanding that he would continue the war by reentering Mexico at some other point. Although it was true that he had not returned, he claimed he had spent his time in the United States working for the republican cause.

Unquestionably, Juárez' legal term of office had expired, yet his retention of the post is justifiable when one considers which man stood the better chance of keeping alive the fight against the Intervention. By 1865 Juárez, through his persistence and determination, had become the nation's symbol of resistance to the French. On the other hand, Ortega's previous flightiness and even on occasion his seeming eagerness to deal with the enemy did little to stamp him as a firm and resolute leader. Even now he still seemed to think that, although the interventionists refused to negotiate with Juárez, they would deal with him. As we have seen, the evidence does not support this assumption; in fact, Maximilian merely viewed the dispute as a means of strengthening his own position.[78] Many others besides Juárez must have had doubts about Ortega's qualifications to hold the presidency at such a time, since Ortega received very little support when he made his bid. Most Mexicans remained loyal to Juárez and justified their position on the ground that it was absolutely necessary to avoid division among the liberals at this critical point.[79] Though Juárez exceeded his constitutional powers he made the correct decision.

Ortega did not return immediately from the United States to push his claim in person, but in November, 1866, he appeared in Texas en route to Mexico for that purpose. The American authorities, wishing to spare Juárez the embarrassment his presence might cause, arrested him and sent him off to New Orleans. After being released, Ortega made his way to Zacatecas where he

78. Corti, *Maximilian*, II, 561.
79. Prieto, Patoni, Negrete, Huerta, and Vega were Ortega's principal supporters. Vega, in San Francisco, was especially willing. He wired Ortega on March 27, 1866: "I have the war material to open campaign through the frontier. . . . Bring all the means at your disposal." Ortega wired back on March 28: "Don't move. I write. [Sic] Affairs here very successful. Write about guns of Patoni." Vega Papers, Vol. III. The telegrams were in English.

arrived in January, 1867. Ortega tried to persuade Governor Miguel Auza to recognize him as president of Mexico, but instead Ortega and General Patoni, who accompanied him, were arrested and jailed.[80] For all practical purposes Ortega's efforts to succeed Juárez ended with his imprisonment.

Juárez had managed the succession crisis without meeting any real opposition, and the lack of support for Ortega indicated an encouraging amount of unity in liberal ranks. The new year brought even more encouraging news to the republicans; in January, 1866, Napoleon III announced his decision to withdraw the French army from Mexico. In February, Maximilian was informed of Napoleon's plans for gradual evacuation of troops beginning in the fall. Bazaine received instructions to draw back very slowly thus giving Maximilian time to build up a Mexican army. Bazaine began his retreat in March, and before the summer ended Matamoros, Monterrey, Saltillo, and Tampico were in the hands of the *juaristas*. Following the republican victories the government was able to leave Paso del Norte on June 10, and its arrival in Chihuahua a week later was the occasion of a happy celebration. In August, news of the Austro-Prussian War improved Juárez' spirits still further for he knew that more than ever the French would want their troops at home.[81] At this stage almost all the news was good; liberal armies continued to gain more ground, and by the end of the year the empire's effective control was confined largely to the central states close to the capital. Juárez took one more step in his journey back to the capital when he left Chihuahua on December 10. After stopping at Durango, which he reached on December 26, he proceeded from there to Zacatecas, where he arrived on January 22, 1867.

Here for the last time the president's safety was threatened when Miramón, in a desperate stab to save the empire, made a completely unexpected move on Zacatecas. In making their escape Juárez and his cabinet, instead of riding in coaches as was their custom, quickly left Zacatecas on horseback and sent the coaches off in a different direction. Miramón naturally followed the carriages and

---

80. Ortega, *Golpe*, 360-361. Sierra points out that Ortega's trip from the border to Zacatecas demonstrated how completely harmless he was, since in all that distance he did not attract a single follower. Justo Sierra, *Juárez*, 491.
81. Juárez, *Archivos privados*, 169.

Intervention   117

by the time the hoax was discovered it was too late, and the pursuit of the men on horseback was unsuccessful. Even Juárez admitted the escape was uncomfortably close; he felt that had they lingered even fifteen minutes more in the city they would have been captured.[82]

By the end of February, Juárez was in San Luis waiting for central Mexico to be brought under control. Maximilian had refused the opportunity to accompany the French as they withdrew and, after deciding to assume personal command of his troops, he shifted his center of operations from the capital to Querétaro. Díaz was now marching on the capital and without French troops it was just a matter of time until both cities fell. When Querétaro finally capitulated, Maximilian became a prisoner and, after a trial to preserve the fiction of legality, the government found him guilty of being a traitor to Mexico and sentenced him to be shot. Juárez received appeals from all over the world to pardon Maximilian but he steadfastly refused to do so. On June 19, 1867, Maximilian, along with Generals Miramón and Mejía, was executed. The government issued a manifesto in which it declared:

> Ferdinand Maximilian von Hapsburg, a Grand-Duke of Austria and an ally of Napoleon III of France, came to Mexico to rob the country of its independence and of its institutions; and, although a mere usurper of the national sovereignty, assumed the title of Emperor. This usurper having been captured by the Republican forces at Querétaro on the 15th of May, 1867, was sentenced to death by a military court martial, with the concurrence of the nation, and was shot for his crimes against the independence of the nation, at Querétaro on the 19th of June, 1867, in company with Generals Miramón and Mejía. Peace be to his ashes.

On July 15, 1867, Juárez made his triumphant entrance into Mexico City.

82. *Ibid.*, 207-208.

Chapter VI

1867-1870

With the defeat of the Intervention, the Mexicans, tired of warfare and disorder, wanted peace and security above all else. For many people the first step toward achieving that goal was the exercise of their right to vote, and after the government had returned to Mexico City they momentarily expected a *convocatoria* (proclamation) setting the date for national elections. But not until the middle of August did the government act, and by that time the press was voicing great concern over the delay. When the proclamation finally appeared on August 14 it did more than merely set the date for the elections of deputies, members of the supreme court, and the president. It gave the clergy the right to vote, allowed them and federal employees to sit as deputies in congress, and eliminated the residence requirement for deputies.[1] In addition the *convocatoria* proposed five constitutional changes.[2] These would establish a senate; give the president a two-thirds suspensive veto; permit in principle all executive reports to congress to be in writing, as opposed to the practice of verbal interpellation of ministers; limit the right of the permanent deputation of congress to call special sessions; and determine the presidential succession beyond the president of the supreme court. Moreover, the *convocatoria* ordered the states to submit the same five points as amendments to their own constitutions, the federal government dis-

---

1. The constitutional requirement that a deputy should be a resident of the district which elected him was generally ignored in practice. As Benítez wrote Díaz: ". . . sometimes there are complaints, but since deputies of all shades of opinion come to congress without fulfilling this requirement, both parties close their eyes and are mutually tolerant." May 31, 1869, Alberto María Carreño, ed., *Archivo del General Porfirio Díaz* (Vols. I-X, México, 1947-1951), VIII, 23. Hereinafter cited as *Archivo Díaz*. The same opinion was expressed in congress by a supporter of the government. P. Tovar, ed., *Historia parlamentaria del cuarto congreso constitucional* (4 vols., México, 1872-1874), IV, 305.

2. D y L, *Legislación*, X, 44-49. While the law enumerated only these five points as suggested constitutional changes, actually the proposal to let clergymen and federal employees serve as deputies was also amending the constitution, since Articles 56 and 57 expressly excluded these two categories from holding seats in the legislature.

pensing them in this case from following the amendment procedures laid down in the state charters.

With the *convocatoria* Lerdo issued a circular explaining the administration's position.³ He defended the government's attempt to change the constitution by popular referendum by arguing that the method provided in the constitution itself was slow and ponderous, and unsuited to the urgency of the present situation. No legal question was involved since the will of the people, freely expressed, was the source of all law and hence superior to any existing law. He defended the specific constitutional changes on the grounds that the executive powers needed to be strengthened in order to balance those held by the legislative branch. When the legislature was everything and the president was powerless before it, Lerdo held, the orderly administration of government was impossible. He denied that the proposals were anything original or new; four of them were in the Constitution of 1824 and he claimed all five were practiced in the United States, from whom Mexico had adopted a great many ideas. Essentially, the government was trying to put a greater distance between the executive and the legislative branch and to insure greater respect for the executive by increasing his power.

Perhaps because he felt that the existence and functioning in the United States of a senate, the executive veto power, and the regulation of the presidential succession were a better argument for these points than anything he could offer, Lerdo did not discuss them at length then. What concerned him most was the revision of legislative functions now in existence, and to the cabinet question he devoted particular attention.

Since the constitution said nothing about the reports of the ministers to congress, Lerdo claimed that the proposal to make them in writing instead of orally would simply be an addition to the organic law rather than a constitutional change. He argued that the procedure to be adopted should depend on the type of government. In a monarchy, where the head of the government held office for life and was not responsible to the chamber, such a system was effective for congressional pressure was the only means of changing an undesirable ministry. But in a republic, the head

3. *Ibid.*, 49-56; summarized in Knapp, *Lerdo*, 126-128.

of the government, being responsible to the people and holding office for a limited term, would not keep a ministry which did not have popular support. Thus under the Mexican system, the legislature did not need the power to force the executive to change his cabinet. While the continuance in office of an incompetent ministry could have unfortunate effects, constant cabinet changes could be equally serious, since without some experience a minister could accomplish little. If congress felt it had just cause it could always indict a cabinet member, but ministers should not be submitted to the indignities which oral questioning in congress so often entailed and which led to public distrust, both of the minister's capabilities and his principles.

While Lerdo agreed that the permanent deputation of Congress should have the power to call an extraordinary session, he stated plainly his belief that the machinery should be made more difficult to operate. He pointed out that as few as seven deputies were sufficient to convoke a special session and recalled the unfortunate experience of 1861 when a handful of deputies ordered an extra session for no other reason than to attack the president.

In defending the extension of the franchise and the right to hold office, Lerdo went on to point out that on July 16, 1864, at Monterrey, the government had removed certain qualifications regarding deputies.[4] Previously, as provided by the constitution, deputies had to reside in the state or territory which elected them, and no clergyman nor federal employees could sit in congress. Lerdo especially stressed that the clergy were citizens and should not be deprived of one of their most important rights.

But the press would have no part of the proposed changes, and the reaction was immediate and violent. With a very few exceptions the newspapers raised such a clamor[5] that Juárez felt it necessary to make a public statement supporting his minister and taking complete responsibility for the proclamation.[6] The amount of opposition must have come as a surprise to the government, and particularly since it came not from the usual sources but also

4. D y L, *Legislación*, IX, 689-690.
5. The newspaper *Orquesta* on September 7, 1867, summed it up very well: "All the papers, every day, every hour, in all their paragraphs . . . devote themselves to nothing but the *convocatoria.*"
6. D y L, *Legislación*, X, 67-68. His statement seemed to have little effect, however, for Lerdo was always regarded as the author.

from partisans of the administration as well. Two governors, León Guzmán of Guanajuato,[7] and Méndez of Puebla[8] both were so violently opposed that the government considered it advisable to remove them from their posts. Cosmes says that the agitation was so great that government employees with ultra-radical ideas resigned their posts which, in a country with a mania for government employment, marked the *summum* of public indignation.[9]

The press put special emphasis on two points: the provision which allowed the clergy to vote and be voted for and the constitutional proposals.[10] In the latter case they objected not only to content but to method. The procedure for changing the constitution was clearly stated in Article 127; to become effective, an amendment needed approval by two-thirds of the deputies present in the chamber and subsequent ratification by a majority of the state legislatures. While Knapp admits that a plebiscite on amendments was unconstitutional, he continues by saying that the *Diario Oficial* pointed out rightfully that the reforms were not attacked on their intrinsic merit but upon the technicality of violating a constitutional procedure.[11] But to those who had fought for years with the Constitution of 1857 as their slogan, the attempt to change it by illegal means was much more than a technicality; it was an attack upon the very foundation of government. Cosío Villegas sums up their attitude by saying that for the victors, after the Reform and the Intervention, the constitution was sacred; it was the cause of the wars, the symbol of victory, and the key to happiness.[12]

Nor was it true that the case was not argued on its merits. Zamacona in *Globo* on September 13 pointed out that the constitutional convention took two ideas as its starting points; the preponderance of the legislative power and the sovereignty of the

7. Guzmán flatly told the president that he would not publish the sections of the *convocatoria* dealing with constitutional reform. Guzmán to Juárez, September 11, 1867. Archivo Juárez.
8. *Siglo*, September 23, 1867.
9. Zamacois, *México*, XIX, 58-59. For the sake of convenience Volumes XIX-XXII, although written by Cosmes, will be cited as above.
10. See, for example, *Siglo, Boletín Republicano,* and *Orquesta* in the fall of 1867.
11. Knapp, *Lerdo*, 123.
12. "Donde está el villano?" *Historia Mexicana*, I, 432. For a more detailed political study see Cosío Villegas, *Historia moderna de México. La república restaurada. La vida política* (México, 1954). This work was published after the completion of the present study and it is more favorable to Juárez.

states. With the decree of August 14, the government had attempted to destroy these two fundamental concepts for it was seeking to concentrate power in its own hands at the expense of the states, and to give the executive absolute supremacy over the legislature. The veto power was one of the instruments the government would use to carry out its plan for one-third of the deputies could prevent congress from overriding the president's veto. "At what time in our history," asked Zamacona, "have we had an executive who did not control one-third of congress?" To insure its control the administration proposed that federal employees be allowed to sit as deputies which meant that "all the bureaucracy could immigrate to the benches of congress." To pass a law over the presidential veto would be impossible.

The arguments over the *convocatoria* were so vigorous largely because they were motivated by a persistent theme: the fear of any increase in the executive power which might lead to a semi-dictatorship. The opposition saw that spectre in every proposal: seats would be political plums, rewarded for support of the administration; federal employees would always vote to uphold the executive since their income depended upon it; the veto would give the president too much control over the legislature. To many Mexicans for whom the federal system was a basic tenet of liberalism, the method proposed for ratification was sufficient in itself to discredit even the most valuable reform. And the timing compounded the injury; by submitting the amendments to the entire electorate when Juárez was so popular after defeating the Intervention, the administration gained an unfair psychological advantage. In short, ever since Independence ambitious executives had been Mexico's affliction.

In spite of the opposition to the *convocatoria* and the fact that Díaz, the popular military hero, was also a presidential candidate, Juárez was returned to office by an overwhelming electoral vote. Probably this outcome signified real public support for Juárez as the symbol of Mexican resistance and nationality, for in future elections he would run into greater difficulties. Compared to a "normal" election, that of 1867 was a rather dull affair for, while there was, of course, interference at the polls, the usual bloody outbursts did not take place.

Although Juárez was reelected, his popularity was not great

enough to carry the changes proposed in the *convocatoria*. When the president gave his speech to the opening session of congress on December 8, he acknowledged the great unpopularity of the suggested amendments.¹³ He conceded that the method of ratification was the subject for as much discussion as the reforms themselves and indicated that he did not believe the government's proposals would carry.¹⁴ The administration had decided, he told the deputies, not to ask congress to count the votes cast on the constitutional questions;¹⁵ instead the government planned to submit bills to the legislature embodying the proposed changes. On December 14 the government introduced its first major proposal for consideration in congress—the five points of the *convocatoria*.¹⁶ Juárez clung stubbornly to his idea that Mexico should have a two-chamber legislature and early in 1870 he personally wrote to the state governors urging them to support the establishment of a senate,¹⁷ but not until Lerdo's presidential administration was the campaign successful. At various times in the next few years administration supporters introduced the amendments, but congress always refused to approve them.

When Juárez returned to Mexico City many liberals expected him to replace the cabinet which had served during the Intervention. In some quarters expectations became demands with the publication of the *convocatoria*, but the outcry did not move Juárez to action. After congress had officially confirmed his election, the entire cabinet resigned so he could have a free hand in choosing his ministers. Juárez promptly dashed the hope for new faces by nominating Lerdo for Relations and Gobernación, Iglesias in Treasury, Balcárcel in Fomento, Mejía in War, and Martínez del Castro in Justice. Congressional debates illustrated the great bitterness aroused by the retention of the old hands and, consequently, the old policy. The constitution stipulated that no deputy could

---
13. Tovar, *Cuarto congreso*, I, 58.
14. *Globo* in its issue for January 2, 1868, stated that the results of 160 electoral districts, with 39 districts still to report, showed 384,355 voted for the reforms, 419,942 against, and 55,942 blank. No authority is cited for its figures. No tally is reported in the congressional record.
15. In its manifesto to the nation, issued January 8, 1868, congress noted that any desirable reforms ought to have all the force and prestige of legality, and for that reason it had refrained from counting the ballots cast on constitutional reforms sought by the *convocatoria*. Tovar, *Cuatro congreso*, I, 165-167.
16. *Ibid.*, 78-79.
17. Letters of March and April, 1870, in Copiadores, Archivo Juárez.

accept a salaried executive appointment without the prior consent of congress, and since Lerdo, Balcárcel, and Iglesias all were deputies, Juárez had to secure congressional permission before they could serve in the ministry. A month later, on January 8, 1868, congress voted to allow them to enter the cabinet, but approval came only after the opposition had bitterly attacked Lerdo.[18]

On January 2, Siglo reported that Iglesias had insisted his health would not permit him to continue in the cabinet, and although Juárez accepted this resignation he would not part with the remaining ministers. Siglo noted pointedly that the advisers responsible for the policies of the dictatorship during the Intervention were still in power. The newspaper, of course, had its sights on Lerdo.[19] From Siglo's point of view the president's decision frustrated many hopes and was one of the first steps in dividing congress and the press into two camps, one supporting, the other opposing the cabinet.

Juárez appointed Matías Romero to replace Iglesias as Minister of the Treasury and assigned Ignacio L. Vallarta to Gobernación. Lerdo was now left with only one portfolio, but it was the key post in the cabinet. Romero's appointment did not imply a shift in policy since he had been associated with the Juárez group throughout the Intervention. The selection of Vallarta was a different matter and it had two important implications. It was taken as an indication, first of all, that some sort of policy change could be anticipated, and secondly, that Juárez was now ready to open the door slightly to people outside the small group of presidential advisers. Vallarta took office on March 23, over two months after his appointment. He demonstrated immediately that he wanted the governmental functions which came under his jurisdiction to be carried out in accordance with the constitution. On April 8 he issued a circular to the state governors recommending the cessation of arbitrary imprisonment, and on the twelfth he sent another emphasizing the need to respect individual guarantees.[20]

18. Tovar, Cuarto congreso, I, 63; 153-162; 163-165. The vote on Lerdo was 68-40. Balcarcel received permission without discussion. Iglesias' resignation came before congress got around to the final vote.
19. Juárez felt, however, that by electing Lerdo and Iglesias to congress, the public showed that it had not lost confidence in the cabinet. Juárez to Luis Terrazas, October 10, 1867. Archivo Juárez.
20. E. Martínez Tamayo, "Un triángulo político," Historia Mexicana, I, 104-106. Circulars in D y L, Legislación, X, 297-300.

If some of the opposition looked upon Vallarta's inclusion in the cabinet as a sort of guarantee of constitutional government, they were soon disillusioned. Juárez had surrendered his extraordinary powers in December at the opening session of congress, but within a few months he was asking for partial restoration. The government on March 5 introduced a bill[21] declaring the law of January 25, 1862,[22] to be in force until actually repealed by congress. When intervention threatened, the government, as part of its preparation to meet the attack, had issued this very punitive decree defining crimes against the nation, public peace and order, and individual guarantees. Persons accused of any of the crimes specified in the law were to be tried without delay by military tribunals and, if found guilty, were subject to immediate and severe penalties from which there was no appeal or pardon. The government was asking congress to reaffirm the law because the Governor of Jalisco had notified it of a serious conspiracy in his state and because of generally unsettled conditions in the country. The opposition in congress immediately declared that the government was really proposing the suspension of individual guarantees since that was also part of the January 25 law.

On March 6, Zamacona attacked the government's proposal in an editorial in *Globo*. He began with an "I-told-you-so" to his readers, recalling that on a number of occasions he had traced the government's movements and had predicted that the final step would be a repetition of the events in mid-1861 when the administration asked congress, in the name of peace and security, to grant the executive power to suspend guarantees. Later came the request to give the executive extraordinary powers. Zamacona warned his readers that the freedom for which the people had fought, and had enjoyed during the past few months, was about to be snatched from them. Professing to be too upset to examine the legal aspects of the government's proposal, he confined himself to saying that if the cabinet persisted in believing, as the *convocatoria* demonstrated, that it was impossible to govern under the existing constitution; if it persisted in declaring, as it had the previous day, that the guarantees and liberties which the constitution gave to the citizens did not have the desired effect of maintaining peace and security, then the

---

21. Tovar, *Cuarto congreso*, I, 528.
22. D y L, *Legislación*, IX, 367-371.

decent thing was not to ask congress to violate the constitution. The thing to do was not to sacrifice the constitution to the cabinet which did not believe in it, but rather to sacrifice the ministry to the constitution. Zamacona recovered quickly and the following day he accused the Minister of Relations, among other things, of using a scare technique in order to get a suspension of guarantees.

The bill reported out on March 9 provided for the retention of the January 25 law, the committee being of the opinion that rebellion and disorder in the states of Yucatán, Guerrero, Sinaloa, Puebla, and Jalisco called for stringent measures.[23] The government needed increased authority not only to deal with conspiracy but also with the kidnapers, thieves, and assassins infesting Mexico's roads and penetrating into the largest cities, even the capital itself. The opposition fought the proposal bitterly, and under Zamacona's leadership forced the government to make a number of very important concessions, one being that individual guarantees would be suspended only until December 31, 1868. Finally on May 8 congress passed a modified law.[24]

Feeling ran very high among the deputies against the bill and against Lerdo, and demands for his dismissal from the cabinet were continuous but the president ignored them. On June 5, however, the opposition received help from an unexpected source when the supreme court joined the political battle. By a seven to five decision, the justices refused to give Lerdo, their colleague on the court, a leave of absence to serve in the cabinet.[25] García Ramírez, Zavala, Velázquez, Lafragua, and Ordaz voted to grant Lerdo his leave; Cardoso, Ogazón, Riva Palacio, Simón Guzmán, León Guzmán, Castillo Velasco, and Altamirano opposed the request.[26] Since most of the justices who made up the majority were either anti-Juárez or anti-Lerdo, the court's decision rested on political considerations rather than on a genuine sentiment that Lerdo's presence was essential to its proper functioning. Newspapers judged the controversy on the same basis. *Globo*, for example, thought the court had acted wisely and considered its refusal the equivalent to a censure of cabinet policy. Papers supporting the government, on

23. Tovar, *Cuarto congreso*, I, 545-548.
24. Plumb, May 25, 1868, to Seward. Mexican Dispatches, Vol. 32. D y L, *Legislación*, X, 319-320.
25. *Orquesta*, June 6, 1868.
26. *Siglo*, June 6, 1868.

the other hand, believed that while the court was within its legal rights in voting as it did, the very important fact remained that the decision restricted the president's freedom in choosing a cabinet member.

But the ruling stood, and Vallarta temporarily assumed the Ministry of Relations in addition to Gobernación. In early September, however, Vallarta's resignation[27] foretold a change in the supreme court's position, and shortly thereafter the court announced that it had voted to reverse itself and to grant Lerdo the requested leave of absence.[28] Ogazón was absent and León Guzmán, Simón Guzmán, Cardoso, and Altamirano remained opposed, but Riva Palacio and Castillo Velasco changed their vote, thus giving Lerdo the necessary majority.[29] Castillo Velasco wrote an open letter explaining quite frankly that his first vote had been a political one. Being in favor of a change in the policy of the cabinet, he felt this objective could be attained by refusing Lerdo permission to serve. He had become convinced, however, that Lerdo's absence had had no effect and that to persist in the refusal would do no more than indicate a purely personal rebuke. He justified his shift in voting by saying that he was not interested in attacking individuals.[30] Certainly this was an extension of the judicial power over the executive which the authors of the Constitution of 1857 had not intended.

The relationship of the court with the other branches of the government arose again in 1869 when the legislature, following executive leadership, attempted to try several of the justices as a result of a court decision which had, in effect, declared the *amparo*[31] law of

27. Vallarta wrote a long letter to Juárez on September 1 explaining clearly his reasons for leaving the cabinet. Most important was Lerdo's animosity toward him for Lerdo believed he was responsible for the supreme court's ruling. Two other factors contributed to his withdrawal from the cabinet: the decision of the court in a case involving Jalisco, his home state, and Juárez' loss of confidence in him. In his letter accepting Vallarta's resignation, Juárez denied any change in his attitude toward him. Martínez Tamayo, "Político."
28. *Siglo*, September 9, 1868.
29. *Globo*, September 10, 1868.
30. *Ibid.*, September 11, 1868.
31. The writ of *amparo* "... is a constitutional suit of a summary nature, the object of which is to protect, in a special case and at the request of an injured party, private persons whose individual rights as established in the Constitution have been violated through laws or acts of the authorities, or when the laws or acts of the Federal authorities injure the sovereignty of the States." J. T. Vance and H. L. Clagett, *A Guide to the Law and Legal Literature of Mexico* (Washington, 1945), 172-173, citing M. Gual Vidal, *Mexican Amparo Proceedings*. Historically, the establishment of the *amparo* in Mexico meant the limitation of the power of the executive and the establishment of

January 20, 1869, unconstitutional. On May 6 in a secret session of congress four deputies presented an accusation against seven justices of the court. The seven were then ordered to appear before congress sitting as a grand jury. But the court, on which the government controlled the votes of only four members as against those of eight independent justices, ruled by an eight to four vote that congress had no right to review the court's decisions when it acted as the supreme judicial power of the federation of Mexico; much less did congress have the right to try members of the court when that body was acting on a purely constitutional question as it had in this case. The federal constitution provided for the independence of the supreme powers of the government; the congressional pretension that it could sit as a judge of the supreme court infringed upon this constitutional concept.

In its statement to congress, the court declared that the basis for the accusation against its members was a decision which the court had rendered in a case of *amparo* brought before the district judge of Sinaloa by a judge from Culiacán and dealing with a violation of individual guarantees. The supreme court had reversed the opinion of the district judge, who held that under the law of January 20 the appeal was inadmissable, and had ordered him to try the case and make his decision according to the law. Article 101 of the constitution gave the court the right and the duty to receive all controversy arising from the laws or from the actions of any authority which violated individual guarantees. A citizen had sought *amparo* for the infringement of those guarantees and the court could not, without being remiss in its duty, have failed to hear a citizen who was exercising a right guaranteed by the constitution. Article 8 of the law of *amparo* denied this appeal in judicial affairs, it was true; but in the first place, no one up to this time could say that the violation of guarantees about which the judge of Culiacán complained was a judicial affair. Besides, even if it were, federal courts not only were within their rights but had the strict obligation to hear the complainant and to protect or aid the citizen if the violation were established. The court further held that in any event Article 8 of the law of *amparo* was contrary to Article 101 of the constitution and, therefore, without force. The constitution pro-

the judiciary as a separate branch of government. The law of January, 1869, is in D y L, *Legislación*, X, 521-525.

vided for a hearing of all complaints charging violation of individual guarantees committed by whatever authority; the law of *amparo* excluded judicial affairs. The court obviously had the right to pass on the case. In concluding its statement the court repeated emphatically that congress had no authority to review judicial decisions.[32] The dignity with which the court conducted itself caused the legislature to call off its exaggerated pretensions.

Shortly afterward the supreme court again declared a law unconstitutional but this time it suffered no attack as the result of its ruling. On April 12 the government had pushed through congress, over bitter protests by the opposition, another law suspending individual guarantees for one year with regard to kidnapers and bandits.[33] After the law was promulgated, Governor Hernández y Hernández of Veracruz refused to enforce it in his state since he considered it unconstitutional. The supreme court upheld this view and the law was never put into effect in Veracruz.[34]

During the Intervention, the government had issued a number of decrees listing the penalties for those guilty of cooperating with the enemy. Since "cooperation," as defined in the decrees, took in a great deal of territory, the question of who was to be punished, and how, came to be an important one after the Intervention had ended. The administration indicated right from the start what its own attitude would be by issuing on July 14, 1867, a decree affecting supporters of the empire which it then held as prisoners in the capital. Many of these individuals were freed, and the severity of sentences imposed by earlier laws upon civilian and military officers was considerably reduced. Later the sentences were lightened still further. A decree on August 12 commuted the penalty of property confiscation into the payment of a fine, and in the months that followed the government issued additional regulations to soften the impact of the laws passed during the emergency.[35] The president affirmed this policy of conciliation in his speech opening the congressional session in December, 1867, when he declared that by making an example at Querétaro of those most guilty, the administration now was in a position to show great clemency to lesser offenders. And he went on to observe that he felt this policy was

32. Zamacois, *México*, XX, 544-553.
33. D y L, *Legislación*, X, 568.
34. Zamacois, *México*, XX, 553-558.
35. D y L, *Legislación*, X, 24-25; 42-43; 65-66; 109-110; 278.

in accord with the generous sentiments of the people.³⁶

That the government actually carried its intentions into effect was apparent from the newspaper reaction. For example, *Orquesta*, which from the beginning had favored a broad amnesty policy, noted on October 10, 1868, that the government had in fact granted the fullest amnesty and most generous pardon. The passing of time had calmed passions, and with each day the punitive measures advocated by some of the extremists became more impossible. While there were a few exceptions, people who had been prominent under the Intervention were now living quietly at home pursuing their businesses or professions undisturbed.

Zarco, who favored stern treatment of those whose loyalty had wavered, used the pages of *Siglo* to attack administration's policy.³⁷ His major complaint was that, instead of bringing the guilty to trial, the executive used its discretionary powers and treated each case individually. Great inequity and injustice resulted from this procedure, and equal crimes did not receive equal punishment. He also felt that just when the law should have been applied most rigorously, it had been relaxed, and he accused the government of being generous and indulgent to the point of granting impunity.³⁸

In the legislature, meanwhile, Mata, Zamacona, Prieto, Benítez and others introduced a bill in December, 1867, granting extensive amnesty.³⁹ On February 6, 1868, congress began debating the majority report on the Mata bill,⁴⁰ but the deputies were too divided to reach any conclusion and the measure was sent back to committee.⁴¹ The whole question took on a new aspect at the next session when Zarco introduced a bill in November designed to grant amnesty for all political crimes committed since July, 1867.

36. Tovar, *Cuarto congreso*, I, 56.
37. See especially *Siglo*, December, 1867, and January, 1868.
38. Zamacona's paper, *Globo*, charged that the government did not want any definite policy set in regard to amnesty since its discretionary powers were a useful club to hold over Intervention supporters.
39. Tovar, *Cuarto congreso*, I, 65-66.
40. Speaking in congress against the majority report, Frías y Soto remarked that ". . . the traitors already have been judged, justly and legally, by the executive. . . . The right to condemn and absolve falls entirely within the executive's powers, and using them, he has commuted punishments and has pardoned individuals and restored them to their places in society." But he went on to add that under the executive there had been a great deal of injustice; while some of the most important traitors walked about peacefully, many others languished in prison. *Ibid.*, 345.
41. *Ibid.*, 327-383.

When the bill was reported out of committee it carried several additional articles, the third stating that those who were still bearing arms against the government could also enjoy the benefits of the law by presenting themselves to their state governors within thirty days after the law was published. The executive had not entered into congressional debates when the deputies had been considering granting amnesty to those who had served the Intervention, but when the committee's bill came up in January, 1869, Iglesias appeared for the government to speak against it.[42] He voiced strong objections, saying that the country was not yet pacified and that men who were at that very moment leading rebellions against the government would automatically be pardoned. In rebuttal, Zarco bitterly denounced the injustice of the administration's stand. He charged that the government was willing to leave unmolested traitors who had attacked Mexican independence by serving the Intervention. Yet it wished to punish those loyal Mexicans whose only aim was to defend the constitution and who had been driven into rebellion by the *convocatoria*. By the close vote of 65-63 the administration forces were able to postpone the discussion.

Not until September 19, 1870, was a bill introduced which finally carried.[43] It included amnesty both for those who had served the Intervention and those who were guilty of political crimes since 1867. The government opposed the measure because of the political amnesty conditions, and in his comments on the legislation, the Secretary of Gobernación stated that the administration did not favor such a broad exemption for political crimes as granted by the bill. But, although the government was against the legislation, congress approved it on October 13,[44] and its passage constituted a great victory for the opponents of the administration. In its final form the law granted amnesty to all individuals who, up to September 19, 1867, had been guilty of treason, sedition, conspiracy, and other crimes against the public order. Not granted amnesty were the regents and their deputies and the generals who had held commands in the imperial army.

Primary elections for deputies were scheduled to begin at the

42. *Ibid.*, III, 611; 737-738; 998-1006.
43. *Diario de los debates. Quinto congreso constitucional de la unión* (4 vols., Mexico, 1871), III, 31 ff.
44. D y L, *Legislación*, XI, 184.

end of June, 1869, and political activity reached such a peak that by February, Benítez was writing to Díaz that the important thing, and the one on which everyone was concentrating, was the forthcoming congressional election.[45] Opposition leaders formed the Constitutional Liberal Party, and in its program the party again attacked the *convocatoria*. The *constitucionalistas* declared that the Constitution of 1857 was the party's symbol and pledged their particular devotion to the rights of man. The program stated that the constitution could not be changed except by following the procedures laid down in the document itself and, as a further thrust at the August 14 proclamation, declared that the states had the inviolable right to regulate their own internal affairs. In addition, they demanded free elections, the establishment of internal security, improved administration in the government, the reduction of the army and the organization of a national guard, and the stimulation of economic development.[46]

The official organ of the opposition was *El Elector*, and *Oposición, Monitor Republicano*, and *Globo* were the other outstanding liberal anti-government papers. For its part, the administration gave its views in the *Diario Oficial, Opinión Nacional*, and *Boquiflojo*. *Siglo* generally defended the government. Very early in the campaign, the opposition began accusing the government of interfering in the elections by the use of bribery and threats, and in spite of official denials the accusations continued with unabated fury during the summer. As a matter of fact, the government intervened very actively in this election,[47] and armed force played a role in the balloting in San Luis Potosí, Puebla, and Jalisco. Even in Mexico City where it might have been assumed that public opinion would exercise a moderating influence, those in opposition to the government were jailed, polling places were taken over by the police, and ballot boxes were stuffed.[48] Consequently, as might be expected, administration candidates were fairly successful. Yet while the op-

---

45. February 24, 1869; *Archivo Díaz*, VII, 226-227.
46. Zamacois, *México*, XX, 699-707. Popular elections were being held for the first time in the two new states which congress had carved from the old state of Mexico: Hidalgo on January 15 and Morelos on April 17, 1869. The *porfiristas* were hopeful that their leader would win the governorship in the state of Mexico, but Mariano Riva Palacio was the successful candidate.
47. More worried than indignant, Benítez wrote Díaz: "I have little hope of being re-elected to congress, since Lerdo is telling his friends that I will be defeated." June 2, 1869. *Archivo Díaz*, VIII, 26.
48. Zamacois, *México*, XX, 754-755. See, also, the opposition press.

position suffered more punishment than it inflicted, it was largely a question of one side's having a greater opportunity than the other. Certainly the Díaz correspondence indicates that the "outs" were trying to make the most of whatever advantages they had.[49]

But in spite of the newspaper polemics the public generally was indifferent to the campaign[50] and, in Zarco's opinion, they were bored as well by the quarreling.[51] When the voting procedure is examined, the reason for public apathy is apparent. The people had no direct vote in selecting their officials; they merely voted for electors. In Tabasco, for example, these electors met at the state capital and, with the governor presiding, cast their ballots by voice vote for deputies to the national congress, the members of the state legislature, and the governor. Since the legislature consisted of only seven members, and the governor appointed all the other officials, he obviously was in a position to dominate the affairs of the state.[52] The example is not atypical and the central government, in turn, frequently was able to dominate the governor.

The split of the pro-government factions into *lerdistas* and *juaristas* began during the elections of 1869.[53] Since the only plausible reason for Lerdo's developing a following of his own was his aspiration to become president, it was plain that Juárez had a competitor within his own administration. In congress, where the two groups were almost equally represented, the cleavage soon became apparent.[54] Shortly after the session opened *Siglo*, in its issue of September 27, deplored the anarchy in the ministerial party as a result of its division into two factions, and the news of the rift continued to appear in the opposition papers. Finally on October 27, the *Diario Oficial*, while not commenting directly, reprinted an item from *Opinión Nacional* denying completely the "rumors" printed by *Globo* and *Monitor Republicano* that the president was having cabinet troubles caused by a disagreement with Lerdo. While actually the trouble was not too serious at the moment, its

49. *Archivo Díaz*, VII & VIII.
50. Reports from American representatives, in the different sections of the country, back to the American Minister in Mexico City. Mexican Dispatches, Vol. 36.
51. *Siglo*, August 3, 1869.
52. Mexican Dispatches, Vol. 36.
53. Zamacois, *México*, XXI, 37-39.
54. Deputy Francisco Mena, September 21, 1869, to Díaz. *Archivo Díaz*, VIII, 79-80. Trinidad García, October 15, 25, November 14, 1869, to Trinidad García de la Cadena. *Periódico Oficial*, Zacatecas, April 30, May 4, 1870.

existence gave the opposition greater confidence and led them to predict future difficulties among administration supporters.⁵⁵

Elections usually added more complications to the generally disturbed relations between the national and state governments, and they tended to confuse still further the already murky political picture within the states themselves. While it might be said that elections aggravated the tendency toward rebellion, that tendency was ever-present and had begun translating itself into action shortly after the Juárez government returned to the capital in the summer of 1867.

But in spite of the fact that disturbances occurred,⁵⁶ the government seemed to be making progress in its goal of pacifying the country. The American representative in Mexico, Edward Lee Plumb, in September, 1868, noted that at no time since Juárez had taken office had Mexico been so quiet. The military and civilian employees were being regularly and promptly paid, which Plumb thought might be one of the most important reasons for the prevailing calm. Travel was still unsafe, however, and in Plumb's opinion conditions would improve only when people found jobs; without any other way to make a living they were driven to crime and rebellion.⁵⁷

The government evidently felt, too, that matters were quite well in hand for on July 13, Mejía, the Secretary of War, had ordered the Governor of Nuevo León to release González Ortega and Patoni from prison, giving as his reason the fact that practically all uprisings had been suppressed and Ortega would not now be much of a threat to public peace.⁵⁸ Upon his release Ortega retired to

55. Mena, November 24, 1869, to Díaz. *Archivo Díaz*, VIII, 95-96. T. García, October 15, 1869, to García de la Cadena. *Periódico Oficial*, Zacatecas, April 30, 1870. Justo Benítez, November 14, 1869, to García de la Cadena. *Ibid.*, May 15, 1870.
56. *Constitucional,* a pro-government paper, on February 10, 1868, listed uprisings in Yucatán, Guerrero, Sinaloa, San Luis Potosí, and the state of Mexico, "to which must be added kidnappings, assassinations, banditry, and the other consequences of public misery." The opposition and the government expressed varying opinions on the state of the nation depending on the circumstances; for example, when the government wanted congress to approve a suspension of guarantees it painted a somber picture, and when it was defending its record against the opposition, things looked considerably brighter.
57. Plumb, September 10, 1868, to Seward. Mexican Dispatches, Vol. 34.
58. *Diario Oficial,* July 21, 1868. Patoni had been offered his release in September, 1867, on the condition that he come to the capital and present himself to the government. He refused to accept the terms, declaring he still thought Juárez was holding office illegally. *Ibid.*

Saltillo and on August 19 issued a statement declaring his intention of retiring completely from politics,[59] thus removing himself as a cause of further rebellion. But an event had already occurred which kept him in the public eye a while longer; on August 18, Patoni was dragged out of bed in Durango at three in the morning and assassinated. The head of the federal troops in the city, General Canto, after first denying any knowledge of the crime, then admitted responsibility for it, saying that he had ordered the execution on secret instructions from the central government. Later he retracted his statement,[60] but the rumor became widespread that the Minister of War had given the orders for the crime. On September 12, Mejía sent a communication to congress[61] in which he described the administration's indignation over the affair and pointed out the energetic steps taken against Canto. He was ousted from his command, jailed, and ordered to Mexico City to be tried. Public sentiment was so great that when he was taken through Zacatecas the populace almost lynched him. The government's action, plus the fact that its supporters in congress voted to have Canto stand trial in the criminal courts, indicated to the people that it had not ordered the execution.[62]

The satisfaction which the administration must have derived from the unusually quiet state of the country did not last long. February, 1869, brought a revolt in Puebla led by Negrete and also an uprising in Tamaulipas. In March came rebellions in the states of Nuevo León and Sinaloa, and to go through the years of 1869 and 1870 would be to catalogue almost every state in the Mexican nation. In a few, such as Guerrero and Jalisco, the disturbances were so prolonged as to be chronic; but everywhere the government was able at least to keep the rebels in check and prevent any real threat to its existence, although it did face a difficult situation when a revolt broke out in San Luis Potosí in December, 1869.

The San Luis revolt should have come as a surprise to no one for ever since the elections the spirit of rebellion seemed to hover

---

59. Zamacois, *México*, XX, 118-124.
60. Tovar, *Cuarto congreso*, III, 371-382. In the session of October 23, 1868, congress sat as a grand jury. This was not, however, a trial. Since Canto was a deputy, and therefore enjoyed the constitutional privilege of a deputy, the voting was on the committee's recommendation that he be turned over to the criminal courts. It was unanimously approved.
61. *Diario Oficial*, September 14, 1868.
62. Zamacois, *México*, XX, 213-217.

over the country. Newspapers reflected the confused and threatening atmosphere and in the words of one deputy:

> Toward the end of the past year a storm was visible on the Mexican horizon. Rumor, vague but persistent, foretold a revolution. . . . Like a sick person who has experienced periods of sharp pain, Mexico could see her illness returning, and six months ago everyone expected that the peace might be broken. People did not want that to happen; it was a presentiment which was painful to contemplate.[63]

The leaders of the San Luis revolt evidently had expected their movement to receive wide support, especially in the surrounding states, and they tried to get Governor Trinidad García de la Cadena of Zacatecas to join them. The latter's agent and accomplice, Trinidad García, deputy to congress, kept advising the governor to be cautious and not to commit himself until he was sure that Zacatecas would be the leader when the revolt was successfully concluded. On January 4, 1870, García wrote from Mexico City advising the governor that the rebellion in Puebla seemed about to end, in which case the Juárez government could devote all its energy to San Luis, with almost certain success.[64]

But on January 8, Governor García issued his plan in which he disavowed Juárez and demanded that the presidency be restored to González Ortega to whom it legally belonged.[65] There was great relief when Ortega issued a statement from Saltillo on January 22 refuting the pretension made in his name. Because of the size of the revolt the administration put two of its top generals, Rocha and Escobedo, in command of the campaign. Although a large battle occurred in February at Lo de Ovejo, it was indecisive but, by the end of March, the rebels were defeated and scattered.

While the government was busy in San Luis, several other plans appeared and the unrest continued with small revolts breaking out constantly. But on the last day of September, 1870, the *Diario Oficial,* noting the end of the recent rebellion in Tamaulipas, ad-

63. Rafael Martínez de la Torre speaking in congress on May 6, 1870. *Quinto congreso,* II, 283.
64. *Ibid.,* 292. The exchange of letters fell into the government's hands when T. García was captured by federal troops. The letters, which seemed to implicate Benítez and Zamacona, caused a veritable scandal. T. García did not attempt to deny their authenticity and he was tried by congress, found guilty, and later imprisoned.
65. *Diario Oficial,* January 15, 1870.

vised its readers that peace was a fact THROUGHOUT THE REPUBLIC. Of that threatening cloud which had formed in San Luis and Zacatecas at the beginning of the year, the last wisp had disappeared.

One can doubt that the administration itself believed such a statement was absolutely true, or even that the comparative quiet would be very prolonged. Some of the reasons for the revolts were political; some were economic. Some men denied the government's authority because they wanted power; a few acted from principle. While every government is subject to criticism, several of the administration's policies made it extremely vulnerable to attack. The *convocatoria* was undoubtedly one of Juárez' worst mistakes for its publication split the liberal party wide open. This is not to say that the break would not have appeared eventually, but perhaps if it had been caused by anything but an attack on the constitution the disruption might not have been so violent.

The administration policy of reserving public offices for its unconditional supporters was another mistake. The members of the bureaucracy, called "the immaculates" by the opposition, became the administration favorites, even to the point where army men frequently were pushed aside. The government also angered the military men on July 23, 1867, when, in an attempt to economize, it cut the size of the army down to 16,000 men.[66] *Siglo* disapproved of the reduction, stating in an article on August 7 that the government should have kept the army on a war footing for another six months. The delay would have given the administration time to work out orderly demobilization rather than turning the army loose to return home, unemployed and discontented. Marcus Ottenburg, the American Consul in Mexico City, reported on August 21, 1867:

> This sudden reduction of the Army has aroused general discontent where every man returns without means to his house left desolate and unproductive during the full period of his absence ... already are the results felt upon the highways where marauders without danger to themselves obtain relief for the immediate wants of life demoralized by habits of a camp.[67]

Mejía, the Minister of War, deserved a great deal of credit for keeping the military in line as well as he did.

66. D y L, *Legislación*, X, 29-30.
67. Mexican Dispatches, Vol. 31.

There is some feeling that Juárez also erred in keeping Lerdo in the top cabinet post even when he was the focus of public censure. On the other hand, this can be viewed as a brilliant piece of political strategy for *el cura* was such a popular target that he deflected the attacks away from the president.

Although the administration had to devote most of its energies and resources to fighting the opposition, both political and military, Juárez made an effort to bring about reforms in the two fields in which he believed Mexico must progress if it were to realize its potential greatness. To improve the educational system and to establish the economy on a sound basis, were goals high on the administration's list and it began to act in both spheres shortly after its return to the capital.

In the fall of 1867, Juárez, eager to reorganize public education on the principles of science and man's ability to obtain the truth, had his Minister of Justice and Public Instruction, Antonio Martínez de Castro, appoint a committee to undertake the task. The five chosen to serve on the committee were Gabino Barreda, Francisco and José Díaz Covarrubias, Ignacio Alvarado, and Eulalio María Ortega.[68] Gabino Barreda was the most interesting personality and was soon to be the leader of the new educational group in Mexico. Born in Puebla in 1818, he had studied in Mexico City and in France where he received a degree in medicine in 1851. During his stay in France he came into contact with the positivist philosophy of Auguste Comte and the six volumes of *Cours de philosophie positive* occupied a preferential place in his library. Barreda's philosophy is best expressed in *De la educación moral* (1863), *Oración cívica* (1867), and *Carta dirigida al C. Mariano Riva Palacio* (1870).

Barreda was especially interested in giving mankind a new set of values through science. Primarily he wanted to direct man's thinking along lines void of dogma and *a priori* assumptions. The stress was upon man. He accepted Comte's views that the human mind has passed through three successive stages: religious, metaphysical, and positive. In Mexico, the church, viewed as a negative

---

68. The basic documents and ideas on education of the period may be found in Martín Luis Guzmán, ed., *Escuelas laicas* (México, 1949); José Fuentes Mares, ed., *Gabino Barreda, Estudios* (México, 1941); and especially in Albert J. Delmez, "The Positivist Philosophy in Mexican Education, 1867-1873," *Americas*, VI, 1.

force, occupied the religious stage; the revolution, the metaphysical; and the emerging liberal forces, the positive stage. In this process the nation was traveling the road to emancipation from such hindrances as the church and the army. Barreda felt that the church had its place in strictly religious affairs, but the state was the institution responsible for ethical standards and, consequently, it had to control education. In this and other ways he felt that ethics and religion could be divorced.[69] According to Delmez:

> Barreda would strive for perfection of the principles of morality through the use of advanced knowledge, that is positive knowledge. This knowledge he would use to discern those habits which are good in man and those which are bad. Having discovered those, he would by the intervention of mental gymnastics exercise the good inclinations, permitting the organs controlling the bad habits to become atrophied through disuse. This is a task for education. It is also the task of education to determine these values or beliefs. In order that these beliefs assume universal validity, they must subject themselves to the rigor of science. This is the positive approach.[70]

Once these principles were adopted Barreda felt that Mexico could progress if some way were found to establish peace and order. Thus the standards became LIBERTY, ORDER, AND PROGRESS. Liberty as the means; order as the base; progress as the end. The base, order, could only be obtained and maintained if there were a high degree of uniformity among thinking people. And education, based upon positive philosophy, would bring about that uniformity. In many ways, then, the liberals had substituted positivism for religion.

Basing their recommendations on these ideas, the committee appointed by Martínez de Castro worked out a plan for education in the Federal District which was adopted by law on December 2, 1867.[71] The curriculum in the primary schools for boys consisted of reading, penmanship, grammar, Spanish, letter writing, arith-

---

69. As another member of the committee put it: ". . . the study of ethics, stripped of all theological origins, sanctions, and objectives, can be reduced to a practical science by the application of laws scientifically deduced from the nature of man and the nature of society." José Díaz Covarrubias in *Diario Oficial*, October 11, 1867.
70. Delmez, "Education."
71. D y L, *Legislación*, X, 193-205.

metic, the decimal system, rudiments of physics, the arts based on chemistry and practical mechanics, linear drawing, morals, physical science, manners, notions of constitutional rights, and the rudiments of history and geography, especially of Mexico. The program for the girls was basically the same with practical hygiene substituted for physical science. In the secondary schools (school for preparatory studies) the course of studies was expanded to include more languages, additional mathematics, and a great deal more science. Primary education was to be free for the poor and compulsory after the age of five.

Delmez comments:

> Here is a plan of education intended to become a pattern for thought and action in revamping the whole system of instruction and, ultimately, of society. It attempts first to provide education vertically, that is, from the primary level to that of preparatory education. Secondly, it tries to provide a comprehensive education by offering a wide variety of subjects. Thirdly, it endeavors to posit science and practicality as the premise for the nature of subject matter. Fourthly, it recognizes the necessity of creating an enlightened society through science. Lastly, it fixes the responsibility of the State in matters of education.[72]

Temporarily, Barreda and his followers used the term "liberal" as signifying progress. Later, however, when elements within the liberal groups disagreed with him, Barreda denounced them for disturbing the foundation of society. The elimination of the dissenters naturally meant that those liberals who remained faithful to Juárez became the true organizers of society and its leaders. With this development liberty began to fade from the trinity, and the stress was upon order so that the end, progress, might be obtained.

The positivists claimed that the educational system of the church bore no relation to the realities of society. The function of education, as they viewed it, was to prepare Mexicans to cope with the world in which they lived, and consequently, a direct relationship existed between education and the country's economy. Commenting on the new education law, José Bustamente expressed the opinion that ethical and material advancement complemented each

---

72. Delmez, "Education."

other, and the result of their interaction would be progress and the welfare of humanity. Bustamante advocated not only a specific educational system to reach the desired goal; as its complement in the economic sphere he endorsed the laissez-faire doctrine for:

> [The] comparison between public instruction and public wealth is not purely and simply a rhetorical figure. The diffusion of knowledge, like the circulation of money, frees many minds of the proletariat; and instruction bears fruit in free minds as does capital in free hands.[73]

With educational reform under way, the necessity for a sound economic basis to government must also be met, and the administration's struggle to revive the economy was begun under conditions that could scarcely have been more difficult. Years of revolution had preceded the bitter War of the Reform which in turn was followed, after only a brief respite, by more years of fighting against a foreign invader. No wonder then that the end of the Intervention found Mexico an economic shambles. Not only had the country suffered the physical devastation common to all wars; the long years of disorder had brought complete economic stagnation.[74] And conditions did not improve during the period under consideration. In a speech in the chamber on September 19, 1870, Deputy Menocal summed up the years since the French defeat:

> The peace so ardently desired by our people has been constantly disturbed; civil war has again flamed in almost every state in the Republic, leaving behind blood, ruin, and misery. Capital either flees from the country or goes into hiding, ruining commerce and cutting off the sources of wealth. Brigandage and kidnapping, inseparable companions of misery, have given the death blow to confidence, which is the basis of property.[75]

Menocal was not exaggerating for the American consuls who reported on economic conditions to the United States Minister in

---

73. *Ibid.* As Elí de Gortari in his "Ciencia positiva política 'científica,'" *Historia Mexicana*, I, 603-616, points out, the whole positivist program was an attempt to impose the then established middle class thinking on all Mexicans.
74. The press was full of reports on the economic situation. The Archivo Juárez in Mexico City is full—too full, and therefore disappointing—of letters from ex-soldiers telling of their participation in the war and describing their present economic trials.
75. *Quinto congreso*, III, 34.

142   *Mexican Politics During the Juárez Regime*

Mexico repeated the same story, with additions. Julius Skelton reported:

> The first merchantile [sic] houses of this capital and Vera Cruz [sic], are free to declare, that the importations do not more than equal one half of those made four, five, six and eight years ago. This results from a want of market. People in the interior and on the coast are not buying goods. Capitalists are, and have been sending money out of the country for investment elsewhere, and others are contenting themselves with letting it lie idle, rather than incur the risk of its total loss.[76]

He went on to explain that the decline in imports stemmed from the decay of agriculture, which in turn was traceable to the insecurity of life and property. Conditions in the interior were no more encouraging. "Never, in the history of the country," wrote the consul in Monterrey,[77] "has there been such an entire stagnation of all business interests. . . . We have had over one hundred bankruptcys during the past year, of men of every branch of business." Furthermore, business in Monterrey was under the additional handicap of having to compete with a great deal of contraband coming in from the Free Zone.[78] From Chihuahua came an equally cheerless account:

> Business is exceedingly dull and silver and gold coin very scarce; commercial distress prevails all over the State; no credit is given to any extent; very hard on retail merchants, who cannot keep up an assortment, and also severely felt by the miners, who formerly paid their working men in goods and made their return in silver, realizing by the operation a large profit. The cause of this decline of credit and fortune is generally attributed to the enormous discount of 60% on the copper coin; the amount of this change circulating in the State exceeds a quarter of a million dollars.[79]

76. August 9, 1869. Mexican Dispatches, Vol. 36.
77. *Ibid.*
78. The Free Zone was first established by the Governor of Tamaulipas in 1858 and approved by the national congress in 1861. Goods imported into this area (Matamoros and five other towns along the Rio Grande) and designed for consumption there were exempt from paying federal import duties. Any imports shipped from these towns into other parts of the republic were supposed to be subject to the regular tariff charges. Ulíses Irigoyen, *El problema económico de las fronteras mexicanas* (2 vols., México, 1935), I, 35-36. Matías Romero opposed the Free Zone but the administration was not able to get congress to repeal the law.
79. September 21, 1869. Mexican Dispatches, Vol. 37.

Administration leaders realized, of course, that economic stability and social stability went hand in hand and that its own life was tied to both. They were willing to use the national government in an attempt to establish a sound economy. In 1867 and 1868 the government renewed the concession for the Veracruz-Mexico City railroad[80] and issued new grants for two more: one from Mexico to Túxpam and the other to extend across the Isthmus of Tehuantepec. Other laws authorized the opening of new roads and the construction of telegraph lines.[81]

After Romero took over the Ministry of the Treasury, he formulated a more definite plan for economic development based upon tariff reform and removal of the crippling restrictions on mining. As he viewed it, Mexico needed three things: immigration, new roads and other internal improvements, and the development of its natural resources. The last was the key for Romero believed that mining would be the agent which would lead to the development of Mexico's other riches and thus to the nation's prosperity. In his words:

> Nature has endowed Mexico with a privileged soil, capable of great development, and the object of the statesman who wishes to assure the prosperity and growth of this nation ought to be to provide for the development of the immense resources which lie buried in its bosom, without encouraging foreign greed so that it tries to take possession of the country.

Or again: "Mining is undisputably the most important source of wealth we have and is also the most susceptible to tremendous development."[82]

As is apparent, when Romero and other administration leaders advocated the capitalistic system for Mexico, they thought in terms

---

80. The tortuous path of the concessions and building of this railroad (not to be completed until 1873) is well told in David M. Pletcher's "The Building of the Mexican Railway," *HAHR*, XXX, 26-62. Antonio Escandón was the leader in obtaining concessions for this railroad from the Mexican government. Of especial concern to the Juárez group was whether to renew the concession granted to Escandón and the Imperial Mexican Railway Company, organized in 1864 by the French. In November, 1867, this was done. An annual subsidy of 560,000 pesos for twenty-five years was given the company. This concession came under fire by Mendiolea and Zamacona in congressional debates and the concession was revised in November, 1868, but no real changes were made.
81. Legislation passed in the years 1867-1868 may be found in D y L, *Legislación*, X, 88-94; 97-101; 137-143; 223-491.
82. Tovar, *Cuarto congreso*, IV, 13-14.

of extractive and commercial rather than industrial capital. The paper, *Voz de México*, expressed the opinion that Mexico ought to have many and varied industries, but the June 15, 1870 issue of the *Diario Oficial* argued back that the money Mexico exported was merchandise and differed in no way from other goods. The most advanced theories of political economy, the writer held, have established that the greatest advantages were to be derived from a high rate both of exports and imports. In this commercial movement, mining countries occupied the most favorable position because it took less work and less time to mine a million pesos than to produce the equivalent in manufactured goods.

To carry out the development program which Romero envisioned took capital, some of which he hoped could be obtained abroad and some of which he wanted the government to raise by administrative and fiscal reforms at home. But the policy of modified isolation toward European countries which Foreign Minister Lerdo adopted tended to discourage their nationals from investing in Mexican enterprises.[83] Any country that had recognized Maximilian's regime was expected to make the advances for renewal of diplomatic relations, which would be carried through only after an equitable adjustment of the old conventions. As a result of Lerdo's policy England withdrew its diplomatic representatives, a state of affairs scarcely encouraging to English investors which continued for a number of years. American investors proved little more eager, although both Juárez and Romero made it plain that they desired American capital.[84]

There was little hope of getting private domestic capital for reasons which Romero explained frankly. He did not think that in any case enough capital existed in Mexico to carry through all the developments needed, but people who did have money lacked sufficient confidence in the country's future to speculate with great amounts of their wealth. In addition, a large number of rich Mexicans, and especially those who had been connected with the Intervention, either had left the country or had sent their capital abroad because they feared a new revolution. But Romero did not

---

83. Knapp, *Lerdo*, 133.
84. See, for example, Juárez, January 27, 1870, to Rosecrans. Copiadores, Archivo Juárez. Romero, July 23, 1869, to Henry Clews. *Diario Oficial*, September 6, 1869.

want only money from the United States; he wanted that "spirit of enterprise" in which he felt the Mexicans were sadly lacking.

In April of 1869 the executive asked congress to approve several bills dealing with tax revision and fiscal policy, and these measures, along with their accompanying expositions, reflected the economic thinking of the administration and the Minister of the Treasury.[85] Their immediate objective was to increase government revenues, but, in addition, Romero felt that most of these proposals, if enacted, would help stimulate commerce and economic activity generally.

Romero, in considering the tax situation in which mining found itself, pointed out that the direct taxes alone on that industry came to almost twenty-five per cent, not of the profits, but of the gross income. He proposed that after July 1, 1870, mines be subject only to one tax, five per cent of their profits. In addition, he asked congress to allow the export of gold and silver bullion tax free and to levy a tax on the export of minted gold and silver: one per cent on the former and eight per cent on the latter. All other national products should be exported free of any tax, federal, state, or municipal.

The *alcabala* had long been deplored and, although its prohibition was made a part of the constitution, many states still depended on it for a good share of their income. Romero, in order to encourage its complete elimination, offered compensation. Any state which had abolished the tax would no longer be required to pay the federal contribution,[86] and all states which repealed the tax in the future would likewise be freed from paying the federal quota. To replace the revenue which would be lost to the national government, the administration proposed eliminating the sale of stamped paper and substituting for it a stamp tax which would cover a much wider range of articles.

The tax on inheritance, graduated on the basis of relationship rather than amount, was purely a revenue measure, but from the small tax he proposed on unexploited property held by large land-

---

85. Tovar, *Cuarto congreso*, IV, 13 ff; also in *Diario Oficial*, April 2, 3, 5, 6, 1869.
86. The federal contribution, much disliked by the states, was decreed on December 16, 1861. D y L, *Legislación*, IX, 338. It was a twenty-five per cent tax on almost all taxes collected, whether by federal, state or municipal officials, which went to the federal treasury. After 1861 the percentage varied.

holders, Romero hoped for other benefits besides an increase in the national revenues. He envisioned that the tax would either stimulate such proprietors to cultivate their land or lead to its transfer to other hands. Eventually it would bring about both an increase in productivity and a gradual subdivision of large estates.

The proposal which created the greatest discussion was Romero's plan for the emission of 18,000,000 pesos in treasury notes. As he pointed out, the government's revenues from customs, on which it largely depended, were heavy for six months and then fell off with the rainy season. He suggested that treasury notes be issued at the beginning of each fiscal year to the amount of the government's anticipated income and that these notes then be used to pay monthly expenses. This would mean that for a change the government could meet its obligations regularly. Another advantage would also accrue from the plan, for one of Mexico's most serious difficulties was the lack of circulating media. Since under the present system—the export of bullion being prohibited—it paid to export coin, money left the country as fast as it was minted.[87] Each time a *conducta* left, the nation faced a veritable monetary crisis. Having another medium of circulation would eliminate many, if not all, of these evils. Apparently, however, not one of his suggestions was enacted into law.[88]

Romero's complaint that the government could not meet its obligations regularly was simply a repetition of what had been said by his predecessors.[89] Since, in general, one-half of the revenue came from the coastal customhouses and that of Mexico City, a government policy which stimulated trade also brought more money to the treasury. So to promote commerce, the government encouraged internal improvements and made an effort to clear the roads of bandits.[90] But equally important, in Romero's opinion, was the complete overhaul of the tariff system.

87. The *Diario Oficial* on September 13, 1870, stated that of the 24,000,000 pesos minted each year twenty-one or twenty-three million were exported.
88. A check of D y L, *Legislación* and the congressional records shows this to be true.
89. Chaotic administrative conditions increased every secretary's frustrations. In February, 1868, Romero had to admit that the department was so disorganized he was unable to figure the income for the fiscal year. *Globo*, February 28, 1868. A much more detailed study of the economy may be found in the recently published work by Francisco R. Calderón, *La vida económica*, Vol. II of Cosío Villegas' *Historia de México* (México, 1955).
90. Laws for 1869 and 1870 are in D y L, *Legislación*, X, 500-783; XI, 34-468.

That the tariff was in need of drastic revision is apparent from reading Plumb's report on the subject.[91] Under the tariff law of 1856 and its subsequent modifications, the following charges were collected:

1. A municipal duty; twelve and one-half per cent upon each package of 200 pounds;
2. A duty of public improvement; twenty per cent on the amount of the import duty. The government was to apply this income to the payment of interest upon capital raised for the construction of railroads;
3. The *internación*, or inland duty; ten per cent on the amount of the import duty which was paid on goods sent from the port of entry into the interior;
4. A counter-register tax; twenty per cent on the amount of the import duty payable upon the arrival of the merchandise at the capital of principal port of destination in the interior;
5. An amortization duty; twenty-five per cent on the amount of the import duty payable to the national treasury in bonds of the public debt.

More exasperating than their multiplicity, Plumb reported, were the frequent changes and modifications of the duties. Often merchants and even government officials themselves did not know what the total charges should be. To illustrate his point he cited some examples. The government had abolished the highway tolls and had changed the duty for the sinking fund. A decree of November 28, 1867,[92] established a special tariff which the customhouses in Mexico City collected, in addition to the regular duties, for the benefit of the municipality. The calculation of tariff charges was such a complex job that as a result trade was left in the hands of the few who were willing to keep up with all the decrees and study them. Simplification and unification were urgently needed.

Early in 1868 the government had appointed a committee to draw up a new tariff[93] and on November 11 the committee made its report.[94] It advocated a system of specific duties and suggested a general reduction of ten per cent on dry goods, groceries, and common hardware. The committee also recommended increasing

91. Mexican Dispatches, Vol. 31. December 12, 1867.
92. D y L, *Legislación*, X, 144-162.
93. Plumb, February 8, 1868, to Seward. Mexican Dispatches, Vol. 32.
94. *Siglo*, November 17, 1868; Plumb, November 20, 1868, to Seward. Mexican Dispatches, Vol. 34.

the free list and abolishing completely the list of prohibited imports. It advised the free export of all products, except for a temporary retention of export duties on silver and gold, coined and in bars. While the committee favored the equal application of the tariff over all the republic and the termination of special privileges, it was willing to grant that the Free Zone might be an exceptional case. The report also recommended that three-fourths of the amount of the duties be paid in drafts to the order of the Minister of the Treasury; that the duties be consolidated; and that the interior customhouses be suppressed.

Although no proof exists that Romero had a hand in preparing the report, certainly the recommendations must have met with his approval. Even before the committee reported, Romero had asked congress to permit the free exportation of ores[95] and his proposal of April 1, 1869, had included some of the changes proposed by the committee.

On December 11, 1868, Romero proposed that congress pass a law which would set broad limits within which the executive would have the power to revise the tariff,[96] and in the April, 1869, proposals he made specific suggestions for tariff revisions. Congress having taken no action, Romero resubmitted his proposal in September, 1869.[97] He commented at the same time that the uncertainty over the tariff question was having a bad effect on commerce and requested congress either to take action itself on the matter or to authorize the administration to proceed with the revision.

Congress decided that to authorize the executive to revise the tariffs would be abdicating its power to enact legislation and, therefore, decided to keep the matter in its own hands. After considerable debate it agreed to ten basic principles on which the new system should be framed and appointed committees to draw up the specific rates.[98] Eventually congress considered a tariff bill, but despite long debates and a great deal of prodding by the administration, the deputies could not agree on any legislation. Tariff reform had to await executive action early in 1872.

95. On October 6, 1868. Tovar, *Cuarto congreso,* III, 217-220.
96. *Ibid.,* 782.
97. *Quinto congreso,* I, 53-54.
98. *Ibid.,* 590 ff.

Chapter VII

THE PRESIDENTIAL ELECTION OF 1871

The battle for possession of the presidency in 1871 had been going on ever since the election of 1867. The hard core of opposition which emerged after the publication of the *convocatoria* never disappeared, and it was this group which backed Díaz in the elections of 1867 and 1871. In congress, the *porfiristas*, often working together with Lerdo's supporters, tried whenever possible to thwart the desires of the president. Opposition newspapers, taking unrestrained advantage of the right to a free press, strove to discredit the administration. Lerdo, on the other hand, did not make public his intention to seek the presidency until a relatively short time before the balloting. But his long tenure and great influence in the cabinet put him in a very strong position which he cannily used to promote his own interests. By taking advantage of his opportunities he had managed to install in office several state governors willing to support his candidacy.

Therefore, although Díaz probably had a much broader popular appeal, the real threat to the *juaristas* was Lerdo's control of certain key offices and officials. Each faction tried to keep firmly in hand the states and municipalities already under its control and to add to the number whenever possible. Where an opponent's grip was too tight to be loosened, the other parties, and particularly the *porfiristas* who controlled relatively few public offices, demanded guarantees to insure free elections and to bar the military from voting areas on election day.

Obviously Lerdo could not remain in the cabinet and run for the same office as his chief. He had asked in July, 1870, and again in September to be relieved,[1] but the separation did not actually occur until after a dispute had arisen over the election of a new city council for the capital in December, 1870. Control of any municipal council was vitally important, for it was the body which supervised local balloting. Thus, if *lerdistas* were in the majority on

1. *Siglo*, January 18, 1871; Lerdo to Mariano Riva Palacio, September 22, 1870, M. Riva Palacio Papers. Lerdo's resignation is summarized in Knapp, *Lerdo*, 148-149.

the council in Mexico City, the assumption was valid that the nine deputies who represented the Federal District and usually had great influence in congress, would be *lerdistas*. When the electoral college met to vote for members of the city council and the *juaristas* discovered they were in the minority, they refused to participate on the grounds that many of the electors carried false credentials. After the *juaristas* had withdrawn, the *lerdistas* proceeded to elect a council, usually referred to as the San Ildefonso Ayuntamiento. The dissidents then met together and, declaring themselves the legal electoral body, they too elected a council. This "plethora of democracy" proved embarrassing to both Lerdo and Juárez for it was a public demonstration of the conflict between the president and the leader of his cabinet. Under the circumstances, the president could not support either of the contending parties, so the cabinet, with Lerdo present, finally decided that the council elected in 1870 should continue in office.[2]

If Lerdo had cherished a hope that the president would retire and that the government machinery would be used to put him in office, the municipal elections undoubtedly disabused him. With the prospect of an automatic succession now completely eliminated, Lerdo again submitted his resignation on January 14, 1871, and Juárez accepted it.[3] The president at this time was experiencing personal sorrow as well as political grief for his wife had died on the second day of January.

There were now two parties, *porfiristas* and *lerdistas*, opposing the reelection of Juárez to whom they both referred as the official candidate. "The Lerdist party assumed the character of its chief, being composed of men of property, a few capitalists, the intelligentsia, the socially prominent, and a minority of the bureaucratic element which Lerdo had erected in governmental posts during his long tenure as chief of cabinet."[4] By far the most important element in the party were men of the legal profession who felt that they

2. *Diario Oficial*, January 19, 1870; Zamacois, *México*, XXI, 745-757.
3. Zamacona makes the following claim in a letter written to Díaz in June, 1871: "In order to get a stable opposition to the administration in congress I conceived of the idea of hastening Lerdo's departure from the cabinet. He had decided to postpone his resignation until the last possible moment, since he realized that the largest part of his resources in the election derived from his official position. However, through the use of certain influences over the *lerdista* party, my plan was successful." *Archivo Díaz*, IX, 145.
4. Knapp, *Lerdo*, 153. One should balance Knapp by reading the description of the party in Zamacois, *México*, XXI, 336-342.

alone were capable of ruling Mexico. Next to Lerdo, the two most influential leaders were Ramón Guzmán and Manuel Romero Rubio. Guzmán, a man of humble origin, was especially close to Lerdo and served as his chief agent in congress. Romero Rubio was a pleasant and well mannered socialite and lawyer whom Lerdo used to smooth out difficulties. Besides these two leaders, Lerdo could count on such outstanding men as Montiel y Duarte, Vidal Castañeda y Nájera, and Dr. Hilarión Frías y Soto. The major newspaper supporting Lerdo was *Siglo XIX*; *Revista Universal* came out openly for him late in the campaign.

Outside of Mexico City Lerdo was quite well entrenched. At one time he could count among his supporters the governors of San Luis Potosí, Morelos, Guanajuato, Hidalgo, Puebla, Michoacán, and Jalisco.[5] Had he been able to retain his control over all these states and the municipal council of Mexico City, he might well have won the election, but after his resignation the *juaristas* were able to raid his preserves effectively.

The *lerdista* program[6] naturally included the policies Lerdo had followed as a cabinet member; for example, that of refusing to reestablish relations with foreign powers except on what was described as "prudent bases." The party made the usual pledges to respect the freedom and sovereignty of the states; to expand the educational system; to enforce the laws; and to respect the individual rights guaranteed by the constitution. Almost half of the points in the program dealt with economic affairs. It listed several steps that a government headed by Lerdo would take to promote and encourage capitalists and free enterprise and to provide the nation with a government free of corruption and economically administered. The *lerdista* platform contained no new ideas and outlined no fresh approach; it more or less recapitulated liberal thinking since the Reform, and the same can be said for the programs presented by the other two candidates.

The *porfiristas* gathered in most of the old *puros* who had opposed Juárez back in 1861-1863, and the ranks were increased

---

5. Based on Knapp, *Lerdo*, 154; *Correo del Comercio*, June 22, 29, 1871; *La Paz*, February 14, 20, 1871. Governor Mariano Riva Palacio of the state of México asserted that friendship for both Juárez and Lerdo would keep him neutral in the election. This was at least a negative triumph for Lerdo. *La Paz*, May 29, 1871.
6. Summarized in Zamacois, *México*, XXI, 761-764.

by a number of dissatisfied office seekers, some military men, and, in general, all those who were disgusted with the other two men. The leader of the party in Mexico City was Justo Benítez and the party included such well known men as Zamacona, Manuel Mendiolea, Ignacio Ramírez, and Ireneo Paz.[7] Díaz came to Mexico City in September, 1870, to take his seat as a deputy but stayed only until December when he retired to his estate in Oaxaca, leaving Benítez to direct party strategy in the capital.

In Mexico City, the newspapers *El Mensajero, El Ferrocarril, La Oposición, El Padre Cobos,* and *Orquesta* backed Díaz. The party was somewhat less well organized in the states but what it counted on was the enactment of laws that would permit a free election for the *porfiristas* believed their candidate was the overwhelming popular favorite.

Their program, printed in *Mensajero,* January 11, 1871,[8] included about the same promises as did the *lerdista* program. In vague terms and imprecise language the *porfiristas* announced their intention to abide by the constitution of 1857 with emphasis upon individual guarantees, free elections, and the proper distribution of authority between the federal and state governments. They promised a government economically administered and free of corruption and one which would improve Mexico's public credit. Under Díaz, the government would search for a way to harmonize the military establishment with democratic principles.

The Juárez party, of course, stood on its record and used the *Diario Oficial* and other papers including *La Paz, Federalista,* and *Correo del Comercio* to remind the voters what it had accomplished. But the programs and the record were merely window dressing. The opposition parties recognized the hard political fact that the administration's control of federal funds and the army gave it a stranglehold on success which neither of them alone was powerful enough to break. This realization led to a marriage of convenience, the formation of a *lerdista-porfirista* bloc in congress. While neither side ever publicly acknowledged the arrangement and Zamacona

7. Ireneo Paz, *Algunas campañas* (3 vols., México, 1884-1886), II and III, has excellent material for the period, and for a study of a "professional" revolutionary these two volumes are invaluable. They must be supplemented by the *Archivo Díaz,* IX, which shows clearly the dissension within the *porfirista* party.
8. See the author's summary in "*EL MENSAJERO* and the Election of 1871 in Mexico," *Americas,* V, 1.

specifically denied it writing in *Mensajero*, the publication of the *Archivo Díaz* gives positive proof of its existence.⁹ Moreover, the press and the congressional debates of the time all indicated that some sort of an agreement existed between the two groups. The *juarista* press continually cited evidence of the operation of such an alliance which it referred to as *la liga,* and congressional voting in the 1871 pre-election session gave support to their charges. It could not have been complete coincidence which so often put *lerdistas* and *porfiristas* on the same side of a question.

Actually the two groups had little in common except their realization that unless they stopped Juárez they had no chance, and each side tried to use the league to achieve its own aims. The *lerdista* goal was to keep the governors supporting Lerdo in power. The governors, who controlled the elections, could swing enough votes from Juárez so that in the final tally no candidate would have the necessary majority with the result that the election would devolve upon congress. In such cases, the existing law provided that every state delegation had one vote in the balloting. The supporters of Lerdo planned to change this procedure to one which would give each individual deputy a vote. Even though Lerdo might receive fewer votes than Juárez in the election, his followers believed that when the contest reached congress, where Lerdo controlled a number of state delegations, that body would choose him president under the new system of voting.¹⁰ Nor was this just wishful thinking. Early in 1871 Lerdo could count on seventy-four deputies and he had a chance of picking up the delegation from the state of México. If he did so he would then have a total of eighty-nine deputies pledged to him.¹¹ Congress rarely had in attendance its total of 220 deputies; usually only about 150 to 160 were present which meant that a bloc of over eighty votes would have a good chance of controlling the election. But these plans involved two difficulties. The first was practical; in order for the scheme to work it was essential that Lerdo retain his influence over the states he controlled. The second was ideological; it meant that Lerdo had to emphasize states' rights in order to make himself president which

9. See especially Zamacona's letter to Díaz written in June, 1871. *Archivo Díaz,* IX, 143-156.
10. Zamacois, *México,* XXI, 735-757.
11. From the states of Jalisco, Michoacán, Puebla, Guanajuato, and México. *Federalista,* May 2, 1871.

contradicted completely his basic political philosophy of centralism.
The *porfiristas* were aware of these calculations, but they too realized that at least temporarily they had to work with the *lerdistas*. The Díaz men believed that their candidate could win only if the elections were free, and they needed *lerdista* support to get legislation through the next session of congress, making it impossible for the administration to control the vote.[12] The program which they designed to block the president's reelection included the enactment of a new electoral law with guarantees for free balloting and, for the same reason, they wanted to repeal the law of the state of siege. Another part of their strategy was to vote a stringent and restrictive budget, particularly in the funds for extraordinary expenses, since they felt the money would be used to put Juárez back into office. They planned to institute in congress a second jury panel to expedite the hearings of the accusations against the ministers and thereby—the assumption being that the ministers would be found guilty—badly cripple what they considered to be the focus of reelectionist intrigue. For their support the *lerdistas* were to be repaid by *porfirista* cooperation on the two questions of the Mexico City council and the state of Guerrero.

Once the two groups had reached an understanding the permanent deputation, composed chiefly of Lerdo supporters, called an extraordinary session of congress for March 6, three weeks before the regular opening date. In addition to the avowed program on which they would cooperate with the *lerdistas* in congress, the *porfiristas* had a private plan of action. Their objective was to weaken as much as possible the elements working for reelection so that Juárez, their most dangerous enemy, could in no case obtain an absolute and decisive majority of the votes. They felt that Lerdo's candidacy, while it had the support of certain governors, absolutely lacked any popular base, and they were sure that some of his supporters would fall from power. Being thus reduced to third place in the competition, Lerdo's followers would support Díaz if the *porfiristas* could succeed in making the *juaristas* and *lerdistas* irreconcilable enemies—something Zamacona admitted he

12. Since the elections were not free, the validity of this assumption was never tested, but the American consuls reporting to the American Minister, Thomas H. Nelson, indicated that they expected Juárez to retain the presidency. Veracruz, Zacatecas, Sonora, Sinaloa, Durango, Jalisco, Tamaulipas, Coahuila, Tabasco, and Colima, according to their calculations, were in the Juárez camp. Mexican Dispatches, Vols. 42 & 43.

had been trying to do for quite a long time.[13] With Juárez lacking a majority and receiving no support from Lerdo, Díaz then would become the next president.

In its preparatory meetings, the special session of congress elected Zamacona president by a vote of 87 to 70, and when the sessions began on March 10 it was evident Juárez was in for a real battle. In his response to Juárez' usual perfunctory welcoming address, Zamacona departed from the equally customary polite reply. He agreed with the president that the country needed peace, but he wanted peace accompanied by freedom which included, particularly in an election year, freedom of the ballot.[14] Zamacona's speech was in keeping with the new spirit which began to manifest itself early in the session and which carried over into the regular session beginning on April 1. Name calling was more common than ever, and the galleries more vociferous in applause and abuse than before.

The first major bill which came up for consideration was the *porfirista* measure to amend the electoral law of 1857 and, from the end of March until its final passage on May 8, it was the deputies' chief topic of debate. The purpose of the law was to guarantee free elections by eliminating the army from the scene. To accomplish that purpose, the legislation provided that all military personnel must vote in their barracks which they were not permitted to leave on election day. To prevent the president from circumventing the law, he was forbidden to call out the troops during the month preceding the election. Federal troops were subject to similar restraints during elections to fill state offices. One section was designed to meet the wishes of the *lerdistas;* it changed the method of congressional balloting for president from voting by delegations to voting by individuals.[15]

Although the bill finally passed despite their efforts, the *juaristas* had one small comfort for their opposition had earned them the sympathies of many army men.[16] The military felt that the legislation was discriminatory, and a number of top army men issued a statement denouncing the law. While it had suffered a defeat in congress, the administration was not ready to stop fighting. When the law was promulgated, the Minister of Gobernación issued an

13. Zamacona, June, 1871, to Díaz. *Archivo Díaz,* IX, 143-156.
14. *Quinto congreso,* IV, 3-6.
15. D y L, *Legislación,* XI, 495-498.
16. Zamacois, *México,* XXI, 834.

accompanying circular in which he termed it a bad piece of legislation and one which discriminated against the army. The circular, which *Mensajero* called seditious, indicated clearly that at best the federal government would make only the feeblest effort to enforce the new legislation.[17]

The supporters of Juárez again found themselves in the minority in the debate on the city council of Mexico City. On March 21 the congressional committee appointed to study the question recommended that the *lerdista* San Ildefonso council be installed as the city's governing body.[18] Administration supporters, adopting the opposition's argument of unconstitutionality, declared the committee's report unacceptable because the constitution forbade interference in municipal affairs. On the final vote, the alliance won by a slender margin of 89 to 88, but they still did not achieve a victory.[19] Juárez took the position that the matter could not be settled by a simple congressional resolution; the deputies would have to pass a law. After considering the president's opinion, congress again ordered him to put the Lerdo group in power, but Juárez refused to change his stand.

Made impatient by the long delay, the *lerdistas* imprudently decided to take action and attempted to take possession of their seats without waiting for the issue to be settled definitely. Their forcible expulsion by the governor of the Federal District caused a sensation, and congress, insisting on its right to intervene, ordered the executive to reinstate the Lerdo group. In the interest of peace, the president complied, but with a protest which he would later recall to his own advantage.[20]

The *porfiristas* were also successful in carrying out another item on their program. They were able to repeal the law of January 21, 1860, which gave the president the power to establish a state of siege if he deemed such action necessary at a time when congress was not in session. As passed on May 24, the new law consisted of a single article which declared the earlier measure unconstitutional. The *juaristas* fought stubbornly against it but the final vote was

17. *Diario Oficial*, May 12-13, 1871.
18. *Quinto congreso*, IV, 99-102.
19. *Ibid.*, 379. Apparently some of the *porfiristas* voted with the Juárez group on this issue. Mendiolea, June 4, 1871, to Díaz. *Archivo Díaz*, IX, 159-163.
20. Nelson, April 29, 1871, to Fish. Mexican Dispatches, Vol. 42.

90 to 60. Actually the administration did not lose a great deal since it could easily declare and enforce a state of siege after congress adjourned at the end of the month. There would be no one to judge its actions until the congress elected in 1871 assembled, and the *juaristas* intended to control that session.[21]

Although on certain questions the opposition was able to work together to defeat the administration, throughout the session the *juaristas* gradually made inroads and weakened the voting strength of the fusion. To some extent the resurgence of *juarista* power can be seen in the case involving Jalisco. During the period when Lerdo was still in the cabinet, the state legislature had removed Governor Gómez Cuervo and had replaced him with its own candidate. When Gómez Cuervo ignored its orders and continued to hold his office, the legislature appealed to the federal government for help in ousting him. Technically the administration, by refusing to intervene in the internal affairs of a state, was carefully observing the federal-state relationship. Actually, however, it gave its support to Gómez Cuervo since the commander of the federal troops in Jalisco continued to recognize him as governor.

But since Gómez Cuervo was a *lerdista* it was only natural that the government should change its policy with Lerdo's withdrawal from the cabinet. Once Lerdo had resigned, Juárez agreed to aid the state legislature, and through the influence of the national government Jesús Camarena was named interim governor in spite of the protests of the *lerdistas*. To weaken Lerdo's influence still further, particularly in Guadalajara, the state legislature declared all town councils illegal whose members had taken office under Gómez Cuervo. To replace these officials new elections were held in May and, since the *juaristas* controlled the polling places, they also won control of the town councils. With the legislature and councils in pro-administration hands, the *lerdistas* would have little chance to win the presidential election. In this case the *porfiristas* remained indifferent for they had no stake in the outcome.[22]

Juárez triumphed not only in the voting on Jalisco but also on questions of lesser importance involving the states of San Luis Potosí and Puebla. The opposition failed, too, in its desire to get closer congressional control of the budget and it was likewise un-

21. Zamacois, *México*, XXI, 916-929.
22. *Ibid.*, 524-576; 795-808; 849; 994-995; 1038.

successful in what was, for all practical purposes, an attempt to impeach Romero.²³ To what extent bribery was responsible for weakening the alliance is unknown, yet it certainly played a part.²⁴ But it was not only the alliance which was proving shaky; divisions were appearing within the Díaz group itself. Zamacona became so disturbed that he called a meeting of the *porfirista* leaders to achieve greater unity in voting²⁵ Those attending agreed to work together, but Benítez, titular head of the group, was not faithful to his word. Zamacona and Mendiolea reported to Díaz that the party lacked unity and that Juárez was picking up strength and getting majorities in congressional voting.²⁶ Both men accused Benítez of not working actively enough to keep up the alliance with the *lerdistas*, and what was worse, he was associating and working with the *juaristas*. Unfortunately we do not have Benítez' letter explaining his actions to Díaz. Zamacona decided he did not have the strength to fight both his friends and his enemies and resigned as editor of *Mensajero*, the principal *porfirista* paper in Mexico City.

While the administration had gained strength in congress and had come through the session with little real damage to its power to control the elections, the Mexico City council remained an important opposition stronghold. This threat to reelection was not permitted to continue very long, however, for after congress adjourned on May 31 the administration felt free to execute its coup. On June 10 the capital received the news. Governor Gabino Bustamante of the Federal District, a *juarista*, announced he had proof that the council intended to control the election by fraudulent means. To prevent a scandal he ordered the suspension of the incumbent body and replaced it with the council elected in 1869.²⁷ As a result of Bustamante's action, real trouble developed between the executive branch and the permanent deputation controlled by the opposition. Bitter exchanges between them went on for four days with the deputation demanding that the *lerdista* council be

23. Nelson, May 29, 1871, to Fish. Mexican Dispatches, Vol. 43.
24. Zamacona, June, 1871, to Díaz. *Archivo Díaz*, IX, 143-156; *Siglo*, April 19, 1871, made similar suggestions.
25. Paz claims that the top leaders of the Díaz group—Benítez, Ignacio Ramírez, Zamacona, Jesús Alfaro, Avila, Felipe Buenrostro, and Mendiolea— met every night to talk matters over. Paz, *Campañas*, III, 27. Apparently either the conferences were not successful or Paz was too optimistic.
26. *Archivo Díaz*, IX, 143-156; 159-163.
27. *Diario Oficial*, June 11, 14, 1871.

reinstated and the governor brought to trial. The Minister of Gobernación replied that Juárez had called upon the governor and that he was now studying the situation. On June 14 the same minister informed Bustamante that, after examining all the legal aspects, the president felt the suspension came within the governor's powers and therefore the administration could not interfere.[28] Although Bustamante died on the same day, Juárez immediately filled the vacancy by appointing Alfredo Chavero who carried on the policy of his predecessor.[29]

The three contending groups fought their political battle not only on the floor of the chamber but they also waged an intensive campaign in the press. Díaz supporters wished to create the impression that they constituted a genuine political party rather than a merely personal following of the general. For that reason they seldom referred to themselves as *porfiristas,* preferring to be called *constitucionalistas.* Since their plan to defeat Juárez depended upon *lerdista* support in congress, the *porfirista* papers seldom attacked Lerdo but rather spent most of their time criticizing the administration. They charged Juárez himself with inactivity and hesitation and they indicted *juaristas* in general for not abiding by the constitution, claiming, as an example, that state governors had been reduced to mere servants of the federal government. The administration was blamed because it had done nothing to relieve the depressed economic conditions and had not put public credit on a sound basis. The *porfiristas* repeatedly charged that favoritism and corruption permeated the government, and the cure they advocated was embodied in their slogan of "No Re-election." To replace the sluggish, inefficient, and corrupt Juárez regime, the Díaz press urged the election of its candidate, a great general who knew the wishes of the people and who would follow the constitution once he gained power.

The *lerdistas* could hardly criticize administration policies carried out during the time Lerdo was serving in the cabinet, but they overcame this handicap by giving their candidate credit for all the achievements in that period. *Siglo* maintained that if Lerdo had not been in the cabinet Mexico might never have survived as a nation. But the *lerdistas* were under no restraints in considering

28. Nelson, June 10, 12, 27, 1871, to Fish. Mexican Dispatches, Vol. 43.
29. *Quinto congreso,* IV, 769-784.

the administration's actions in the months since Lerdo's resignation. They attacked the government for its illegal and unconstitutional procedures in meddling in state and municipal politics and otherwise trying to control the forthcoming elections.

The *juaristas* devoted their greatest efforts to splitting the alliance. To nettle the *porfiristas* they drew up a balance sheet with all the credit on Lerdo's side; the Díaz group was reminded that its return from the cooperation project was zero. Since Lerdo controlled some of the state governors and had more of a political machine than Díaz, the *juaristas* concentrated their major efforts on Lerdo. The ex-minister's long tenure in the cabinet caught them in the same dilemma as it did their opponents, and they adopted the same solution in reverse. In their version, Lerdo had been responsible for all the poor decisions while the president had made those which were wise and good. The pro-Juárez papers also kept insisting that the reactionary group was supporting Lerdo and that he could not afford to disown them since that would be equivalent to renouncing his candidacy. But even so, the pages of *Federalista* reflected the *juaristas'* problems in trying to attack Lerdo after his previous close association with Juárez.

The partisan press campaigned on a very low level, especially as election time approached; and the papers were willing to use practically any rumor, no matter how malicious, to injure opposition candidates. Probably the *porfirista* press was the worst, but there was little to choose among them.

The primary elections were held in June and the electors chosen at that time met the following month to vote for president and deputies to congress. Before the final result was known, each side claimed victory but the complete tally gave Juárez 5,837 votes, Díaz 3,555, and Lerdo 2,874. Since no candidate had received an absolute majority, the final decision rested with congress. The *juaristas* had been most successful in electing deputies for they returned approximately 105 men to congress, an increase of about twenty over the previous session.[30]

The time between the announcement of the election results and the reconvening of congress in September was an uneasy interval for the feeling prevailed that Díaz was ready to revolt if he did not win. As a matter of fact, no decision had been reached for the

30. Zamacois, *México*, XXII, 19-20.

porfirista party was divided on methods. All of them wanted to see their candidate in office, but one faction was determined to use force if necessary to grasp their objective; the other was intent on achieving the goal by peaceful and constitutional means. For this reason they suggested recreating the congressional alliance with the *lerdistas*. If the latter agreed to vote for Díaz, the supporters of Díaz planned to reward them with government offices.[31] In early September, Díaz himself seemed inclined to follow a policy of conciliation and the government, working through Matías Romero, was doing its best to keep him in that mood. Yet Díaz knew at this time that his brother Félix, Governor of Oaxaca, had already begun stocking guns and ammunition, and the two had established a code for their correspondence.[32]

But the Juárez group watched not so much the actions of Díaz as of the *lerdistas* for if a rebellion did take place they wanted to be certain that the Lerdo supporters would at least remain neutral. Although the *lerdistas* did not later resort to violence as did Díaz, still the *Diario Oficial* from July to September reflected *juarista* uncertainty as to the *lerdista's* future course. In fact, in July the *Diario Oficial* reported that *Siglo* was calling on Oaxaca and Puebla to join in a show of strength against the government. When *Siglo* ultimately rejected revolution as an acceptable course, the *Diario* observed on August 25 that the editorial came as a great surprise. *Revista Universal,* another Lerdo organ, echoed *Siglo's* views and, although the government's paper welcomed their statements, an undercurrent of mistrust still remained in the *Diario's* comments.

As the day approached for congress to assemble one thing was certain: the alliance was now broken.[33] This fact and the increased number of Juárez deputies assured the president of reelection. From September 1 to September 15 the preparatory junta of congress met to organize the new session. Its discussions dealt chiefly with the appointment of the credentials committee which would study disputed election returns and recommend the seating of deputies. The orators had lost none of their fire during the summer recess, and Zamacona continued his violent denunciations of the pro-administration faction. However, under Sánchez Azcona's lead-

31. Ezequiel Montes, August 20, 1871, to Díaz. *Archivo Díaz,* IX, 251-254.
32. *Ibid.,* 234-235; 255-259; 286-290.
33. *Diario Oficial,* August 31, 1871.

ership, the *juaristas* in congress were able to get control of the committee. After the sessions officially opened on September 16, congress devoted the next month almost exclusively to considering the credentials of deputies. Several test votes in the chamber gave early proof that the *juaristas* controlled enough deputies to block whatever parliamentary maneuvers the *porfiristas* might attempt. The Díaz supporters seem to have had two objectives: they wanted to block any vote for the presidency, and they wanted full blame for a revolt, if it came, to rest on Juárez. During the credentials debates, congress was really an open forum for denouncing the *juaristas*. Díaz men tried hard to show that the administration's election methods were illegal and that the procedure for seating deputies was equally so.[34]

The *porfiristas* were not alone in protesting the manner in which deputies were seated; the *lerdistas* did too. As September wore on, *Siglo's* complaints grew increasingly bitter, and by the last day of the month the paper was saying that the responsibility for any revolt which might occur would lie with the *juaristas*. Yet *Siglo* weighed its aversion to both the *juaristas*' present tactics and the *porfiristas*' threatened revolution and concluded that, while it could not support the latter, neither could it work with the government. Therefore it counseled abstention and a "wait and see" attitude. At least the *juaristas* seemed to have achieved their objective of keeping Lerdo's followers neutral.

The point was an important one for before September ended the disturbances the government had been anticipating occurred. On September 28, the Minister of War informed congress he had received news of a revolt in Nuevo León led by General Treviño, and two days later *Federalista* reported outbreaks in Sinaloa and San Luis Potosí. The big news, however, came on October 1 when several military men led by General Negrete attempted a coup d'etat at the Ciudadela in Mexico City. They had spent a good deal of money on their preparations but General Sóstenes Rocha, commander of the government forces, was ready to meet them and the uprising was stamped out quickly and completely.

On October 12 congress declared Juárez the legally elected president. He would not begin serving his new term until December 1

---

34. *Diario de los debates. Sexto congreso constitucional de la unión* (4 vols., México, 1871-1873), I, 75-271.

and few people, except the government which was preparing for it, really expected any trouble from Díaz until after that date. They believed Díaz would wait until Juárez took the oath, after which he would claim that the president held office illegally. But many of Díaz' supporters had been planning the revolt since July,[35] and their intrigue reached its climax early in November with the Plan of La Noria. The Plan was published in Mexico City on November 13.

Díaz charged in his Plan that the indefinite and controlled reelection of the president was endangering the national institutions, citing as examples the fact that congress and the supreme court had become mere tools of the executive. The same situation prevailed in some states where the federal government had replaced the legally constituted authorities with its own followers. Federal troops kept these men in power, and the army in general was forced to serve as an instrument of the people's oppression. Although federal revenues were sufficient to meet the country's expenses, "the ineptitude of some, the favoritism of others, and the corruption of all" had ruined Mexican prosperity. The justification for rebellion against these evil forces was that they could be removed in no other way. If the opposition had lost the elections fairly, it would have been content to wait and try again, but under present conditions it had no alternative but to resort to arms. Díaz adopted as his motto the Constitution of 1857 and electoral freedom; his program: less government and more liberty.

To carry out the program Díaz outlined a specific plan of action for what he termed a reconstruction of the government.[36] In the "reconstructed" government the election of the president was to be by direct individual voting, and no one could be a candidate who during one year preceding the election had held any authority or office whose functions extended over the whole national territory. The president must submit to congress for confirmation the appointment of secretaries of the cabinet and other officials having a yearly salary of 3,000 pesos or more. Under the new government,

35. Paz, *Campañas*, III, 63-76.
36. Apparently Díaz drew up the Plan but Benítez changed it completely. Paz and others found it much too verbose and forced some changes. *Ibid.*, 76-78. The Plan of La Noria may be found in practically any book on Mexican history. As convenient as any is Vol. X of the *Archivo Díaz*, 43-48. Daniel Cosío Villegas has an excellent study on the Plan in his *Porfirio Díaz en la revuelta de la Noria* (México, 1953).

congress would guarantee to the town councils their rights and revenues so they would be free and independent. The Plan also promised the establishment of trial by jury, the elimination of the sales tax, and the amendment of the tariff laws. The body responsible for carrying out the reconstruction would be a convention composed of three representatives from each state chosen by direct vote of the people. The first task of this body would be to choose a provisional president who could, under no circumstances, be the commander of the revolutionary forces. After completing this task, the convention would devote itself to providing Mexico with an organic law.

It was this part of the Plan which cost Díaz much support. For above all else, people in Mexico wanted constitutional government and, although Díaz seemed to be calling for just that, his plan actually overthrew the constitution by providing that the convention select a provisional president. The Constitution of 1857 stated that when a president, for any reason, did not complete his term of office, the presidency should pass to the president of the supreme court. Consequently, if Juárez were to be removed, Lerdo would be his legal successor. But Díaz was not interested in promoting Lerdo's fortunes and, under the circumstances, his own desire for the presidency could not be satisfied without setting aside constitutional procedure. The Lerdo supporters, in turn, could not support a plan which eliminated their leader.

The reaction to this pronouncement was not enthusiastic. Plumb, then living in Mexico City, wrote of its reception:

> It appears it has been the deliberate intention of the Porfirio Diaz party, in any case, if not successful in the election, to appeal to arms, and notwithstanding the high opinion we had formed of that person, he has proven to be utterly without political capacity, character or patriotism. For several months there have been constant rumors that there would be a revolution of which he would be the head but so high has been the estimation entertained of him personally that there has been great reluctance to believe that this could prove to be true. . . .
> On November 13 there reached here a proclamation issued at La Noria. It has caused a profound sensation, and I may also say, almost universal disgust, so great even that very many at first refused to credit its authenticity. Only one paper has come out in its defense. In the manifesto, Diaz,

while pretending to sustain the Constitution, sets it aside entirely. And going back of the times even of Santa Anna, he proposed nothing less than a pure military dictatorship.

The result of La Noria has been to force a union between the Lerdo and Juarez parties and unite all who are opposed to anarchy and a return to the era of military pronouncements. These people are now supporting the government and this has rendered impossible the permanent triumph of the revolution.[37]

On the day the Plan reached Mexico City, congress began debating the grant of extraordinary powers to the president. Díaz supporters who were still attending the sessions used all kinds of devices to prevent a vote on the measure, and understandably so, for the increased executive powers might be used against them. On November 16, amid great confusion in congress, the *porfiristas* walked out in protest against a ruling of the chair, only to return the next day to continue the bitter debate. Not until December 1 did congress approve the measure.[38]

37. Plumb, Mexico City, November 18, 1871, to Babcock. Plumb Papers.
38. *Sexto congreso*, I, 383; 453-454.

Chapter VIII

THE LAST TERM

On the same day that congress voted him extraordinary powers, Juárez appeared in the chamber to take the oath of office. The *porfirista* deputies refused to participate officially in the ceremony and watched from the galleries, their abstention being designed to signify their protest against the legality of the elections. Almost all the *lerdistas*, however, were in their chairs on the floor of congress.[1] In his short inaugural address devoted to the turbulent internal conditions, the president made pointed references to Díaz without once mentioning his name. Juárez declared that the rebels wanted to return to the militarism and the personalism which had proved so disastrous in the past, and he expressed his firm belief that the country would not accept any plan to overthrow the institutions established at such great sacrifices.

Mexicans might have had some difficulty in sharing their president's optimism for while the administration could count on reliable support in Oaxaca, even though it was the Díaz stronghold, the story was quite different in the interior and on the northern frontier. Subduing the rebels was made more difficult by the fact that they tended to make it a guerrilla war rather than to meet the federal troops in large scale battles. But the administration was not entirely unprepared, and early in January, 1872, government forces moved into Oaxaca and after some skirmishes were able to take the capital without a fight. The death of Félix Díaz, the governor, which occurred shortly afterward virtually ended the revolt in that state. In the north, General Rocha defeated Treviño's troops early in March, yet while the rebellion was weakened considerably by the administration's local successes, the final sparks would not be extinguished until the Lerdo administration.

Congress had ended its first session on December 15, 1871, and when it reconvened for the second session on April 1, 1872, the deputies listened to President Juárez read his address consisting of the usual dry recitation of facts.[2] He informed them that the gov-

1. *Federalista*, December 2, 1871.
2. *Sexto congreso*, II, 5-7.

ernment had successfully put down the La Noria rebellion and had done so without resorting to forced loans, extraordinary taxation, or other exactions. But while it was true that the government had crushed the chief revolt, minor guerrilla warfare still continued, and the president felt compelled to ask congress for an extension of the extraordinary powers granted him the previous December. He defended his past use of this increased authority, saying that he had never abused his power and had only declared states of siege when such action was absolutely necessary. Besides giving the deputies a résumé of the government's activities during the recess, the president also recommended two constitutional changes, listing first the creation of a Senate. Not less important in his estimation was a revision of constitutional procedure so that, no matter what the circumstances, there would always be a legal successor to the presidency.

The following day Minister of the Treasury Romero submitted his report, an extensive and important document dealing not only with current fiscal affairs but also including plans for improving Mexico's economic situation.[3] Romero explained how the government was able to meet the increased military expenditures without raising taxes: the cost of the civil lists had been reduced; taxes were collected more efficiently; the date for payment of certain direct taxes had been moved up; and salaries of the customs officials had been raised. But the most important source of revenue to meet immediate expenses was a new type of contract with the minting houses which, among other things, allowed the mints to export gold and silver in bullion. For this privilege the mints were willing to pay the government 300,000 pesos.

Although Romero believed the export of bullion would bring long term benefits to the Mexican economy, he emphasized the change in the tariff laws as the most important innovation. He used a good part of his report to develop the idea that under the extra powers granted to the executive, the president had the power to promulgate a new tariff law without consulting congress. The administration had promulgated the law on January 1, 1872, and had set July 1, 1872, as the date on which it was to go into effect.[4] By

---

3. *Ibid.*, 10-46.
4. Zamacona apparently had foreseen the administration's intention to promulgate the tariff, for he had introduced a resolution in the previous session of

submitting the decree to congress, however, the executive gave that body plenty of time to debate the proposed tariff. Romero also reported on three other changes put through by the administration: a new stamp tax was substituted for the old stamped paper; the tax on coined money was to be paid at the point of production instead of at the point of export; and merchants were permitted to transport foreign goods across the country for reexport.

Without delay the administration sought the enactment of two laws granting the government powers it claimed were indispensable if the country were to be pacified. On April 2 the Minister of Gobernación introduced a resolution asking for the extension of the law of December 2, 1871, giving the president additional powers through the suspension of guarantees; the following day the government requested extension of the law on kidnaping and banditry of May 18, 1871.[5] Congress approved the second bill on May 23 but, as usual, the proposal to continue the president's extraordinary powers provoked vehement debate.

Zamacona's arguments against the bill probably summarized quite accurately the feeling of the opposition. Ever since the Constitution of 1857 had nominally gone into effect, Zamacona charged, Mexico had lived under a dictatorship for the administration maintained that without extraordinary powers the restoration of peace and order was impossible. The government had been able to find no other method for meeting emergencies than to ask for an extension of its dictatorial powers, using the excuse that as long as the opposition persisted in armed rebellion ordinary constitutional procedures were insufficient to cope with the situation. In Zamacona's opinion such reasoning condemned the nation to a vicious circle; cut off from winning control of the government through legal channels, revolution offered anti-administration elements their only opportunity to attain power. The only solution, he pleaded, was free government under the constitution. Although the opposition attacked the bill violently, the administration had a safe majority and on May 17 the chamber approved the legislation by a vote of 95 to 37.

Before the debate began on the resolution to extend the presi-

congress to the effect that the grant of powers to the executive did not allow him to enact a new tariff. The resolution was not admitted. *Ibid.*, I, 636.
5. *Ibid.*, II, 9-10; 174-175.

dent's extraordinary powers, the opposition had tried to replace this bill with a counterproposal of its own. On April 11 the *porfiristas*, joined by Romero Rubio of the Lerdo group, introduced a bill calling for an end to the states of siege which the administration had imposed on five states. The key article was really the second which declared that no one in the Mexican Republic had the power to suspend the operation of the federal constitution and of the laws emanating from it, except as provided by Article 2 of the constitution itself. On April 20 the opposition followed with another resolution suspending the operation of laws issued by the Secretary of the Treasury under the grant of extra powers to the executive until congress had revised them. The first proposal was buried in committee; congress briefly discussed the second in connection with the tariff but it was not given any serious consideration.

Although the opposition was unsuccessful in putting its own measures through congress, it was powerful and vocal enough to force changes in administration bills, particularly the budget and tariff laws. The budget was introduced in April and throughout that month the opposition had Romero under fire. On May 1, in replying to charges of having personally profited from his government post, Romero suggested that a formal accusation be made so that congress, sitting as a grand jury, could decide his innocence or guilt.[6] Romero did not get his trial but he and his policies continued under strong attack.

The new tariff law was the subject of much controversy, in the press as well as in the chamber, and as the debate went on, the budget and other legislation all became tied in with the tariff measure. The new law[7] made few fundamental changes in tariff rates. For as Romero explained in a circular[8] accompanying the law, the president felt that in view of the prevailing crisis the time was not an auspicious one for radical changes in the existing tariff; rather the task of the executive was to simplify and codify. Romero summed up the improvements which resulted from the new law. It combined the various duties on imported merchandise into a single charge and fixed import duties at a given amount, using an *ad valorem* basis only in cases where a specific duty could not be set.

6. *Ibid.*, 246-247; 464; 482-488; 604-613; 779; 855.
7. D y L, *Legislación*, XII, 6-87.
8. *Ibid.*, 3-6.

The new tariff listed various articles not included in the old schedule and thus avoided the inconveniences of arbitrary imposts previously collected on such goods. It completely abolished the prohibited list and increased the free list, exempting these articles from any payment whereas the old tariff law had only freed them in part. Another forward step in stimulating commerce was the abolition of the onerous restrictions upon the internal circulation of foreign goods which had paid importation duties. In addition, by establishing the decimal metric system the tariff law carried out the provisions of the law of March 15, 1857. The law also authorized the export of precious metals in bullion, subject only to the restrictions imposed by the government's contracts with the lessees of the mints.

The new tariff law indicated a trend toward centralization of economic authority. Article 19 particularly was bound to create trouble for it provided that foreign merchandise should pay no charges beyond those established in the tariff schedule. Such a prohibition eliminated the duties which states or municipalities were charging on imports entering the area under their jurisdiction. Also subject to much criticism was that section which removed the export tax on gold and silver in bullion. The government did, however, bow to pressure in retaining the Free Zone.

The states of Jalisco and Guanajuato petitioned congress to amend Article 19 of the tariff, and on May 8, Deputy Lemus, a member of the opposition, introduced a bill declaring null and void the decrees of the Minister of the Treasury, known as the laws on stamps, tariff, and direct taxes. He tried to get a suspension of debate on all other matters so that his measure could be considered immediately, but by the very close margin of 67 to 66 the deputies rejected his proposal.[9]

The vote pointed up the great dissatisfaction with the law as it stood and in recognition of opposition strength, administration supporters on the same day introduced a resolution of their own calling for modifications in the tariff law. Their bill authorized the states to levy a tax of not more than five per cent on the import duties established by the tariff law of January 1, 1872. The tax would be collected when the foreign goods reached their ultimate destination,

9. *Sexto congreso*, II, 675.

with the revenues to be spent locally. Of the money collected from this five per cent tax in the Federal District and in the Territory of Lower California, three per cent would go to the Federal Treasury and the remainder would go to the District and the Territory. The bill also repealed Article 78 of the law of January 1 which permitted untaxed export of gold and silver, minted or in bullion. It established an export tax of four per cent of the value of these metals and continued in force the taxes on assaying, smelting, and minting decreed by the law of December 24, 1871.

The next day, May 9, Romero appeared before congress to defend the government's promulgation of the new tariff. Romero considered first the executive's power to take such a step and the circumstances which made it imperative that he do so. He cited the law of December 1, 1871, as clear proof of authority, for under this law congress delegated to the executive its legislative powers in matters relating to the departments of Treasury and War, an action made necessary by the revolt then underway. To wage war the government obviously had to have money, but it did not resort this time to the customary forced loans. Its extraordinary powers enabled the administration to raise the necessary revenue by contracts which were not harmful to the national treasury and by the reorganization and simplification of existing taxes. These measures, none of which could be called irregular, brought excellent results, although naturally the rebels criticized them, as did deputies who had opposed the grant of power in December. It was natural, too, that a bill should be introduced into congress to declare null and void the steps taken by the government by virtue of powers granted under the December law. Approval of such a measure by congress would have deplorable results, particularly if it interfered with contracts which the government had signed. Under such circumstances confidence in the good faith of the executive would be lost and, if another emergency arose, money would not be forthcoming because of the expectation that congress would reverse the executive decrees.

One of the main objectives in granting the extra powers was to enable the government to raise money, and specific authorization was included to impose new taxes. Certainly the tariff was a tax which produced revenue for the treasury, and therefore it was clearly included within the scope of the law. The objection had been raised that the new tariff had produced no resources for the treasury in the worst days of the revolt. Romero dismissed such arguments as being based on pure supposition. When the revolt broke out, the rebels had such strong support that the government felt it must prepare for a long struggle. The most efficient way to provide a regular income during all this time was to decree a new tariff law.

Romero then came to the point in his argument that the law of December 1 gave the executive power to change the tariff. He recalled that when the law was debated in the previous session of congress, Zamacona had presented an addition which specifically barred the executive from using his extraordinary powers to promulgate a new tariff. Congress refused to approve the motion, clearly implying that it considered it unwise to hamper the executive in his exercise of the power they were granting him.

Aside from the problem of increasing the federal revenues, another circumstance made the establishment of a new tariff schedule imperative. In 1868 the executive had suggested a new tariff law, and since that time merchants engaged in foreign trade were hampered in their business by uncertainty over what changes might be forthcoming. The executive had felt that this indecision was responsible for the sharp decline in maritime revenues and had often made its opinion known to the legislature. Romero reminded the deputies that early in 1870 congress had made considerable progress in writing a tariff law of its own but by failing to complete the task had increased the uncertainty of the traders.

After establishing the executive's authority to issue a new tariff law, Romero went on to explain why the administration had taken the step. The executive felt he had found a method of bringing the government more money through additional revenue from increased customs receipts, while at the same time providing other advantages. A new tariff law would benefit foreign commerce, would accelerate the development of sources of national wealth, and would simplify both the administration of the treasury and the operations of importing and exporting.

In spite of all the benefits which the government expected after the law had been given a chance to function, some were displeased with its provisions. Romero then considered the three main objections. He had explained in an earlier appearance before congress that the complaints of a large increase in the duties were not based on fact, and he now repeated that although the tariff looked higher, this was due to the incorporation of all duties into one charge.

State governments protested that the new law invaded their sovereignty by prohibiting them from taxing imports, with the result that state treasuries would suffer a great loss of revenue. Romero pointed out that Article 19 of the new law merely restated the prohibition embodied in Part I of Article 112 of the constitution: no state could tax imports without the consent of congress, a prohibition largely ignored. Thus the tariff law did not prevent states from collecting revenue in this manner; it merely obliged them to comply with the constitutional provision for obtaining congressional permission to put such a tax into effect. Under the new law all such state import taxes would be uniform throughout the country, and merchants would no longer puzzle over different rates in different areas. But Romero was quite sure that the states would not suffer financially with the enactment of the new tariff. The bill before congress authorizing the states to collect up to five per cent on the quotas of the new tariff on foreign goods consumed locally would certainly equal, if it did not exceed, a given state's income from similar taxes under the old system.

Romero expressed his surprise over the introduction of a resolution in congress moving repeal of the entire tariff and the other treasury laws promulgated while the executive had extraordinary powers. The reason given for introducing the bill was that the state of Guanajuato had petitioned for such legislation. But, the minister declared, according to his information all the Guanajuato petition sought was the repeal of Article 19. Such action would, at the same time, repeal Part I of Article 112 of the constitution. Furthermore, since Guanajuato had indicated its willingness to accept the substitute of the five per cent tax, repeal of the law would, in Romero's opinion, ultimately do the state more harm than good.

Finally, Romero replied to the objections against the free export of precious metals, which he considered the most important section of the new law. He felt that the mining industry, in order to prosper, had to be freed of the obstacles hampering its development. The new law had removed some of these restrictions, and as a result not only mining but the nation as a whole, and the national treasury, would profit. In Romero's opinion, mining was the industry which Mexico could most easily and quickly exploit on a large scale, and he felt that an increase in mineral output would in turn affect all the other aspects of Mexican production. Romero regarded it as impossible at the moment to attempt a great increase in agricultural production because of the scarcity of farm labor. Nor did he think that industrial development was the solution to Mexico's problems. Manufacturing undoubtedly had a place in Mexico's future, but for the present the minister pinned his hopes on the mines. Labor was always available because of the high wages and the location of the mines in healthy areas. Due to the fact that mineral products bulked very little and were easily shipped, the industry could expand without any immediate need to improve transportation facilities such as would be required by increased agricultural production. The mining industry would soon take a prominent place in the economy if it were freed from the trammels that had prevented its full development. Chief among these obstacles were the prohibitions on the export of bullion and the heavy tax on mining. Permitting free export would be a big step in the rehabilitation of this vital industry.

As the session moved into late May, neither the budget nor the tariff had received congressional approval. Although on May 7, by a vote of 64 to 50, the budget had been approved in general, the government did not fare so well in the debate on specific items. Since congress was to close its session on May 31, on May 28 the administration made an urgent appeal to congress for action.[10]

On the final day of the session the deputies approved a compromise measure which continued in effect for 1872-1873 the budget of the previous fiscal year. It repealed Articles 19 and 83 of the January tariff law and, in the Federal District and in Lower California, continued the collection of the sales tax at the rate of six per cent on imported goods, the revenues to be divided between the government and Lower California in the ratio provided by the existing law. Silver, in bullion or in coin, would be subject upon export to a tax of five per cent of its value, and gold would pay one-half per cent, with the taxes on assaying, smelting, and coinage to continue as established by the law of December 24, 1871. To compensate for these additions and increases the tariff rates were reduced ten per cent.[11] While the administration had been defeated

10. *Ibid.*, 663; 678; 685-714; 903.
11. D y L, *Legislación*, XII, 202.

on a number of points, at least the plan for a unified tariff had not been disturbed.

On the last day of the session, Juárez made his final speech before congress.[12] It was a short summary of what congress had done, as were most of his speeches closing congressional sessions. He did, however, suggest that at its next session congress might turn to constitutional reforms.

A few days later, on June 8, Mariscal, Castillo Velasco, and Romero resigned from the cabinet. The entire cabinet had presented its resignation after congress had reelected Juárez in October, but the outbreak of serious revolts and later the stormy congressional sessions had made them reconsider. With the adjournment of congress, the three ministers again offered their resignations which the president now accepted. In reorganizing the ministry, Juárez offered posts to José María Lafragua in Relations; Francisco Gómez del Palacio in Gobernación, Francisco Mejía in Treasury, and Joaquín Ruiz in Justice.[13]

Although pro-administration papers spoke highly of the new ministers, the general reaction was one of censure and disapproval. On June 11, *Siglo* published a caustic editorial on the character and political ideas of Lafragua, Gómez del Palacio, and Mejía, reserving its sharpest criticisms for the latter. While the paper had nothing but praise for Ruiz, it predicted that unless he were willing to compromise his principles regarding constitutional government he would clash constantly with Ignacio Mejía, the Minister of War. Even the little comfort *Siglo* found in the Ruiz appointment did not last very long for he ultimately refused the president's offer because of a disagreement over government policy.[14] Ruiz believed that before the administration initiated any measure under the extraordinary powers granted to the executive, all the ministers should discuss and approve whatever action was contemplated. Juárez held that such a procedure was unnecessary; that since he alone held the executive power it was sufficient for him to consult only the minister directly involved. Unable to agree with this interpretation, Ruiz decided not to enter the cabinet.

Undoubtedly the cabinet was composed of unimportant men who

12. *Sexto congreso*, II, 943.
13. *Diario Oficial*, June 10, 1872.
14. Zamacois, *México*, XXII, 292-295; *Siglo*, June 23, 1872.

lacked the qualifications to deal firmly and boldly with the prevailing chaos. Every newspaper, both pro- and anti-administration, including the *Diario Oficial* itself which tended to gloss over the unsettled conditions, carried endless accounts of the small uprisings which broke out continuously and of roving bands of thieves, kidnapers, and marauders, as well as of rebellion in Yucatán, trouble in Hidalgo, revolt in Puebla. The financial crisis grew worse and agriculture continued to deteriorate. The misery of the poorer classes was deepened by the growing shortage of circulating media, and *Federalista* on June 20 wrote a strong editorial opposing the suggestion that business houses close on Sunday to give their workers a day of rest. The lower classes, *Federalista* argued, did not have enough money to buy their food a day in advance.

The president had little opportunity to test the effectiveness of his dictatorial power in restoring peace and order. "At daybreak on the morning of the 19th [July], the inhabitants of this capital were startled by the roar of artillery, followed by a gun each quarter of an hour, which indicated the death of the head of the government."[15] Juárez had been ill for two days, but without alarming symptoms; the end came suddenly with a severe attack similar to the one he had suffered in October, 1870. A state funeral was held; the procession lasted two hours and Mexicans lined the streets to pay their last tribute.

15. July 24, 1872, Mexican Dispatches, Vol. 46.

The approach in this study has been a consideration of the national political scene, and it is apparent even from this limited scope that the leaders of the Reform were successful in introducing certain aspects of democratic capitalism. They undoubtedly achieved their aim of circumscribing the economic and political power of the church, and they introduced republican institutions along with free speech and a free press. Many of the political leaders were probably ardent believers of the laissez-faire philosophy. Yet equality before the law, capitalism itself, free elections, and many of the other fundamental theses of the Reform Program never took root, never developed to any great extent. Above all else, Mexico did not get away from personalism in politics.

BIBLIOGRAPHY

UNPUBLISHED MATERIAL

Archivo Juárez, Biblioteca Nacional, Mexico City.
Ignacio Comonfort Papers, Texas.
Juan Antonio de la Fuente, Correspondencia, 1856-1863, Texas.
Manuel Doblado Typescripts, Texas.
Documentos relativos a la reforma, 1850-1867, Texas.
León Guzmán, El partido constitucional, la 2a y 3a época del Presidente D. Benito Juárez, Texas.
Francisco Mejía, Epocas, hechos y acontecimientos de mi vida, Texas.
Jesús González Ortega Typescripts, Texas.
Edward L. Plumb Papers, Stanford.
Mariano Riva Palacio Papers, Texas.
Vicente Riva Palacio Papers, Texas.
Jesús Terán Typescripts, Texas.
United States National Archives, Dispatches from Mexico, Volumes 27-40; Consular Dispatches from Paso del Norte and Veracruz. Microfilm.
Plácido Vega Papers, California (Berkeley).

Doctoral Dissertations

Brown, Robert B., "Guns Over the Border: American Aid to the Juárez Government During the French Intervention," University of Michigan, 1951.
Cadenhead, I. E., "González Ortega and Mexican National Politics," University of Missouri, 1950.
Caldwell, E. M., "The War of 'La Reforma' in Mexico, 1858-1861," University of Texas, 1935.
Frazer, Robert W., "Matías Romero and the French Intervention in Mexico," University of California, Los Angeles, 1941.

Miscellaneous

List of books in Juárez' library in Oaxaca. Supplied the author by J. F. Iturribarría.

PUBLISHED MATERIALS

Abbott, G. D., *Mexico and the United States: Their Mutual Relations and Common Interests.* New York, 1869.
Aguilar, G. F., *Los presupuestos mexicanos desde los tiempos de la colonia hasta nuestros días.* México, 1940.
Aguilar de Bustamante, J., *Ensayo político, literario, teológico dogmático.* México, 1862.
Alfaro y Piña, L., *Relación descriptiva de la fundación . . . de las iglesias y conventos de México. . . .* México, 1863.
Altamirano, Ignacio, *Aires de México.* México, 1940.
―――, *Discursos de. . . .* México, 1934.
―――, *Historia y política de México, 1821-1882.* México, 1947.
Alvarez, Diego, *El ciudadano General Diego Alvarez a sus conciudadanos.* Acapulco, 1868.
Alvarez, Ignacio, *Estudios sobre la historia general de México.* 6 vols., Zacatecas, 1875-1877.
Alvarez, Melchor, *Historia documentada de la vida pública del Gral. José Justo Alvarez.* México, 1905.
Alvensleven, M., *With Maximilian in Mexico.* London, 1867.
Amador, E., *Bosquejo histórico de Zacatecas.* 2 vols., Zacatecas, 1943.

Archivo Histórico Diplomático Mexicano. Especially:
  Vol X, *Notas de Don Juan Antonio de la Fuente Ministro de México, cerca de Napoleon III*
  Vol. XIII, *El Tratado Mon-Almonte*
  Vol. XVII, *Las relaciones diplomáticas de México con Sud-América.*
  Vol. XXV, *Don Juan Prim y su labor diplomática en México*
  Vol. XXVIII, *La labor diplomática de D. Manuel María de Zamacona como Secretario de Relaciones Exteriores*
  Segunda Series. Vol. I, *La misión confidencial de Don Jesús Terán en Europa, 1863-1865.*
Archivo Mexicano. Colección de leyes, decretos, circulares y otros documentos. 6 vols., México, 1856-1862.
Arrillaga, Basilio J., *Recopilación de leyes, decretos, bandos.* . . . 9 vols., México, 1861-1866.
Arróniz, Marcos, *Manual del viajero en Méjico o compendio de la historia de la ciudad de Méjico.* Paris, 1858.
Bancroft, H. H., *History of Mexico.* 6 vols., San Francisco, 1883-1888.
Banda, L., *Estadística de Jalisco . . . en los años de 1854 a 1863.* Guadalajara, 1866.
Basch, S., *Recuerdos de México.* México, 1870.
Bassols, N., *Leyes de reforma que afectan al clero.* Puebla, 1902.
Baz, G., *Vida de Benito Juárez.* México, 1874.
———, and Gallo, E. L., *History of the Mexican Railway.* México, 1876.
Baz, Juan J., *Artículos diversos.* . . . México, 1861.
Beals, C., *Porfirio Díaz, Dictator of Mexico.* Philadelphia, 1932.
Benjamin, R. L., "Marcus Ottenbourg, United States Minister to Mexico," *American Jewish Historical Society,* XXXII, 1931.
Bianchi, A. G., ed., *Correspondencia de Juárez y Montluc.* México, 1905.
Binkley, R. C., *Realism and Nationalism, 1852-1871.* New York, 1935.
Blanchot, C., *Memoires L'Intervention Francaise en Mexique.* 3 vols., Paris, 1911.
Blasio, José L., *Maximilian Emperor of Mexico. Memoirs of His Private Secretary.* New Haven, 1934.
British Foreign and State Papers, 1853-1872.
Buenrostro, Felipe, *Historia del primero y segundo congresos constitucionales de la República Mexicana.* 9 vols., México, 1874-1882.
———, *Historia del segundo congreso constitucional de la República Mexicana, que funcionó en los años de 1861, 62 y 63.* México, 1874.
Bulnes, Francisco, *El verdadero Juárez y la verdad sobre la intervención y el imperio.* México, 1904.
———, *Juárez y las revoluciones de Ayutla y de la Reforma.* México, 1905.
Burke, U. R., *A Life of Benito Juárez.* London, 1894.
Cadenhead, I. E., "González Ortega and the Presidency of Mexico," *HAHR,* XXXII, No. 3.
Calderón, Francisco R., *La vida económica.* Vol. II of Cosío Villegas, *Historia moderna de México.* Mexico, 1955.
Callahan, James M., *American Foreign Policy in Mexican Relations.* New York, 1932.
Callcott, W. H., *Church and State in Mexico, 1822-1857.* Durham, 1926.
———, *Liberalism in Mexico, 1857-1929.* Stanford, 1931.
———, *Santa Anna, The Story of an Enigma who once was Mexico.* Norman, 1936.
Cambre, Manuel, *La guerra de tres años en el estado de Jalisco.* Guadalajara, 1892.
Carrion, A., *Historia de la ciudad de la Puebla de los Angeles.* 2 vols., México, 1897.
Castañeda, C. E., ed., *La guerra de reforma según el archivo del General D. Manuel Doblado, 1857-1860.* San Antonio, 1930.

Bibliography 181

Circular a todos los sacerdotes de la diócesis . . . de Guadalajara. Guadalajara, 1859.
Colección de leyes, decretos y circulares expedidas por el Supremo Gobierno de la República, 1863-1867. 3 vols., México, 1867.
Comunicaciones cambiadas entre el Ministro de Justicia . . . y el . . . Obispo de Guadalajara con motivo de la ley de . . . 25 de junio de 1856. Guadalajara, 1857.
Correspondence Relative to the Present Conditions of Mexico Communicated to the House of Representatives by the Department of State. Washington, 1862.
Corti, E., *Maximilian and Charlotte of Mexico.* 2 vols., New York, 1928.
Cosío Villegas, Daniel, "Donde está el villano?", *Historia Mexicana*, I, No. 3.
———, *Historia moderna de México. La República restaurada. La vida política.* México, 1954.
———, "Historia y prejuicio," *Historia Mexicana*, I, No. 1.
———, *La cuestión aranceleria en México.* México, 1932.
———, *Porfirio Díaz en la revuelta de la Noria.* México, 1953.
———, "Ya viene la bola!", *Historia Mexicana*, II, No. 2.
Couto, José B., *Obras de. . . .* México, 1898.
Cuevas, P. Mariano, ed., *Diario de sucesos notables de Don José Ramon Malo, 1832-1864.* 2 vols., México, 1948.
———, *Historia de la iglesia en México.* Vol. V, El Paso, 1928.
Daran, V., *El General Miguel Miramón.* México, 1887.
Dawson, Daniel, *The Mexican Adventure.* London, 1935.
Decorme, Gerardo, *Historia de la Compañía de Jesús en la república mexicana durante el siglo XIX.* 2 vols., Guadalajara, 1914-1921.
Delmez, Albert J., "The Positivist Philosophy in Mexican Education, 1867-1873," *Americas*, VI, No. 1.
Diario de los debates. Quinto congreso constitucional de la unión. 4 vols., México, 1871.
———. *Sexto congreso constitucional de la unión.* 4 vols., México, 1871-1873.
Didapp, J. P., *Partidos políticos de México.* México, 1903.
Dios Peza, Juan de, *Epopeyas de mi patria.* México, 1904.
Documentos para la historia contemporánea de México. 2 vols., México, 1867-1868.
Dublán, Manuel, and Lozano, José María, eds., *Legislación mexicana o colección completa de las disposiciones legislativas expedidas desde la independencia de la república.* 34 vols., México, 1876-1904.
Elton, J. F., *With the French in Mexico.* London, 1867.
Evans, A. E., *Our Sister Republic: A Gala Trip Through Tropical Mexico in 1869-1870.* Hartford, 1870.
Foix, Pere, *Juárez.* México, 1949.
Frazer, R. W., "Latin-American Projects to Aid Mexico During the French Intervention," *HAHR*, August, 1948.
———, "Maximilian's Propaganda Activities in the United States, 1865-1866," *HAHR*, February, 1944.
———, "The Ochoa Bond Negotiations of 1865-1867," *Pacific Hist. Rev.*, XI, No. 4.
———, "The United States, European, and West Virginia Land Company," *Pacific Hist. Rev.*, XIII, No. 2.
———, "Trade Between California and the Belligerent Powers During the French Intervention in Mexico," *Pacific Hist. Rev.*, XV, No. 4.
Frías y Soto, H., *Juárez glorificado y la Intervención y el Imperio ante la verdad histórica.* México, 1905.
Fuentes Mares, José, ed., *Gabino Barreda, Estudios.* México, 1941.
Galindo y Galindo, Miguel, *La gran década nacional, o relación histórica de la guerra de reforma, intervención extranjera y gobierno del Archiduque Maximiliano, 1857-1867.* 3 vols., México, 1904.

García, Genaro, ed., *Documentos inéditos o muy raros para la historia de México*. Especially:
Vols. I, IV, XIII, *Correspondencia secreta de los principales intervencionistas mexicanos*
Vol. XI, *Don Santos Degollado*. . . .
Vols. XIV, XVI, XVII, XVIII, XX, XXII, XXIV, XXVII, XXX, XXXIII, *La intervención francesa en México según el archivo del Mariscal Bazaine*
Vol. XXIII, *El sitio de Puebla en 1863*
Vol. XXVI, *La revolución de Ayutla según el archivo del General Doblado*
Vol. XXXI, *Los gobiernos de Alvarez y Comonfort según el archivo del General Doblado*
—————, *Juárez. Refutación a Don Francisco Bulnes*. México, 1904.
García Granados, R., *Historia de México desde la restauración de la república en 1867, hasta la caída de Porfirio Díaz*. México, 1936.
—————, *La Constitución de 1857 y los leyes de Reforma en México. Estudio histórico-sociológico*. México, 1906.
Gardiner, C. H., "Foreign Travelers' Accounts of Mexico, 1810-1910," *Americas*, VIII, No. 3.
—————, "The Mexico-Toluca Railroad and Lottery," *Inter-American Economic Affairs*, II, No. 4.
Gibaya y Patrón, Antonio, *Comentario crítico, histórico, auténtico a las revoluciones sociales de México*. 5 vols., México, 1926-1934.
González, A. R., *Historia del estado de Aguascalientes*. México, 1881.
González Navarro, M., *Vallarta y su ambiente político jurídico*. México, 1949.
Gortari, Elí de, "Ciencia positiva política 'científica,' " *Historia Mexicana*, I, No. 4.
Gropp, A. E., *Union List of Latin American Newspapers in the United States*. Washington, 1953.
Guzmán, Martín Luis, ed., *Escuelas laicas*. México, 1949.
Hall, F., *The Laws of Mexico*. San Francisco, 1885.
Handbook of Latin American Studies.
Hanna, K. A., "The Roles of the South in the French Intervention in Mexico," *Journal of Southern History*, XX, No. 1.
Historia de la revolución de México contra la dictadura del General Santa-Anna, 1853-1855. México, 1856.
Hyde, M., *Mexican Empire: The History of Maximilian and Carlota of Mexico*. London, 1946.
Iglesias, José M., *Autobiografía de*. . . . México, 1893.
—————, *Revistas históricas sobre la intervención francesa en México*. 3 vols., México, 1867-1869.
Iglesias Calderón, F., *El egoismo norte-americano durante la intervención francesa*. México, 1905.
—————, *Las supuestas traiciones de Juárez*. México, 1907.
Irigoyen, Ulíses, *El problema económico de las fronteras mexicanas*. 2 vols., México, 1935.
Iturribarría, Jorge F., *Historia de Oaxaca, 1821-1854*. 3 vols., 1935-1939.
Johnson, Richard A., *The Mexican Revolution of Ayutla, 1854-1855*. Rock Island, 1939.
Juárez, Benito Pablo, *Archivos privados*, see Puig Casauranc.
—————, *Flor y latigo ideario político*. México, 1944.
"Juárez y los Te Deums oficiales," *Boletín del Archivo General de la Nación*, IX, No. 4.
Ker, A. M., *Mexican Government Publications. A Guide to the More Important Publications of . . . Mexico, 1821-1936*. Washington, 1940.
Knapp, Frank A., "Parliamentary Government and the Mexican Constitution of 1857," *HAHR*, XXXIII, No. 1.

Bibliography 183

———, "The Apocryphal Memoirs of Sebastián Lerdo de Tejada" *HAHR*, XXXI, No. 1.
———, *The Life of Sebastián Lerdo de Tejada, 1823-1889.* Austin, 1951.
Lempriere, C., *Notes in Mexico in 1861 and 1862.* London, 1862.
Lerdo de Tejada, Miguel, *Cuadro sinóptico de la repúblicana mexicana en 1856 formado en vista de los últimos datos oficiales.* . . . México, 1856.
McBride, G. M., *The Land Systems of Mexico.* New York, 1923.
McCaleb, W. F., *The Public Finances of Mexico.* New York, 1921.
McCornack, R. B., "Un amigo de México," *Historia Mexicana*, I, No. 4.
Manning, William R., ed., *Diplomatic Correspondence of the United States: Inter-American Affairs, 1831-1860.* 12 vols., Washington, 1932-1939. Especially Vol. IX.
María Carreño, Alberto, ed., *Archivo del General Porfirio Díaz.* Vols. I-X, México, 1947-1951.
Martínez Tamayo, E., "Un triángulo político," *Historia Mexicana*, I, No. 1.
Mateos, José María, *Historia de la masonería en México desde 1806 hasta 1884.* México, 1884.
Memorias of Hacienda, Justicia, and Relaciones of the Mexican Government. México, 1857-1872.
Mills, W. W., *Forty Years at El Paso, 1858-1898.* El Paso?, 1901.
Moore, J. Preston, "Correspondence of Pierre Soulé: The Louisiana Tehuantepec Company," *HAHR*, XXXII, No. 1.
Muro, M., *Historia de San Luis Potosí.* Vol. III, San Luis Potosí, 1910.
Murray, Paul, *Tres norteamericanos y su participación en el desarrollo del tratado McLane-Ocampo, 1856-1860.* Guadalajara, 1946.
National Archives, *List of File Microcopies of the National Archives.* Washington, 1950.
Ocaranza, F., ed., *Juárez y sus amigos.* 2 vols., México, 1939-1942.
Ortega, José G., *El golpe de estado de Juárez.* México, 1941.
Owsley, F. L., *King Cotton Diplomacy. Foreign Relations of the Confederate States of America.* Chicago, 1931.
Parra, P., *Estudio histórico-sociológico sobre la Reforma en México.* México, 1906.
Payno, Manuel, *Memoria sobre la revolución de diciembre de 1857 y enero de 1858.* México, 1860.
———, *México y sus cuestiones financieras con la Inglaterra, la España y la Francia.* México, 1862.
Paz, Ireneo, *Algunas campañas.* 3 vols., México, 1884-1886.
———, ed., *Los hombres prominentes de México.* México, 1888.
Pérez Verdía, L., *Historia particular del estado de Jalisco.* Vol. III, Guadalajara, 1911.
Perkins, Dexter, *Hands Off. A History of the Monroe Doctrine.* Boston, 1942.
———, *The Monroe Doctrine, 1826-1867.* Baltimore, 1933.
Phipps, H., *Some Aspects of the Agrarian Question in Mexico.* Austin, 1925.
Planchet, R., *La cuestión religiosa en México o sea vida de Benito Juárez.* Rome, 1906.
Pletcher, David M., "A Prospecting Expedition Across Central Mexico, 1856-1857," *Pacific Hist. Rev.*, XXI, No. 1.
———, "General William S. Rosecrans and the Mexican Transcontinental Railroad Project," *Miss. Valley Hist. Rev.*, XXXVIII, No. 4.
———, "México, campo de inversiones norteamericanas: 1867-1880," *Historia Mexicana*, II, No. 4.
———, "The Building of the Mexican Railway," *HAHR*, XXX, No. 1.
Pola, Angel, ed., *Discursos y manifiestos de Benito Juárez.* México, 1905.
———, *Miscelánea de Benito Juárez.* México, 1906.
———, *Obras Completas de D. Melchor Ocampo.* 3 vols., México, 1900-1901.
Portilla, Anselmo de la, *Méjico en 1856 y 1857. Gobierno del General Comonfort.* New York, 1858.
Prieto, G., *Colección de poesías escogidas.* México, 1897.

——, *Lecciones de historia patria escritas para los alumnos del colegio militar.* México, 1893.
——, *Memorias de mis tiempos.* 2 vols., México, 1948.
Puig Casauranc, J. M., ed., *Archivos privados de D. Benito Juárez y D. Pedro Santacilia.* México, 1928.
Rabasa, Emilio, *La organización política de México. La constitución y la dictadura.* Madrid, 1917?
Ramírez, Ignacio, *Obras de. . . .* 2 vols., México, 1889.
Riva Palacio, V., ed., *México a través de los siglos.* Vol. V by José M. Vigil, *La Reforma.* México, 1940.
Rivera, A., *La reforma y el segundo imperio.* México, 1904.
Rivera Cambas, M., *Historia antigua y moderna de Jalapa y de las revoluciones del estado de Veracruz.* 5 vols., México, 1869-1871.
Roeder, R., *Juárez and His Mexico.* 2 vols., New York, 1947.
Roel, S., ed., *Correspondencia particular de D. Santiago Vidaurri, Tomo Primero, Juárez-Vidaurri.* Monterrey, 1946.
Romero, Matías, ed., *Correspondencia de la Legación Mexicana en Washington durante la Intervención Extranjera.* 10 vols., México, 1870-1892.
——, *Mexico and the United States. . . .* New York, 1908.
Ruiz, E., *Biografía del ciudadano Melchor Ocampo.* México, 1893.
——, *Historia de la guerra de intervención en Michoacán.* México, 1940.
Ruiz, Manuel, *Ministro constitucional de la suprema corte de justicia de la nación.* México, 1868.
Ruiz Castaneda, M., *Periodismo político de la reforma en la ciudad de México, 1854-1861.* México, 1950.
Scholes, Walter V., "A Revolution Falters: Mexico, 1856-1857," *HAHR,* XXXII, No. 1.
——, "Church and State at the Mexican Constitutional Convention, 1856-1857," *Americas,* IV, No. 2.
——, "El liberalismo reformista," *Historia Mexicana,* II, No. 3.
——, "EL MENSAJERO and the Election of 1871 in Mexico," *Americas,* V, No. 1.
Sheridan, P. H., *Personal Memoirs of. . . .* 2 vols., New York, 1888.
Sierra, Justo, *Juárez, su obra y su tiempo.* México, 1948.
Sierra Casasús, C., "Altamirano íntimo," *Historia Mexicana,* I, No. 1.
Silva Herzog, J., "Economic Ideas in Mexico in the Constitutional Congress of 1857," *Social Sciences in Mexico,* May, 1947.
——, *El pensamiento económico en México.* México, 1947.
Skinner, J. E. H., *After the Storm; or Jonathan and His Neighbors in 1865-6.* 2 vols., London, 1866.
Sosa, F., *Biografías de mexicanas distinguidos.* México, 1884.
Tovar, P., ed., *Historia parlamentaria del cuarto congreso constitucional.* 4 vols., México, 1872-1874.
Trens, M. B., *Historia de Veracruz.* Vol. V, México, 1950.
Turlington, E. W., *Mexico and Her Foreign Creditors.* New York, 1930.
United States Congress. 37th Congress. 2nd Session. Document No. 100.
United States. Department of State. *Foreign Relations.* Washington, D.C., 1862-1872.
Valades, José C., *Don Melchor Ocampo. Reformador de México.* México, 1954.
Valdés, M., *Memorias de la guerra de reforma.* México, 1913.
Vance, J. T., and Clagett, H. L., *A Guide to the Law and Legal Literature of Mexico.* Washington, 1945.
Villaseñor y Villaseñor, A., *Obras de. . . .* 2 vols., México, 1897-1906.
Zamacois, Niceto de, *Historia de Méjico desde sus tiempos mas remotos hasta nuestros días.* 22 vols., Barcelona, 1878-1903. Vols. 19-22 of this set were written by F. G. Cosmes.
Zarco, Francisco, ed., *Historia del congreso estraordinario constituyente de 1856 y 1857.* 2 vols., México, 1857.
Zayas Enríquez, Rafael de, *Benito Juárez, su vida su obra.* México, 1906.
Zea, L., *El positivismo en México.* México, 1943.

NEWSPAPERS AND JOURNALS

(Unless otherwise designated they are from Mexico City.)

El Amigo del Pueblo, 1861.
El Boletín de la Sociedad Mexicana de Geografía y Estadística.
El Boletín de Noticias, 1860-1861.
El Boletín Republicano, 1867.
El Constitucional, 1867-1868.
El Constituyente, (Oaxaca), 1856.
El Correo del Comercio, 1871-1872.
La Cruz, 1855-1857.
El Diario de Avisos, 1856-1860.
El Diario del Imperio, 1865-1866.
El Diario Oficial (Including *Periódico Oficial* of the Intervention Period), 1863-1872.
El Eco de Ambos Mundos, 1872.
El Eco Nacional, 1857-1858.
El Estandarte Nacional, 1856-1857.
La Estrella de Occidente, (Ures), 1859-1860.
El Federalista, 1871-1872.
El Globo, 1867-1869.
El Mensajero, 1871.
El Monitor Republicano, 1868-1870.
La Nación, 1856-1857.
La Orquesta, 1861-1869.
Los Padres del Agua Fría, 1856.
El Pájaro Verde, 1861-1863.
El Pensamiento Nacional, 1855-1856.
El Periódico Oficial, (Zacatecas), 1869-1870.
El Siglo Diez y Nueve, 1855-1858, 1861-1863, 1867-1872.
El Socialista, 1871-1872.
La Sociedad, 1855-1856.
La Voz de México, 1870-1872.

INDEX

Alcalde, Joaquín M., 93-94
Altamirano, Ignacio, 81
Alvarez, Juan,
    Leader of revolt against Santa Anna, 3
    Acting President, 4-6
Amnesty Law, 129-131
Arriaga, Ponciano, 14

Balcárcel, Blas, 74, 84
Barreda, Gabino, 138-140
Bazaine, F. A., 99-102, 111, 116
Benítez, Justo, 130, 132, 152, 158

Carrera, Manuel, 4
Castañeda, Marcelino, 13
Church-state relations,
    General liberal views, 2
    Ley Juárez, 5-6
    Question of religious toleration in constitutional convention, 11-14
    Ley Lerdo, 14-16, 22
    Pesado's views on, 17-20
    Conservative reaction to Constitution of 1857, 21-22
    Liberal manifesto, 1859, 43-46
    Reform Laws, 47-50
    Expulsion of archbishop and bishops, 1861, 57
    Actions of radical liberals, 1862-1863, 88-89
Churchwell, William M., 33-34
Club de la Reforma,
    Opposition to Juárez, 58-59, 68-70
Comonfort, Ignacio,
    Revolt against Santa Anna, 3-4
    In Alvarez cabinet, 5
    Acting President, 6-11, 20-21
    President, 22-24
    Returns to Mexico, 90-91
    Enters Juárez cabinet, 95-98

Congressional elections, 1869, 131-133
Conservatives,
    Revolt against Comonfort, 7-8
    Reaction to Ley Lerdo, 15
    General political position, 17-20
    Government under Zuloaga and Miramón, 28-33, 37-40
    Disunity under Maximilian, 111
Constitutional Convention, 1856-1857,
    Differences with president, 8-9
    Rights of man, 11
    Trial by jury, 11
    Debate on religious toleration, 11-14
    Ley Lerdo, 14-15
    Monopolies, 17
Convocatoria, August 14, 1867, 118-123, 132
Corwin, T., 73, 78

Degollado, Santos,
    Commander of the liberal army, 27-30, 37-38, 40-42
    Position on Reform Laws, 52-53
    Death of, 72
De la Fuente, José Antonio, 36, 57, 77-78, 90, 99
De la Rosa, Luis, 6
Díaz, Isidro, 58-59
Díaz, Porfirio, 91, 106, 122, 132, 149-165
Doblado, Manuel,
    Revolt against Santa Anna, 3
    Opposes Plan of Tacubaya, 24
    In Juárez cabinet, 1857, 26-27
    Position, 1861-1863, 74, 83-87, 89-90
    Disagreement with Zarco and Juárez at San Luis Potosí, 92-97
    Attempts to get Juárez to resign, 100-102

Economic conditions and attempted reforms after Intervention, 141-148
Education,
 Introduction of positivism, 138-141
Escandón, Antonio, 67

Foreign relations of Mexico,
 Conservative government, 1858-1860, 31-32
 With France, 74-79, 86-88, 90-91, 99-102, 116-117
 With Great Britain, 38, 41, 74-80, 86-87, 144
 With Spain, 74-79, 86-87
 With United States, 33-37, 76-80, 109-111
Forsyth, John, 31 32
France,
 See Foreign relations of Mexico

Gamboa, José Antonio, 12-13
García de la Cadena, Trinidad, 136
Great Britain,
 See Foreign relations of Mexico
Gutiérrez de Estrada, José M., 75-76
Guzmán, León, 26, 71, 73, 121
Guzmán, Ramón, 151

Iglesias, José María, 97-98, 100, 103-104, 131

Juárez, Benito,
 Revolt against Santa Anna, 3
 In Alvarez cabinet, 5
 Ley Juárez, 5-6
 Refusal to publish Comonfort's Organic Statute, 9
 In Comonfort cabinet, 23
 Assumes temporary presidency, 24
 Biographical sketch, 25-26
 Moves government to Veracruz, 26-28
 Liberal government in Veracruz: relations with Vidaurri, 29, Mc-

Juárez, Benito—(Continued)
 Lane-Ocampo Treaty, 33-37, attempted British mediation, 38-39, relations with liberal military leaders, 40-42, manifesto of the government, 43-50, position on Reform Laws, 51-55
 Liberal government, 1861-1863: amnesty question, 57-59, radical cabinet, 59-61, economic reforms, 67, presidential campaign, 68-69, 72, relations with Ortega, 69-70, 81-83, radical liberal opposition, 72-73, 81-84, suspension of payments on foreign debts, 74-80, relations with Doblado, 84-85, 89-90
 Intervention: disagreements with other liberals, 92-98, attempts to get president to resign, 100-102, trouble with Vidaurri, 102-105, government in Chihuahua and Paso del Norte, 107-116, Ortega's attempt to become president, 111-116
 Reelected president, 122-123
 Amnesty law, 129-130
 Split with Díaz, 131-132
 Split with Lerdo, 133-134
 Revolts against, after Intervention, 135-137, 162
 Presidential election, 1871, 149-162
 Final term as president, 166-175

Lafragua, José María, 6, 175
Lerdo de Tejada, Miguel,
 Possible presidential candidate, 1858, 22
 Position on McLane-Ocampo Treaty, 35-36
 Position on proposed British mediation, 38-40
 Position on Reform Laws, 51-55
 Presidential campaign, 1861, 68-69, 72

Index

Lerdo de Tejada, Sebastián,
  Refuses to enter Juárez cabinet, 1861, 74, 84
  Rejection of Wyke-Zamacona Treaty, 80
  Enters Juárez cabinet, 95-98
  Interpretation of presidential term of office, 112
  Defense of *Convocatoria*, 118-120
  Political attacks on, 122, 124, 126-127
  Presidential election, 1871, 133-134, 149-162
Ley Juárez, 5-6
Ley Lerdo, 14-16
Liberal thought,
  Views on democratic capitalism, 1-3
  Theory of government, 10-11
  Religious toleration, 11-14
  Ley Lerdo, 14-16
  Need of immigration, 2, 12-13, 17
  Manifesto of 1859, 43-47
  Reform Laws, 47-53
  Government program, 1861, 61
  Educational policy, 138-141
  Economic thought after Intervention, 143-148, 167-168
Liberals,
  Division among, 3, 8-9, 11-14, 50-59, 68-70, 72-73, 81-84, 92-98, 120-123, 131-132

McLane, Robert, 33-36
McLane-Ocampo Treaty, 33-37
Mata, José María, 33, 36-37, 50, 70
Mathew, George B., 38, 41
Maximilian, Ferdinand, 111, 116-117
Mejía, Ignacio, 134, 137, 175
Mendiolea, Manuel, 152, 158
Miramón, Miguel, 28-33, 37-40, 116-117
Mon-Almonte Treaty, 32

Napoleon III, 76-77, 111, 116
Núñez, José H., 74-75, 90, 95-97

Ocampo, Melchor,
  In Alvarez cabinet, 5
  In Juárez cabinet, 26
  Negotiations with McLane, 33-37
  Position on Reform Laws, 50-55
  Laws to punish conservatives, 56-57
  Opposition to Miguel Lerdo, 1861, 68
  Death of, 71
Ortega, González,
  In War of Reform, 41-42
  In Juárez cabinet, 1861, 60-61
  Presidential campaign, 1861, 68-69, 72
  Resignation from cabinet, 69-71
  Elected Chief Justice, 73
  Further disagreements with Juárez, 1861, 81-84
  Letter to Saligny, 88
  Commander of army in Puebla, 90-91
  Attempt to get Juárez to resign, 100-102
  Defeat at Majoma, 107
  Claim to presidency, 111-116
  Released from prison, 134-136

Parrodi, Anastasio, 24, 27
Patoni, José María, 107, 116, 134-135
Payno, Manuel, 6, 23
Paz, Ireneo, 152
Pesado, J. J., 17-20
Plan of Tacubaya, 23
Plumb, Edward Lee, 134, 147, 164
Prieto, Guillermo,
  Cabinet positions, 5, 26, 60
  Saves life of Juárez, 26-27
  Attempt to improve financial position of government, 62-63
  Attempt to clarify land titles, 64-65
  Resignation from cabinet, 1861, 70
  Split with Juárez, 113-114, 130

Quiroga, Julián, 106-107

Ramírez, Ignacio, 8-9, 16, 60, 152
Reform Laws, 43-55
Riva Palacio, Vicente, 66, 72, 93
Romero Matías,
   Mexican representative in the United States, 78, 109-110
   Secretary of Treasury, 124
   Plans for economic reform, 143-148, 167-174
   Resigns cabinet post, 175
Romero Rubio, Manuel, 151, 169
Ruiz, Manuel,
   In Comonfort cabinet, 23
   In Juárez cabinet, 26, 38
   Relates responsibility for Reform Laws, 50-53

Seward, William, 78-79, 109
Siliceo, Manuel, 6, 99
Spain,
   See Foreign relations of Mexico
Supreme Court of Mexico, 126-129

Terán, Jesús, 85, 90, 94, 109

United States,
   See Foreign relations of Mexico

Uraga, José López, 93-96, 98-100, 105-106

Vallarta, Ignacio L., 124-125, 127
Vega, Plácido, 110
Vidaurri, Santiago, 3-4, 8-9, 29, 89, 102-105

War of Reform, 25-42
Wyke, Charles, 79-80, 86-87
Wyke-Zamacona Treaty, 80

Yañez, José M., 6

Zamacona, Manuel María de,
   Minister of Relations, 74-75, 79-80, 84
   Disagreement with Doblado, 92-97
   Attack on *Convocatoria*, 121-122
   General criticism of Juárez, 125-126, 130, 168-169
   Supports Díaz for president, 152, 154-155, 158
Zamora, Manuel, 28
Zaragosa, Ignacio, 70-71, 87, 90
Zarco, Francisco, 6, 60, 69, 92-97, 130-131
Zuloaga, Felíz, 23, 28-29, 32